Cram101 Textbook Outlines to accompany:

Nurse Anesthesia

John J. Nagelhout, Karen L. Plaus, 4th Edition

A Content Technologies Inc. publication (c) 2012.

Learning System

Cram101 Textbook Outlines is a learning system. The notes in this book are the highlights of your textbook, you will never have to highlight a book again.

How to use this book. Take this book to class, it is your notebook for the lecture. The notes and highlights on the left hand side of the pages follow the outline and order of the textbook. All you have to do is follow along while your instructor presents the lecture. Circle the items emphasized in class and add other important information on the right side. With Cram101 Textbook Outlines you'll spend less time writing and more time listening. Learning becomes more efficient.

Cram101.com Online

Increase your studying efficiency by using Cram101.com's practice tests and online reference material. It is the perfect complement to Cram101 Textbook Outlines. Use self-teaching matching tests or simulate in-class testing with comprehensive multiple choice tests, or simply use Cram's true and false tests for quick review. Cram101.com even allows you to enter your in-class notes for an integrated studying format combining the textbook notes with your class notes.

Visit **www.Cram101.com**, click Sign Up at the top of the screen, and enter **DK73DW14432** in the promo code box on the registration screen. Your access to www.Cram101.com is discounted by 50% because you have purchased this book. Sign up and stop highlighting textbooks forever.

Nurse Anesthesia
John J. Nagelhout, Karen L. Plaus, 4th

CONTENTS

CRAM101

Chapter 1. PART I: Chapter 1 - Chapter 18

Endocrine system	The Endocrine system is a system of glands, each of which secretes a type of hormone to regulate the body. The field of study that deals with disorders of endocrine glands is endocrinology, a branch of the wider field of internal medicine. The Endocrine system is an information signal system much like the nervous system.
Fresh frozen plasma	The term Fresh frozen plasma refers to the liquid portion of human blood that has been frozen and preserved quickly after a blood donation and will be used for blood transfusion. The capitalized term Fresh frozen plasma is the proper name in the United States for the fluid portion of one unit of human blood that has been centrifuged, separated, and frozen solid at −18 °C (−0.4 °F) (or colder) within 8 hours of collection. Other single-donor plasma units, either frozen or liquid, are substituted for Fresh frozen plasma. Indications for these products are similar to those for Fresh frozen plasma with the exception heat-sensitive proteins in the plasma, such as factor V, and the term is often used to mean any transfused plasma product.
Histamine	Histamine is a biogenic amine involved in local immune responses as well as regulating physiological function in the gut and acting as a neurotransmitter. Histamine triggers the inflammatory response. As part of an immune response to foreign pathogens, Histamine is produced by basophils and by mast cells found in nearby connective tissues.
Florence Nightingale	Florence Nightingale, OM, RRC was an English nurse, writer and statistician. She came to prominence during the Crimean War for her pioneering work in nursing, and was dubbed `The Lady with the Lamp` after her habit of making rounds at night to tend injured soldiers. Nightingale laid the foundation of professional nursing with the establishment, in 1860, of her nursing school at St Thomas`s Hospital in London, the first secular nursing school in the world.
Ignaz Semmelweis	Dr. Ignaz Semmelweis discovered in 1847 that hand-washing with a chlorinated-lime solution reduced the incidence of fatal childbed fever tenfold in maternity institutions. However, the reaction of his contemporaries was not positive; his subsequent mental disintegration led to his being confined to an insane asylum, where he died in 1865. Semmelweis`s critics claimed his findings lacked scientific reasoning.
Anesthesia	Anesthesia has traditionally meant the condition of having sensation blocked or temporarily taken away. This allows patients to undergo surgery and other procedures without the distress and pain they would otherwise experience. The word was coined by Oliver Wendell Holmes, Sr.

Chapter 1. PART I: Chapter 1 - Chapter 18

Epidural	Epidural or extradural hematoma (haematoma) is a type of traumatic brain injury (TBI) in which a buildup of blood occurs between the dura mater (the tough outer membrane of the central nervous system) and the skull. The dura mater also covers the spine, so Epidural bleeds may also occur in the spinal column. Often due to trauma, the condition is potentially deadly because the buildup of blood may increase pressure in the intracranial space and compress delicate brain tissue.
Guideline	`Guideline` is the NATO reporting name for the Soviet SA-2 surface-to-air missile. A Guideline is any document that aims to streamline particular processes according to a set routine. By definition, following a Guideline is never mandatory (protocol would be a better term for a mandatory procedure).
Perspective	Perspective erspective in the graphic arts, such as drawing, is an approximate representation, on a flat surface , of an image as it is seen by the eye. The two most characteristic features of perspective are that objects are drawn: · Smaller as their distance from the observer increases · Foreshortened: the size of an object`s dimensions along the line of sight are relatively shorter than dimensions across the line of sight . Linear perspective works by representing the light that passes from a scene through an imaginary rectangle (the painting), to the viewer`s eye. It is similar to a viewer looking through a window and painting what is seen directly onto the windowpane.
Nurse anesthetist	A Nurse anesthetist is a registered nurse and advanced practice nurse who has acquired additional education to administer anesthesia. In the United States, education is overseen by the American Association of Nurse anesthetists AANurse anesthetist Council on Accreditation of Nurse Anesthesia Educational Programs. The Nurse anesthetist`s education and official title vary in different nations.
Assertive community treatment	Assertive community treatment is a highly intensive and integrated approach for community mental health service delivery. Assertive community treatment programs serve people whose symptoms of mental illness result in severe functional difficulties that interfere with their ability to achieve personally meaningful recovery goals in several major areas of life: working, having friends, living independently, and so forth. The defining characteristics of Assertive community treatment include:

· a clear focus on those participants (clients) who require the most help from the service delivery system;

· an explicit mission to promote the participants' independence, rehabilitation, and recovery, and in so doing to prevent homelessness and unnecessary hospitalization;

· a primary emphasis on home visits and other in vivo (out-of-the-office) interventions, eliminating the need to transfer learned behaviors from an artificial rehabilitation or treatment setting to the 'real world';

· a participant-to-staff ratio that is low enough to allow the Assertive community treatment 'core services team' to perform virtually all of the necessary rehabilitation, treatment, and community support tasks themselves in a coordinated and efficient manner -- unlike traditional case managers, who broker or 'farm out' most of the work to other professionals;

· a 'total team approach' in which all of the staff work with all of the participants;

· an interdisciplinary assessment and service planning process that typically involves a psychiatrist and one or more nurses, social workers, substance abuse specialists, vocational rehabilitation specialists, and peer recovery specialists (individuals who have had personal, successful experience with the recovery process);

· a willingness on the part of the team to take ultimate professional responsibility for the participants' well-being in all areas of community functioning, including most especially the 'nitty-gritty' aspects of everyday life;

· a conscious effort to help people avoid crisis situations in the first place or, if that proves impossible, to intervene at any time of the day or night to keep crises from turning into unnecessary hospitalizations; and

· a promise to work with people on a time-unlimited basis, as long as they demonstrate a continuing need for this highly intensive and integrated form of professional help.

Medical Device

A Medical device is a product which is used for medical purposes in patients, in diagnosis, therapy or surgery. If applied to the body, the effect of the Medical device is primarily physical, in contrast to pharmaceutical drugs, which exert a biochemical effect. Specific regional definitions of Medical device vary slightly as detailed below.

Chapter 1. PART I: Chapter 1 - Chapter 18

Medical Practice	A Medical practice or practice of medicine is the practice of medicine, as performed by a medical practitioner--a physician (medical doctor). Typically, practicing medicine involves giving a diagnosis, prescribing a treatment for medical condition.
	In developed countries, only qualified persons--those with the appropriate licensure, certification, or registration with a relevant body, often governmental--are legally permitted to practice medicine.
Trauma	Trauma can represent:
	· Physical Trauma, an often serious and body-altering physical injury, such as the removal of a limb
	· Blunt Trauma, a type of physical Trauma caused by impact or other force applied from or with a blunt object
	· Penetrating Trauma, a type of physical Trauma in which the skin or tissues are pierced by an object
	· Psychological Trauma, an emotional or psychological injury, usually resulting from an extremely stressful or life-threatening situation
	· Post-cult Trauma, the intense emotional problems that some members of cults and new religious movements experience upon disaffection and disaffiliation
	· Trauma team, a group of healthcare workers who attend to seriously ill or injured casualties who arrive at a hospital emergency department
	· Trauma center, a hospital equipped to provide comprehensive emergency medical services to patients suffering Traumatic injuries
	· Trauma, a character associated with Avengers: The Initiative in the Marvel Universe
	· Trauma a psychological thriller directed by Marc Evans and starring Colin Firth

· Trauma a horror film directed by Dario Argento

· Trauma a medical drama set in San Francisco

· Also see Troma Entertainment, a film company specializing in independent, horror, and exploitation films

· Trauma Studios, an American computer game development company

· Trauma Center (series), a surgical based video game.

· `Day Twelve: Trauma`, a song by Ayreon on the album The Human Equation

· `Trauma` (song) by Ayumi Hamasaki

· Trauma by rapper/producer DJ Quik

· Trauma Records, a record label

· Trauma an American Heavy-metal band

· Trauma Flintstone, drag performer and actress

· Baltimore Trauma, professional paintball team from North Carolina

Risk factor

A Risk factor is a variable associated with an increased risk of disease or infection. Risk factors are correlational and not necessarily causal, because correlation does not imply causation. For example, being young cannot be said to cause measles, but young people are more at risk as they are less likely to have developed immunity during a previous epidemic.

Chapter 1. PART I: Chapter 1 - Chapter 18

Depression	Depression is a term that can refer to a wide variety of abnormal variations in an individual`s mood. If changes in an individual`s mood are persistent and cause distress or impairment in functioning, then a mood disorder may be present. Individuals with mood disorders experience extremes of emotions, for example sadness, that are higher in intensity and longer in duration than normal.
Frontier Nursing Service	The Frontier Nursing Service provides healthcare services to rural, underserved populations and educates nurse-midwives. The Service maintains six rural healthcare clinics in eastern Kentucky, the Mary Breckinridge Hospital, the Mary Breckinridge Home Health Agency, the Frontier School of Midwifery and Family Nursing and the Bed and Breakfast Inn at Wendover, Kentucky. This was founded by Mary Breckenridge.
Lark	Lark is a term used to describe a person who usually gets up early in the morning and goes to bed early in the evening. Other terms are "morning person" and "early bird". The lark is primarily diurnal, which explains the choice of the word "lark" for people who may sleep from around 10 p.m. to 6 a.m. Larks tend to feel most energetic just after they get up in the morning.
Syndrome	In medicine and psychology, the term syndrome refers to the association of several clinically recognizable features, signs (observed by a physician), symptoms (reported by the patient), phenomena or characteristics that often occur together, so that the presence of one feature alerts the physician to the presence of the others. In recent decades the term has been used outside of medicine to refer to a combination of phenomena seen in association. The term syndrome derives from its Greek roots and means literally `run together`, as the features do.
Rush	· Rush (name), a surname and given name · Rush (Thorpe Park), an amusement park ride in Surrey, UK · Rush, any of the grass-like plants in the Juncaceae family · Rush (psychology), a sudden pleasurable effect induced by a psychoactive drug

· Rush, Dublin

· Rush, Colorado

· Rush, Kentucky

· Rush, New York

· Rush, Ohio

· Rush City, Minnesota

· Rush (band), a Canadian rock band

· Rush (album), its 1974 rock album

· Rush (Darude album), a 2003 trance album

· Rush (Dean Geyer album), a 2007 pop album

· Rush (Poisonblack single), a 2006 goth rock song

· `Rush` (Aly ' AJ song), a 2005 pop song

· `Rush` (BAD song), a 1991 alternative dance song

· `Rush` (The Pillows song), a 1999 Japanese-rock song

· `Rush`, a 1993 song by Depeche Mode on Songs of Faith and Devotion

· `Rush`, a 2005 song by MYMP on Beyond Acoustic

· Rush Rush, 1991 Paula Abdul song

· Rush (1983 film), a science fiction film directed by Anthony Richmond

CRAMIOI

· Rush (1991 film), a crime film directed by Lili Fini Zanuck

· Rush (1970s TV series), a 1970s Australian historical drama

· Rush (2008 TV series), an Australian police drama

· Rush (video game series), an arcade racing series

· Rush (video game), series edition for PlayStation Portable

· Rush (computer and video games), an attack strategy

· Rush (Mega Man), a character from the video game series

· August Rush, a 2007 film

· Rush (American football), a tactic in American Football

· Rush (Australian Rules football), a tactic in Australian Rules football

· Rush, in croquet, a roquet whose aim is to move the target ball a significant distance

· USS William R. Rush, the name of more than one United States Navy ship .

Chlordiazepoxide

Chlordiazepoxide, is a sedative/hypnotic drug and benzodiazepine derivative. It is marketed under the trade names Klopoxid, Librax (also contains clidinium bromide), Libritabs, Librium, Mesural, Multum, Novapam, Risolid, Silibrin, Sonimen, Tropium, and Zetran.

Chlordiazepoxide was the first benzodiazepine to be synthesised and the discovery of Chlordiazepoxide was by pure chance.

Chapter 1. PART I: Chapter 1 - Chapter 18

Lorazepam	Lorazepam, initially marketed under the brand names Ativan and Temesta, is a benzodiazepine drug with short to medium duration of action. It has all five intrinsic benzodiazepine effects: anxiolytic, amnesic, sedative/hypnotic, anticonvulsant and muscle relaxant. It is a powerful anxiolytic, and, since its introduction in 1977, Lorazepam`s principal use has been in treating the symptom of anxiety.
Triazolam	Triazolam is a benzodiazepine derivative drug. It possesses pharmacological properties similar to that of other benzodiazepines, but it is generally only used as a sedative to treat insomnia. In addition to the hypnotic properties Triazolam possesses, amnesic, anxiolytic, sedative, anticonvulsant and muscle relaxant properties are also present.
Medicaid	Medicaid is the United States health program for eligible individuals and families with low incomes and resources. It is a means tested program that is jointly funded by the states and federal government, and is managed by the states. Among the groups of people served by Medicaid are certain eligible U.S. citizens and resident aliens, including low-income adults and their children, and people with certain disabilities.
Hospital	· Jean Manco, The Heritage of Mercy · Last Resort: Hospital Care in Canada (an illustrated historical essay) · Medieval Hospitals of England, by Rotha Mary Clay (1909 book, now in the public domain) · Directory and Ranking of more than 17000 Hospitals worldwide · Haute Autorité de santé or French National Authority for Health
Oliguria	Oliguria is the decreased production of urine. The decreased production of urine may be a sign of dehydration, renal failure, hypovolemic shock or urinary obstruction/urinary retention. It can be contrasted with anuria, which represents a more complete suppression of urination.

19

Chapter 1. PART I: Chapter 1 - Chapter 18

Anesthesiologist	An anaesthetist also 'anaesthesiologist,' is a medical doctor trained to administer anesthesia (e.g. a drug) and manage the medical care of patients before, during, and after surgery. According to Mosby's Medical Dictionary, 8th edition, 2009, anesthetist is a general term used to describe a health care professional trained to administer anesthesia to their patients. In addition, the source defines an Anesthesiologist is a physician who completes an accredited residency program in anesthesiology.
Trisomy	A Trisomy is a genetic abnormality in which there are three copies, instead of the normal two, of a particular chromosome. A Trisomy is a type of aneuploidy (an abnormal number of chromosomes). Most organisms that reproduce sexually have pairs of chromosomes in each cell, with one chromosome inherited from each parent.
Scope of practice	Scope of practice is a terminology used by state licensing boards for various professions that defines the procedures, actions, and processes that are permitted for the licensed individual. The Scope of practice is limited to that which the law allows for specific education and experience, and specific demonstrated competency. Each state has laws, licensing bodies, and regulations that describe requirements for education and training, and define Scope of practice.
Role	A Role or a social Role is a set of connected behaviors, rights and obligations as conceptualized by actors in a social situation. It is an expected or free or continously changing behavior and may have a given individual social status or social position. It is vital to both functionalist and interactionist understandings of society. Social Role posits the following about social behavior: · The division of labor in society takes the form of the interaction among heterogeneous specialized positions, we call Roles. · Social Roles included appropriate and permitted forms of behavior, guided by social norms, which are commonly known and hence determine the expectations for appropriate behavior in these Roles. · Roles are occupied by individuals, who are called actors. · When individuals approve of a social Role (i.e., they consider the Role legitimate and constructive, they will incur costs to conform to Role norms, and will also incur costs to punish those who violate Role norms.

Chapter 1. PART I: Chapter 1 - Chapter 18

21

Go to **Cram101.com** for Interactive Practice Exams for this book or virtually any of your books.
And, **NEVER** highlight a book again!

Chapter 1. PART I: Chapter 1 - Chapter 18

	· Changed conditions can render a social Role outdated or illegitimate, in which case social pressures are likely to lead to Role change.
	· The anticipation of rewards and punishments, as well as the satisfaction of behaving prosocially, account for why agents conform to Role requirmeets.
Pharmacokinetics	Pharmacokinetics is a branch of pharmacology dedicated to the determination of the fate of substances administered externally to a living organism. In practice, this discipline is applied mainly to drug substances, though in principle it concerns itself with all manner of compounds ingested or otherwise delivered externally to an organism, such as nutrients, metabolites, hormones, toxins, etc.
	Pharmacokinetics is often studied in conjunction with pharmacodynamics.
Minimum alveolar concentration	Minimum alveolar concentration , or potency, of anaesthetic vapours; in simple terms, it is defined as the concentration of the vapour in the lungs that is needed to prevent movement (motor response) in 50% of subjects in response to surgical (pain) stimulus. Thus, it is actually a median value; the use of minimum would appear to be descended from the original paper in which the concept appeared, although the term there was minimal alveolar concentration. The concept was introduced in 1965.
Licensure	Licensure refers to the granting of a license, which gives a `permission to practice.` Such licenses are usually issued in order to regulate some activity that is deemed to be dangerous or a threat to the person or the public or which involves a high level of specialized skill. The danger and skill elements inspire governments not to allow a free-for-all, but to regulate the activity, and licensing is a well-established and convenient method of regulation. Licensing includes such things as pilot and driving licenses, licenses to play professional sports, etc.
AIDS	AIDS: Acquired immune deficiency syndrome
	HIV: Human immunodeficiency virus
	CD4+: CD4+ T helper cells
	CCR5: Chemokine (C-C motif) receptor 5
	CDC: Centers for Disease Control and Prevention
	WHO: World Health Organization

PCP: Pneumocystis pneumonia

TB: Tuberculosis

MTCT: Mother-to-child transmission

HAART: Highly active antiretroviral therapy

Acquired immune deficiency syndrome or acquired immunodeficiency syndrome (AIDS) is a disease of the human immune system caused by the human immunodeficiency virus (HIV).

STI/STD: Sexually transmitted infection/disease
This condition progressively reduces the effectiveness of the immune system and leaves individuals susceptible to opportunistic infections and tumors. HIV is transmitted through direct contact of a mucous membrane or the bloodstream with a bodily fluid containing HIV, such as blood, semen, vaginal fluid, preseminal fluid, and breast milk.

Nurses

· EMTs and Paramedics work closely with emergency and critical care Nurses to stabilize life-threatening trauma and medical emergencies and to provide a seamless transfer of care from incoming ambulances to awaiting medical/surgical teams.

· Technicians: , certified medication aides in the US, are trained to administer medications in a long-term care setting. There are also phlebotomy technicians, who perform venipuncture; surgical technologist (US), and technicians trained to operate most kinds of diagnostic and laboratory equipment, such as X-ray machines, electrocardiographs, and so forth.

Evidence-based practice

· Epidemiology

· Evidence-based design

· Evidence-based management

· Evidence-based medicine

Chapter 1. PART I: Chapter 1 - Chapter 18

· Evidence-based pharmacy in developing countries

· Dynamic treatment regimes

· Dale AE (2005). `Evidence-based practice: compatibility with nursing`. Nurs Stand 19 (40): 48-53.

Fan death

Fan death is a South Korean urban legend which states that an electric fan, if left running overnight in a closed room, can cause the death of those inside (by suffocation, poisoning,). Fans manufactured and sold in Korea are equipped with a timer switch that turns them off after a set number of minutes, which users are frequently urged to set when going to sleep with a fan on. The specifics behind belief in the myth of fan-death often offer several explanations for the precise mechanism by which the fan kills.

Accreditation

Accreditation is a process in which certification of competency, authority, or credibility is presented.

Organizations that issue credentials or certify third parties against official standards are themselves formally accredited by Accreditation bodies (such as UKAS); hence they are sometimes known as 'accredited certification bodies'. The Accreditation process ensures that their certification practices are acceptable, typically meaning that they are competent to test and certify third parties, behave ethically, and employ suitable quality assurance.

Blood

Blood is a specialized bodily fluid that delivers necessary substances to the body's cells -- such as nutrients and oxygen -- and transports waste products away from those same cells.
In vertebrates, it is composed of Blood cells suspended in a liquid called Blood plasma. Plasma, which comprises 55% of Blood fluid, is mostly water (90% by volume), and contains dissolved proteins, glucose, mineral ions, hormones, carbon dioxide (plasma being the main medium for excretory product transportation), platelets and Blood cells themselves.

Blood pressure

Blood pressure is the pressure (force per unit area) exerted by circulating blood on the walls of blood vessels, and constitutes one of the principal vital signs. The pressure of the circulating blood decreases as it moves away from the heart through arteries and capillaries, and toward the heart through veins. When unqualified, the term Blood pressure usually refers to brachial arterial pressure: that is, in the major blood vessel of the upper left or right arm that takes blood away from the heart.

Clinical	Clinical can refer to:
	· clinical medical practice
	· Clinic
	· Illness
	· clinical waste, segregated for safety or security
	· clinical medical professions
	· clinical psychology
	· clinical examination; see Physical examination
	· clinical conditions, diagnosed from clinical examination alone

· clinical death

· clinical research

· clinical governance of patient care within a health system

· clinical trial, research involving patients

· clinical linguistics, linguistics applied to speech therapy .

Clinical monitoring	Clinical monitoring - Oversight and administrative efforts that monitor a participant`s health during a clinical trial. The government and other clinical trial funding agencies require data and safety monitoring boards to oversee clinical trials. They want to be certain that safety measures are in place to protect participants.
Health	At the time of the creation of the World Health Organization (WHO), in 1948, Health was defined as being `a state of complete physical, mental, and social well-being and not merely the absence of disease or infirmity`. This definition invited nations to expand the conceptual framework of their Health systems beyond issues related to the physical condition of individuals and their diseases, and it motivated us to focus our attention on what we now call social determinants of Health. Consequently, WHO challenged political, academic, community, and professional organizations devoted to improving or preserving Health to make the scope of their work explicit, including their rationale for allocating resources.
Health Care	Health care , refers to the treatment and management of illness, and the preservation of health through services offered by the medical, dental, complementary and alternative medicine, pharmaceutical, clinical laboratory sciences , nursing, and allied health professions. Health care embraces all the goods and services designed to promote health, including `preventive, curative and palliative interventions, whether directed to individuals or to populations`.

Chapter 1. PART I: Chapter 1 - Chapter 18

	Before the term Health care became popular, English-speakers referred to medicine or to the health sector and spoke of the treatment and prevention of illness and disease.
Joint	A Joint is the location at which two or more bones make contact. They are constructed to allow movement and provide mechanical support, and are classified structurally and functionally.
	Joints are mainly classified structurally and functionally.
Joint Commission	The Joint Commission, formerly the Joint Commission on Accreditation of Healthcare Organizations (Joint CommissionAHO), is a private sector United States-based not-for-profit organization. The Joint Commission operates voluntary accreditation programs for hospitals and other health care organizations. The Joint Commission accredits nearly 16,000 health care organizations and programs in the United States.
Res ipsa loquitur	Res ipsa loquitur is a common law theory on the use of circumstantial evidence in tort liability on a negligence theory. The term comes from Latin and means `the thing itself speaks,` but is more often translated `the thing speaks for itself.` The Latin sentence is found in Cicero`s speech Pro Milone . The theory allows the plaintiff to use circumstantial evidence to meet the burden of proof in negligence cases for only the first two elements: duty and breach.
Social Security	The term Social Security has several uses.
	· Social Security - the general concept of providing welfare
	· Social Security - a play by Andrew Bergman
	· Social Security - system of welfare payments in Australia
	· Social Security
	· Social Security - the United States retirement/disability program
	· Social Security Administration - the agency which administers the U.S. program
	· Social Security number - an identification number used in the U.S. to track individuals for taxation purposes

· Social Security Trust Fund - the financial accounts for the U.S. retirement program

· South African Social Security Agency - an Agency of the South African Government .

Dent v. West Virginia	Dent v. West Virginia, 129 U.S. 114 (1889), was an important United States Supreme Court case involving the reputable practice of physicians and state laws in the late nineteenth century. Frank Dent was a physician of the Eclectic sect, a group which accepted and taught the conventional medical science of the time. However, in the area of therapeutics, the Eclectics carried on a rigorous campaign against excesses of drugging and bleeding, which were still practices used by many physicians at the time.
Punitive Damages	Punitive damages are damages intended to reform or deter the defendant and others from engaging in conduct similar to that which formed the basis of the lawsuit. Although the purpose of Punitive damages is not to compensate the plaintiff, the plaintiff will in fact receive all or some portion of the punitive damage award. Punitive damages are often awarded where compensatory damages are deemed an inadequate remedy.
Consent	Consent refers to the provision of approval or assent, particularly and especially after thoughtful consideration. Consent can be either express or implied. For example, participation in a contact sport usually implies Consent to contact by other participants, when contact is permitted by the rules of the sport.
Informed consent	Informed consent is a legal condition whereby a person can be said to have given consent based upon a clear appreciation and understanding of the facts, implications and future consequences of an action. In order to give Informed consent, the individual concerned must have adequate reasoning faculties and be in possession of all relevant facts at the time consent is given. Impairments to reasoning and judgement which would make it impossible for someone to give Informed consent include such factors as severe mental retardation, severe mental illness, intoxication, severe sleep deprivation, Alzheimer's disease, or being in a coma.

Chapter 1. PART I: Chapter 1 - Chapter 18

Transfusion	Blood Transfusion is the process of transferring blood or blood-based products from one person into the circulatory system of another. Blood Transfusions can be life-saving in some situations, such as massive blood loss due to trauma, or can be used to replace blood lost during surgery. Blood Transfusions may also be used to treat a severe anaemia or thrombocytopenia caused by a blood disease.
Brace	· Brace (orthopaedic), a device used to restrict or assist body movement
	· Back Brace, a device limiting motion of the spine
	· Milwaukee Brace, a kind of back Brace used in the treatment of spinal curvatures
	· Cervical collar, also called a neck Brace, used to restrict neck movement
	· Dental Braces, a device used to reposition teeth
	· Brace (tool), a hand tool
	· Brace (theatre), a stabilizer for a piece of scenery
	· A reinforcement used in architecture, such as in timber framing
	· Brace position, a body stance used to prepare for a crash
	· The { and } symbols, also known as Braces
	· Curly bracket programming language, a programming language that uses Braces.
	· Military Brace, a body posture primarily used in military schools
	· Braces (clothing), known in American English as suspenders, elastic fabric straps used to support trousers
	· Brace (singer) , a Dutch singer

· Braces (sailing), the lines used to rotate the yards around the mast .

Extracorporeal

An Extracorporeal medical procedure is a medical procedure which is performed outside the body.

A procedure in which blood is taken from a patient's circulation to have a process applied to it before it is returned to the circulation. All of the apparatus carrying the blood outside the body is termed the Extracorporeal circuit.

· Hemodialysis

· Hemofiltration

· Plasmapheresis

· Apheresis

· Extracorporeal membrane oxygenation (ECMO)

· Cardiopulmonary bypass during open heart surgery.

Lithotripsy

Extracorporeal Shock Wave Lithotripsy is the non-invasive treatment of kidney stones (urinary calculosis) and biliary calculi (stones in the gallbladder or in the liver) using an acoustic pulse. Lithotripsy and the lithotriptor were developed in the early 1980s in Germany by Dornier Medizintechnik GmbH , and came into widespread use with the introduction of the HM-3 lithotriptor in 1983. Within a few years, ESWL became a standard treatment of calculosis.

It is estimated that more than one million patients are treated annually with ESWL in the USA alone.

Chapter 1. PART I: Chapter 1 - Chapter 18

Intentional tort	An Intentional tort is a category of torts that describes a civil wrong resulting from an intentional act on the part of the tortfeasor. The term negligence, on the other hand, pertains to a tort that simply results from the failure of the tortfeasor to take sufficient care in fulfilling a duty owed, while strict liability torts refers to situations where a party is liable for injuries no matter what precautions were taken. As a matter of public policy, damages available for Intentional torts tend to be broader and more generous than for negligent torts.
Levobupivacaine	Levobupivacaine is a local anaesthetic drug belonging to the amino amide group. It is the S-enantiomer of bupivacaine. Levobupivacaine hydrochloride is commonly marketed by AstraZeneca under the trade name Chirocaine.
Levorphanol	Levorphanol is an opioid medication used to treat severe pain. It is the laevorotary stereoisomer of the synthetic morphinan (Dromoran) and a pure opioid agonist, first described in Germany in 1946 as an orally active morphine-like analgesic. Morphinan is the parent drug and prototype of a large series of opioid and/or NMDA antagonists and opioid agonists used in medicine including nalbuphine, butorphanol, dextromethorphan, and others.
Labor law	Labor law is the body of laws, administrative rulings, and precedents which address the legal rights of, and restrictions on, working people and their organizations. As such, it mediates many aspects of the relationship between trade unions, employers and employees. In Canada, employment laws related to unionized workplaces are differentiated from those relating to particular individuals.
Rule	A rule is: · Rewrite rule, in generative grammar and computer science · Standardization, a formal and widely-accepted statement, fact, definition, or qualification · Operation, a determinate rule (method) for performing a mathematical operation and obtaining a certain result (Mathematics, Logic) · Unary operation

Chapter 1. PART I: Chapter 1 - Chapter 18

· Binary operation

· rule of inference, a function from sets of formulae to formulae (Mathematics, Logic)

· rule of thumb, principle with broad application that is not intended to be strictly accurate or reliable for every situation. Also often simply referred to as a rule

· Moral, an atomic element of a moral code for guiding choices in human behavior

· Heuristic, a quantized `rule` which shows a tendency or probability for successful function

· A regulation, as in sports

· A Production rule, as in computer science

· Procedural law, a ruleset governing the application of laws to cases

· A law, which may informally be called a `rule`

· A court ruling, a decision by a court

· In the U.S. Government, a regulation mandated by Congress, but written or expanded upon by the Executive Branch.

· Norm (sociology), an informal but widely accepted rule, concept, truth, definition, or qualification (social norms, legal norms, coding norms)

· Norm (philosophy), a kind of sentence or a reason to act, feel or believe

· `rulership` is the concept of governance by a government:

· Military rule, governance by a military body

· Monastic rule, a collection of precepts that guides the life of monks or nuns in a religious order where the superior holds the place of Christ

· Slide rule

· `rule,` a song by Ayumi Hamasaki

· `rule,` a song by rapper Nas

· `rules,` an album by the band The Whitest Boy Alive

· rules: Pyaar Ka Superhit Formula, a 2003 Bollywood film

· ruler, an instrument for measuring lengths

· rule, a component of an astrolabe, circumferator or similar instrument

· The rules, a bestselling self-help book

· rule Project (Run Up-to-date Linux Everywhere), a project that aims to use up-to-date Linux software on old PCs

· rule engine, a software system that helps managing business rules

· Ja rule, a hip hop artist

· R.U.L.E., a 2005 greatest hits album by rapper Ja rule

· `rules,` a KMFDM song

Medical record

A Medical record, health record, or medical chart is a systematic documentation of a patient`s medical history and care. The term `Medical record` is used both for the physical folder for each individual patient and for the body of information which comprises the total of each patient`s health history. Medical records are intensely personal documents and there are many ethical and legal issues surrounding them such as the degree of third-party access and appropriate storage and disposal.

Chapter 1. PART I: Chapter 1 - Chapter 18

Agonist	An Agonist is a chemical that binds to a receptor of a cell and triggers a response by the cell. An Agonist often mimics the action of a naturally occurring substance. An Agonist produces an action.
General anaesthetic	A General anaesthetic drug is an anaesthetic drug that brings about a reversible loss of consciousness. These drugs are generally administered by an anesthesia provider in order to induce or maintain general anaesthesia to facilitate surgery. Drugs given to induce or maintain general anaesthesia are either given as: · Gases or vapors (inhalational anaesthetics) · Injections (intravenous anaesthetics) Most commonly these two forms are combined, with an injection given to induce anaesthesia and a gas used to maintain it, although it is possible to deliver anaesthesia solely by inhalation or injection.
Local	Local usually refers to something nearby, or in the immediate area. It may be used in many ways, some of which are related to this general meaning, others which are not: .
Local anesthetic	A Local anesthetic is a drug that causes reversible local anesthesia and a loss of nociception. When it is used on specific nerve pathways (nerve block), effects such as analgesia and paralysis can be achieved. Clinical Local anesthetics belong to one of two classes: aminoamide and aminoester Local anesthetics.

Cram101

Chapter 1. PART I: Chapter 1 - Chapter 18

Opioid	An Opioid is a chemical that works by binding to Opioid receptors, which are found principally in the central nervous system and the gastrointestinal tract. The receptors in these two organ systems mediate both the beneficial effects and the side effects of Opioids. The analgesic effects of Opioids are due to decreased perception of pain, decreased reaction to pain as well as increased pain tolerance.
Pharmacodynamics	Pharmacodynamics is the study of the physiological effects of drugs on the body or on microorganisms or parasites within or on the body and the mechanisms of drug action and the relationship between drug concentration and effect. One dominant example is drug-receptor interactions as modeled by $$L + R \leftrightarrow L \cdot R$$ where L=ligand (drug), R=receptor (attachment site), reaction dynamics that can be studied mathematically through tools such as free energy maps. Pharmacodynamics is often summarized as the study of what a drug does to the body, whereas pharmacokinetics is the study of what the body does to a drug.
Pharmacology	Pharmacology is the study of drug action. More specifically, it is the study of the interactions that occur between a living organism and exogenous chemicals that alter normal biochemical function. If substances have medicinal properties, they are considered pharmaceuticals.
Retroperitoneal	The retroperitoneum (or extraperitoneum) is the anatomical space in the abdominal cavity behind (retro) the peritoneum. It has no specific delineating anatomical structures. Organs are Retroperitoneal if they only have peritoneum on their anterior side. The retroperitoneam can be further subdivided into the: · Perirenal space · Anterior pararenal space · Posterior pararenal space

Structures that lie behind the peritoneum are termed `Retroperitoneal`.

Measurement

In science, Measurement is the process of obtaining the magnitude of a quantity, such as length or mass, relative to a unit of Measurement, such as a meter or a kilogram. The term can also be used to refer to the result obtained after performing the process.

The word `Measurement` is derived from the Greek word `metron` which means a limited proportion.

Burn

A burn is a type of skin injury that may be caused by heat, electricity, chemicals, light, radiation, or friction. Most burns only affect the skin (epidermal tissue and dermis). Rarely deeper tissues, such as muscle, bone, and blood vessel can also be injured.

Data collection

Data collection is a term used to describe a process of preparing and collecting data - for example as part of a process improvement or similar project. The purpose of Data collection is to obtain information to keep on record, to make decisions about important issues, to pass information on to others. Primarily, data is collected to provide information regarding a specific topic.

Data collection usually takes place early on in an improvement project, and is often formalised through a Data collection plan which often contains the following activity.

· Pre collection activity - Agree goals, target data, definitions, methods

· Collection - Data collection

· Present Findings - usually involves some form of sorting analysis and/or presentation.

Procedures

An ASC is a health care facility that specializes in providing surgery, including certain pain management and diagnostic (e.g., colonoscopy) services in an outpatient setting. Overall, the services provided can be generally called procedures. In simple terms, ASC-qualified procedures can be considered procedures that are more intensive than those done in the average doctor`s office but not so intensive as to require a hospital stay.

Chapter 1. PART I: Chapter 1 - Chapter 18

Number needed to treat	The Number needed to treat (NNT) is an epidemiological measure used in assessing the effectiveness of a health-care intervention, typically a treatment with medication. The NNT is the number of patients who need to be treated in order to prevent one additional bad outcome (i.e. the number of patients that need to be treated for one to benefit compared with a control in a clinical trial). It is defined as the inverse of the absolute risk reduction.
Humans	Humans commonly refers to the species Homo sapiens , the only extant member of the Homo genus of bipedal primates in Hominidae, the great ape family. However, in some cases the term is used to refer to any member of the genus Homo.
	Humans have a highly developed brain, capable of abstract reasoning, language, introspection, and problem solving.
National Commission for the Protection of Human Subjects of Biomedical and Behavioral Research	National Commission for the Protection of Human Subjects of Biomedical and Behavioral Research was the first public national body to shape bioethics policy in the United States.
	Formed in the aftermath of the Tuskegee Experiment scandal, the Commission was created in 1974 as Title II of the National Research Act. It was part of the United States Department of Health, Education, and Welfare (DHEW) until 1978.
Nuremberg Code	The Nuremberg Code is a set of research ethics principles for human experimentation set as a result of the Subsequent Nuremberg Trials at the end of the Second World War. In August 1947, the judges delivered their verdict in the `Doctors` Trial` against Karl Brandt and several others. They also delivered their opinion on medical experimentation on human beings.
TIC	A Tic is a sudden, repetitive, nonrhythmic, stereotyped motor movement or vocalization involving discrete muscle groups. Tics can be invisible to the observer, such as abdominal tensing or toe crunching. Common motor and phonic Tics are, respectively, eye blinking and throat clearing.
Constipation	Constipation, costiveness,) experiences hard feces (faeces) that are difficult to expel. This usually happens because the colon absorbs too much water from the food. If the food moves through the gastro-intestinal tract too slowly, the colon may absorb too much water, resulting in feces that are dry and hard.

CRam101

Chapter 1. PART I: Chapter 1 - Chapter 18

Institutional review board	An Institutional review board , also known as an independent ethics committee (IEC) or ethical review board (ERB) is a committee that has been formally designated to approve, monitor, and review biomedical and behavioral research involving humans with the aim to protect the rights and welfare of the research subjects. In the United States, the Food and Drug Administration (FDA) and Department of Health and Human Services (specifically Office for Human Research Protections) regulations have empowered Institutional review boards to approve, require modifications in planned research prior to approval, or disapprove research. An Institutional review board performs critical oversight functions for research conducted on human subjects that are scientific, ethical, and regulatory.
Biotransformation	Biotransformation is the chemical modification (or modifications) made by an organism on a chemical compound. If this modification ends in mineral compounds like CO_2, NH_3^+ or H_2O, the Biotransformation is called mineralisation. Biotransformation means chemical alteration of chemicals such as (but not limited to) nutrients, amino acids, toxins, or drugs in the body.
Vaporization	Vaporization of an element or compound is a phase transition from the liquid or solid phase to gas phase. There are three types of Vaporization: evaporation, boiling and sublimation. Evaporation is a phase transition from the liquid phase to gas phase that occurs at temperatures below the boiling temperature at a given pressure.
Geriatric anesthesia	Geriatric anesthesia is the branch of medicine that studies anesthesia approach in elderly. The perioperative care of elderly patients differs from that of younger patients for a number of reasons. Some of these can be attributed to the changes that occur in the process of aging, but many are also caused by diseases that accompany seniority.
Obstetric	Obstetrics is the surgical specialty dealing with the care of women and their children during pregnancy, childbirth and postnatal. Midwifery is the non-medical equivalent. Veterinary Obstetrics is the same concept for veterinary medicine.
Carbon dioxide	Carbon dioxide is a chemical compound composed of two oxygen atoms covalently bonded to a single carbon atom. It is a gas at standard temperature and pressure and exists in Earth`s atmosphere in this state. CO_2 is a trace gas being only 0.038% of the atmosphere.

Chapter 1. PART I: Chapter 1 - Chapter 18

Selective relaxant binding agent	Selective Relaxant Binding Agents (Selective Relaxant Binding Agents) are a new class of drugs that selectively encapsulates and binds neuromuscular blocking agents (NMBAs). The first drug introduction of an Selective Relaxant Binding Agent is sugammadex. Sugammadex is a modified gamma cyclodextrin that specifically encapsulates and binds the aminosteroid NMBAs: rocuronium>vecuronium>>pancuronium.
Effective dose	An Effective dose in pharmacology is the amount of drug that produces a therapeutic response in 50% of the people taking it, sometimes also called Effective dose-50. In radiation protection it is an estimate of the stochastic effect that a non-uniform radiation dose has on a human. In pharmacology, Effective dose is the median dose that produces the desired effect of a drug.
Interaction	Interaction is a kind of action that occurs as two or more objects have an effect upon one another. The idea of a two-way effect is essential in the concept of Interaction, as opposed to a one-way causal effect. A closely related term is interconnectivity, which deals with the Interactions of Interactions within systems: combinations of many simple Interactions can lead to surprising emergent phenomena.
Lethal dose	A Lethal dose is an indication of the lethality of a given substance or type of radiation. Because resistance varies from one individual to another, the `Lethal dose` represents a dose (usually recorded as dose per kilogram of subject body weight) at which a given percentage of subjects will die. The most commonly-used lethality indicator is the Lethal dose$_{50}$ (or Lethal dose50), a dose at which 50% of subjects will die.
Pollutant Standards Index	The Pollutant Standards Index provides a uniform system of measuring pollution levels for the major air pollutants. It is based on a scale devised by the United States Environmental Protection Agency (USEPA) to provide a way for broadcasts and newspapers to report air quality on a daily basis. The Pollutant Standards Index is reported as a number on a scale of 0 to 500 and is the air quality indicator.
Diuretic	A Diuretic is any drug that elevates the rate of urination and thus provides a means of forced diuresis. There are several categories of Diuretics. All Diuretics increase the excretion of water from bodies, although each class does so in a distinct way.
Structure-activity relationships	Structure-activity relationships (SAR) are the traditional practices of medicinal chemistry which try to modify the effect or the potency (i.e. activity) of bioactive chemical compounds by modifying their chemical structure. Medinical chemists use the techniques of chemical synthesis to insert new chemical groups into the biomedical compound and test the modifications for their biological effects.

	This enables the identification and determination of the chemical groups responsible for evoking a target biological effect in the organism.
Insulin	Insulin is a hormone that is central to regulating the energy and glucose metabolism in the body. Insulin causes cells in the liver, muscle, and fat tissue to take up glucose from the blood, storing it as glycogen in the liver and muscle. Insulin stops the use of fat as an energy source.
Bronchoscopy	Bronchoscopy is a technique of visualizing the inside of the airways for diagnostic and therapeutic purposes. An instrument (bronchoscope) is inserted into the airways, usually through the nose or mouth, or occasionally through a tracheostomy. This allows the practitioner to examine the patient's airways for abnormalities such as foreign bodies, bleeding, tumors, or inflammation.
Lipid	Lipids are a broad group of naturally-occurring molecules which includes fats, waxes, sterols, fat-soluble vitamins (such as vitamins A, D, E and K), monoglycerides, diglycerides, phosphoLipids, and others. The main biological functions of Lipids include energy storage, as structural components of cell membranes, and as important signaling molecules. Lipids may be broadly defined as hydrophobic or amphiphilic small molecules; the amphiphilic nature of some Lipids allows them to form structures such as vesicles, liposomes, or membranes in an aqueous environment.
Solubility	Solubility is the property of a solid, liquid, or gaseous chemical substance called solute to dissolve in a liquid solvent to form a homogeneous solution. The Solubility of a substance strongly depends on the used solvent as well as on temperature and pressure. The pressure also affects the solution whether it is gas or liquid, like temperature.
Bioavailability	In pharmacology, Bioavailability is used to describe the fraction of an administered dose of unchanged drug that reaches the systemic circulation, one of the principal pharmacokinetic properties of drugs. By definition, when a medication is administered intravenously, its Bioavailability is 100%. However, when a medication is administered via other routes (such as orally), its Bioavailability decreases (due to incomplete absorption and first-pass metabolism).

Chapter 1. PART I: Chapter 1 - Chapter 18

Intrathecal	Intrathecal is an adjective that refers to something that happens inside the spinal canal. For example, Intrathecal immunoglobulin production means production of this substance in the spinal cord.
	As other example, an Intrathecal injection (often simply called `Intrathecal`) is an injection into the spinal canal (Intrathecal space surrounding the spinal cord), as in a spinal anaesthesia or in chemotherapy or pain management applications.
Bioequivalence	Bioequivalence is a term in pharmacokinetics used to assess the expected in vivo biological equivalence of two proprietary preparations of a drug. If two products are said to be bioequivalent it means that they would be expected to be, for all intents and purposes, the same. Birkett (2003) defined Bioequivalence by stating that, 'two pharmaceutical products are bioequivalent if they are pharmaceutically equivalent and their bioavailabilities (rate and extent of availability) after administration in the same molar dose are similar to such a degree that their effects, with respect to both efficacy and safety, can be expected to be essentially the same.
Sign	A sign is an entity which signifies another entity. A natural sign is an entity which bears a causal relation to the signified entity, as thunder is a sign of storm. A conventional sign signifies by agreement, as a full stop signifies the end of a sentence.
Sublingual Administration	Sublingual, literally `under the tongue`, from Latin, refers to the pharmacological route of administration by which drugs diffuse into the blood through tissues under the tongue. Many pharmaceuticals are designed for Sublingual administration, including cardiovascular drugs, steroids, barbiturates, enzymes, and increasingly, vitamins and minerals.
	When a chemical comes in contact with the mucous membrane beneath the tongue, or buccal mucosa, it diffuses through it.
Perfusion	In physiology, Perfusion is the process of nutritive delivery of arterial blood to a capillary bed in the biological tissue.`
	Tests of adequate Perfusion are a part of patient triage performed by medical or emergency personnel in a mass casualty incident.

Perfusion can be calculated with the following formula, where Pa is mean arterial pressure, Pv is mean venous pressure, and R is vascular resistance:

$$F = \frac{P_A - P_V}{R}$$

The term `Pa - Pv` is sometimes presented as `ΔP`, for the change in pressure.

The terms `Perfusion` and `Perfusion pressure` are sometimes used interchangeably, but the equation should make clear that resistance can have an effect on the Perfusion, but not on the Perfusion pressure.

Drug metabolism	Drug metabolism is the metabolism of drugs, their biochemical modification or degradation, usually through specialized enzymatic systems. This is a form of xenobiotic metabolism. Drug metabolism often converts lipophilic chemical compounds into more readily excreted polar products.
Metabolism	Metabolism is the set of chemical reactions that happen in living organisms to maintain life. These processes allow organisms to grow and reproduce, maintain their structures, and respond to their environments. Metabolism is usually divided into two categories.
Hydrocodone	Hydrocodone or dihydrocodeinone is a semi-synthetic opioid derived from two of the naturally occurring opiates, codeine and thebaine. Hydrocodone is an orally active narcotic analgesic (pain reliever) and antitussive (cough suppressant). It is commonly available in tablet, capsule, and syrup form, and is often compounded with other analgesics like paracetamol or ibuprofen.
Enzyme	Enzymes are mainly proteins, that catalyze (i.e., increase the rates of) chemical reactions. In enzymatic reactions, the molecules at the beginning of the process are called substrates, and the Enzyme converts them into different molecules, called the products. Almost all processes in a biological cell need Enzymes to occur at significant rates.
DRESS syndrome	`DRESS syndrome stands f) with Eosinophilia and Systemic Symptoms. It is also known as Drug Hypersensitivity Syndrome. The symptoms of DRESS syndrome usually begin 1 to 8 weeks after exposure to the offending drug.
Capacitance	

Chapter 1. PART I: Chapter 1 - Chapter 18

In electromagnetism and electronics, Capacitance is the ability of a body to hold an electrical charge. Capacitance is also a measure of the amount of electric charge stored (or separated) for a given electric potential. A common form of charge storage device is a parallel-plate capacitor.

Disease

A Disease or medical condition is an abnormal condition of an organism that impairs bodily functions, associated with specific symptoms and signs. It may be caused by external factors, such as invading organisms, or it may be caused by internal dysfunctions, such as autoimmune Diseases.
In human beings, `Disease` is often used more broadly to refer to any condition that causes pain, dysfunction, distress, social problems, and/or death to the person afflicted, or similar problems for those in contact with the person.

Gender

Gender is the wide set of characteristics that are seen to distinguish between male and female entities, extending from one`s biological sex to, in humans, one`s social role or Gender identity. As a word, it has more than one valid definition. In linguistics, it refers to characteristics of words.

Polymorphism

Polymorphism in biology occurs when two or more clearly different phenotypes exist in the same population of a species -- in other words, the occurrence of more than one form or morph. In order to be classified as such, morphs must occupy the same habitat at the same time and belong to a panmictic population (one with random mating).

Polymorphism is common in nature; it is related to biodiversity, genetic variation and adaptation; it usually functions to retain variety of form in a population living in a varied environment.

Genetics

Genetics a discipline of biology, is the science of heredity and variation in living organisms. The fact that living things inherit traits from their parents has been used since prehistoric times to improve crop plants and animals through selective breeding. However, the modern science of Genetics, which seeks to understand the process of inheritance, only began with the work of Gregor Mendel in the mid-nineteenth century.

Computed tomography

Computed tomography is a medical imaging method employing tomography created by computer processing. Digital geometry processing is used to generate a three-dimensional image of the inside of an object from a large series of two-dimensional X-ray images taken around a single axis of rotation.

Chapter 1. PART I: Chapter 1 - Chapter 18

	Computed tomography produces a volume of data which can be manipulated, through a process known as `windowing`, in order to demonstrate various bodily structures based on their ability to block the X-ray/Röntgen beam.
Cardiac output	Cardiac output (Q) is the volume of blood being pumped by the heart, in particular by a ventricle in a minute. This is measured in dm^3 min^{-1} (1 dm^3 equals 1000 cm^3 or 1 litre). An average Cardiac output would be 5L.min^{-1} for a human male and 4.5L.min^{-1} for a female.
Dose concentration	Dose concentration is the measure of the ratio of the mass of the drug to the volume that contains it, often measured in units of moles/m^3.
Ventilation	Ventilation is the intentional movement of air from outside a building to the inside. It is the V in HVAC. With clothes dryers, and combustion equipment such as water heaters, boilers, fireplaces, and wood stoves, their exhausts are often called vents or flues -- this should not be confused with Ventilation. The vents or flues carry the products of combustion which have to be expelled from the building in a way which does not cause harm to the occupants of the building.
Air embolism	An Air embolism is a pathological condition caused by gas bubbles in a vascular system. The most common context is a human body, in which case it refers to gas bubbles in the bloodstream (embolism in a medical context refers to any large moving mass or defect in the blood stream). However Air embolisms may also occur in the xylem of vascular plants, especially when suffering from water stress.
Blood flow	Blood flow is the flow of blood in the cardiovascular system. It can be calculated by dividing the vascular resistance into the pressure gradient. Mathematically, Blood flow is described by Darcy's law (which can be viewed as the fluid equivalent of Ohm's law) and approximately by Hagen-Poiseuille equation.
Cerebral blood flow	Cerebral blood flow is the blood supply to the brain in a given time. In an adult, Cerebral blood flow is typically 750 millitres per minute or 15% of the cardiac output. This equates to 50 to 54 millilitres of blood per 100 grams of brain tissue per minute.

Chapter 1. PART I: Chapter 1 - Chapter 18

Cardiovascular system	The circulatory system is an organ system that passes nutrients (such as amino acids and electrolytes), gases, hormones, blood cells, etc. to and from cells in the body to help fight diseases and help stabilize body temperature and pH to maintain homeostasis. This system may be seen strictly as a blood distribution network, but some consider the circulatory system as composed of the Cardiovascular system, which distributes blood, and the lymphatic system, which distributes lymph.
Respiratory system	The respiratory system`s function is to allow gas exchange to all parts of the body. The space between the alveoli and the capillaries, the anatomy or structure of the exchange system, and the precise physiological uses of the exchanged gases vary depending on the organism. In humans and other mammals, for example, the anatomical features of the respiratory system include airways, lungs, and the respiratory muscles.
Kidney	The Kidneys are paired organs, which have the production of urine as their primary function. Kidneys are seen in many types of animals, including vertebrates and some invertebrates. They are an essential part of the urinary system, but have several secondary functions concerned with homeostatic functions.
Kidneys	The Kidneys are paired organs, which have the production of urine as their primary function. Kidneys are seen in many types of animals, including vertebrates and some invertebrates. They are an essential part of the urinary system, but have several secondary functions concerned with homeostatic functions.
Liver	The liver is a vital organ present in vertebrates and some other animals. It has a wide range of functions, including detoxification, protein synthesis, and production of biochemicals necessary for digestion. The liver is necessary for survival; there is currently no way to compensate for the absence of liver function.
Barbiturates	Barbiturates are drugs that act as central nervous system depressants, and, by virtue of this, they produce a wide spectrum of effects, from mild sedation to total anesthesia. They are also effective as anxiolytics, hypnotics and as anticonvulsants. They have addiction potential, both physical and psychological.
Coma	In medicine, a Coma is a profound state of unconsciousness. A Comatose person cannot be awakened, fails to respond normally to pain or light, does not have sleep-wake cycles, and does not take voluntary actions. Coma may result from a variety of conditions, including intoxication, metabolic abnormalities, central nervous system diseases, acute neurologic injuries such as stroke, and hypoxia.

Chapter 1. PART I: Chapter 1 - Chapter 18

Chemical structure	A Chemical structure includes molecular geometry, electronic structure and crystal structure of a chemical compound. Molecular geometry refers to the spatial arrangement of atoms in a molecule and the chemical bonds that hold the atoms together. Molecular geometry can range from the very simple, such as diatomic oxygen or nitrogen molecules, to the very complex, such as protein or DNA molecules.
Pain management	Pain management is the medical discipline concerned with the relief of pain. Acute pain, such pain resulting from trauma, often has a reversible cause and may require only transient measures and correction of the underlying problem. In contrast, chronic pain often results from conditions that are difficult to diagnose and treat, and that may take a long time to reverse.
Etomidate	Etomidate is a short acting intravenous anaesthetic agent used for the induction of general anaesthesia and for sedation for short procedures such as reduction of dislocated joints and cardioversion. It was discovered at Janssen Pharmaceutica in 1964. Etomidate, a hypnotic is a carboxylated imidazole derivative.
Ketamine	Ketamine is a drug used in human and veterinary medicine developed by Parke-Davis (today a part of Pfizer) in 1962. Its hydrochloride salt is sold as Ketanest, Ketaset, and Ketalar. Pharmacologically, Ketamine is classified as an NMDA receptor antagonist. At high, fully anesthetic level doses, Ketamine has also been found to bind to opioid µ receptors and sigma receptors.
Propofol	Propofol is a short-acting, intravenously administered hypnotic agent. Its uses include the induction and maintenance of general anesthesia, sedation for mechanically ventilated adults, and procedural sedation. Propofol is also commonly used in veterinary medicine.
Alprazolam	Alprazolam, also known under the trade names Xanax, Xanor, Alprax, and Niravam, is a highly potent short-acting drug of the benzodiazepine class. It is primarily used to treat moderate to severe anxiety disorders (e.g., social anxiety disorder) and panic attacks, and is used as an adjunctive treatment for anxiety associated with moderate depression. It is also available in an extended-release form, Xanax XR, both of which are now available in generic form.
Flurazepam	Flurazepam is a drug which is a benzodiazepine derivative. It possesses anxiolytic, anticonvulsant, sedative and skeletal muscle relaxant properties. It produces a metabolite with a very long half-life (40-250 hours), which may stay in the bloodstream for up to four days.

Chapter 1. PART I: Chapter 1 - Chapter 18

Midazolam	Midazolam is a short-acting drug in the benzodiazepine class that is used for treatment of acute seizures and for inducing sedation and amnesia before medical procedures. It has potent anxiolytic, amnestic, hypnotic, anticonvulsant, skeletal muscle relaxant, and sedative properties. Midazolam has a fast recovery time and is the most commonly used benzodiazepine as a premedication for sedation; less commonly it is used for induction and maintenance of anesthesia.
Nodes of Ranvier	Nodes of Ranvier are the gaps (approximately 1 micrometer in length) formed between the myelin sheaths generated by different cells. A myelin sheath is a many-layered coating, largely composed of a fatty substance called myelin, that wraps around the axon of a neuron and very efficiently insulates it. At Nodes of Ranvier, the axonal membrane is uninsulated and therefore capable of generating electrical activity.
Peripheral	A Peripheral is a device attached to a host computer but not part of it whose primary functionality is dependent upon the host, and can therefore be considered as expanding the host`s capabilities, while not forming part of the system`s core architecture. Examples are printers, scanners, tape drives, microphones, speakers, webcams, and cameras. Whether something is a Peripheral or part of a computer is not always clearly demarcated; a video capture card inside a computer case is not part of the core computer but is contained in the case.
Schwann cell	Schwann cells are glia of the peripheral nervous system (PNS). They are involved in many important aspects of peripheral nerve biology; the conduction of nervous impulses along axons, nerve development and regeneration, trophic support for neurons, production of the nerve extracellular matrix and presentation of antigens to T-lymphocytes. Charcot-Marie-Tooth disease (CMT), Guillain-Barré syndrome (GBS), schwannomatosis and chronic inflammatory demyelinating polyneuropathy (CIDP) are all neuropathies involving Schwann cells.
Schwann cells	Schwann cells are glia of the peripheral nervous system (PNS). They are involved in many important aspects of peripheral nerve biology; the conduction of nervous impulses along axons, nerve development and regeneration, trophic support for neurons, production of the nerve extracellular matrix and presentation of antigens to T-lymphocytes. Charcot-Marie-Tooth disease (CMT), Guillain-Barré syndrome (GBS), schwannomatosis and chronic inflammatory demyelinating polyneuropathy (CIDP) are all neuropathies involving Schwann cells.

Chapter 1. PART I: Chapter 1 - Chapter 18

Electrophysiology	Electrophysiology is the study of the electrical properties of biological cells and tissues. It involves measurements of voltage change or electric current on a wide variety of scales from single ion channel proteins to whole organs like the heart. In neuroscience, it includes measurements of the electrical activity of neurons, and particularly action potential activity.
Evoked Potential	An Evoked potential is an electrical potential recorded from the nervous system of a human or other animal following presentation of a stimulus, as distinct from spontaneous potentials as detected by electroencephalography (EEG) or electromyography (EMG).
	Evoked potential amplitudes tend to be low, ranging from less than a microvolt to several microvolts, compared to tens of microvolts for EEG, millivolts for EMG, and often close to a volt for ECG. To resolve these low-amplitude potentials against the background of ongoing EEG, ECG, EMG and other biological signals and ambient noise, signal averaging is usually required. The signal is time-locked to the stimulus and most of the noise occurs randomly, allowing the noise to be averaged out with averaging of repeated responses.
Lung	The Lung or pulmonary system is the essential respiration organ in air-breathing animals, including most tetrapods, a few fish and a few snails. In mammals and the more complex life forms, the two Lungs are located in the chest on either side of the heart. Their principal function is to transport oxygen from the atmosphere into the bloodstream, and to release carbon dioxide from the bloodstream into the atmosphere.
Membrane	A Membrane is a layer of material which serves as a selective barrier between two phases and remains impermeable to specific particles, molecules, or substances when exposed to the action of a driving force. Some components are allowed passage by the Membrane into a permeate stream, whereas others are retained by it and accumulate in the retentate stream.
	Membranes can be of various thickness, with homogeneous or heterogeneous structure.
Membrane potential	Membrane potential is the voltage difference (or electrical potential difference) between the interior and exterior of a cell. All animal cells are surrounded by a plasma membrane composed of a lipid bilayer with many diverse protein assemblages embedded in it. The fluid on both sides of the membrane contains high concentrations of mobile ions, of which sodium (Na^+), potassium (K^+), chloride (Cl^-), and calcium (Ca^{2+}) are the most important.
Nerve	A Nerve is an enclosed, cable-like bundle of peripheral axons (the long, slender projections of neurons). A Nerve provides a common pathway for the electrochemical Nerve impulses that are transmitted along each of the axons. Nerves are found only in the peripheral nervous system.

Chapter 1. PART I: Chapter 1 - Chapter 18

Neuron	A neuron is an electrically excitable cell that processes and transmits information by electrochemical signaling, via connections with other cells called synapses. neurons are the core components of the nervous system, which includes the brain, spinal cord, and peripheral ganglia. A number of specialized types of neurons exist: sensory neurons respond to touch, sound, light and numerous other stimuli affecting cells of the sensory organs that then send signals to the spinal cord and brain.
Methemoglobinemia	Methemoglobinemia is a disorder characterized by the presence of a higher than normal level of methemoglobin (metHb) in the blood. Methemoglobin is a form of hemoglobin that does not bind oxygen. When its concentration is elevated in red blood cells, tissue hypoxia can occur.
QRS complex	The QRS complex is a recording of a single heartbeat on the ECG that corresponds to the depolarization of the right and left ventricles. Ventricles contain more muscle mass than the atria, therefore the QRS complex is considerably larger than the P wave. The His/Purkinje specialised muscle cells coordinate the depolarization of both ventricles, the QRS complex is 80 to 120 ms in duration represented by three small squares or less, but any abnormality of conduction takes longer and causes widened QRS complexes.
Ropivacaine	Ropivacaine is a local anaesthetic drug belonging to the amino amide group. The name Ropivacaine refers to both the racemate and the marketed S-enantiomer. Ropivacaine hydrochloride is commonly marketed by AstraZeneca under the trade name Naropin.
Epinephrine	Epinephrine is a hormone and neurotransmitter. When produced in the body it increases heart rate, contracts blood vessels and dilates air passages and participates in the `fight or flight` response of the sympathetic nervous system. It is a catecholamine, a sympathomimetic monoamine produced only by the adrenal glands from the amino acids phenylalanine and tyrosine.
Tetracaine	Tetracaine is a potent local anesthetic of the ester group. It is mainly used topically in ophthalmology and as an antipruritic, and it has been used in spinal anesthesia. In biomedical research, Tetracaine is used to alter the function of calcium release channels (ryanodine receptors) that control the release of calcium from intracellular stores.
Nerve block	Regional Nerve blockade, or more commonly Nerve block, is a general term used to refer to the injection of local anesthetic onto or near nerves for temporary control of pain. It can also be used as a diagnostic tool to identify specific nerves as pain generators. Permanent Nerve block can be produced by destruction of nerve tissue.

Chapter 1. PART I: Chapter 1 - Chapter 18

Symptoms	A symptom is a departure from normal function or feeling which is noticed by a patient, indicating the presence of disease or abnormality. A symptom is subjective, observed by the patient, and not measured. Symptoms may be chronic, relapsing or remitting.
Fentanyl	Fentanyl -- brand names include Actiq, Durogesic, Duragesic, Fentora, Onsolis, Sublimaze and Instanyl -- is a synthetic primary μ-opioid agonist commonly used to treat chronic breakthrough pain and is commonly used in pre-procedures. It is approximately 100 times more potent than morphine, with 100 micrograms of Fentanyl approximately equivalent to 10 mg of morphine and 75 mg of pethidine (meperidine) in analgesic activity. It has an LD_{50} of 3.1 milligrams per kilogram in rats, 0.03 milligrams per kilogram in monkeys, and an undetermined LD_{50} in humans.
Diascordium	In pre-modern medicine, Diascordium is a kind of electuary, or opiate, first described by Fracastorius, and denominated from the dried leaves of scordium, which is an ingredient therein. The other ingredients are red roses, bole, storax, cinnamon, cassia lignea (coarse bark of Cinnamomum cassia), dittany, tormentil roots, bistort, gentian, galbanum, amber, terra sigillata, opium, long pepper, ginger, mel rosatum, and malmsey. It was used against malignant fevers, the plague, worms, colic, to promote sleep, and resist putrefaction.
Intraocular pressure	Intraocular pressure is the fluid pressure of the aqueous humor inside the eye. Intraocular pressure is mainly determined by the coupling of the production of aqueous humor and the drainage of aqueous humor mainly through the trabecular meshwork located in the anterior chamber angle. Intraocular pressure is measured with a tonometer.
Alfentanil	Alfentanil is a potent but short-acting synthetic opioid analgesic drug, used for anaesthesia in surgery. It is an analogue of fentanyl with around 1/10 the potency of fentanyl and around 1/3 of the duration of action, but with an onset of effects 4x faster than fentanyl. It is an OP3 mu-agonist.
Codeine	Codeine or methylmorphine is an opiate used for its analgesic, antitussive, and antidiarrheal properties.

Codeine is a natural alkaloid found in opium poppy, a plant in the papaveraceae family. Opium poppy has been cultivated and utilized throughout human history for a variety of medicinal (analgesic, anti-tussive, anti-diarrheal..).

Pethidine

Pethidine or meperidine (USAN) ; Petidin Dolargan ; Dolestine; Dolosal; Dolsin; Mefedina) is a fast-acting opioid analgesic drug. In the United States and Canada, it is more commonly known as meperidine or by its brand name Demerol.

Pethidine was the first synthetic opioid synthesized in 1932 as a potential anti-spasmodic agent by the chemist Otto Eislib.

Pentazocine

Pentazocine is a synthetically-prepared prototypical mixed agonist-antagonist narcotic (opioid analgesic) drug of the benzomorphan class of opioids used to treat mild to moderately severe pain. Pentazocine is sold under several brand names, such as Fortral, Talwin NX (with the mu-antagonist naloxone, will cause withdrawal in opioid dependent persons), Talwin, Talwin PX (without naloxone), Fortwin (Lactate injectable form) and Talacen (with acetaminophen). This compound may exist as one of two enantiomers, named (+)-Pentazocine and (-)-Pentazocine.

Remifentanil

Remifentanil is a potent ultra short-acting synthetic opioid analgesic drug. It is given to patients during surgery to relieve pain and as an adjunct to an anaesthetic. Remifentanil is used for sedation as well as combined with other medications for use in general anesthesia.

Buprenorphine

Buprenorphine is a semi-synthetic opiate with partial agonist actions at the mu opioid receptor and ORL1/nociceptin receptor and antagonist actions at other opioid receptors. Buprenorphine hydrochloride was first marketed in the 1980s by Reckitt ' Colman (now Reckitt Benckiser) as an analgesic, available generally as Temgesic 0.2 mg sublingual tablets, and as Buprenex in a 0.3 mg/ml injectable formulation. In October 2002, the Food and Drug Administration (FDA) of the United States of America additionally approved Suboxone and Subutex, Buprenorphine`s high-dose sublingual pill preparations for opioid addiction, and as such the drug is now also used for this purpose.

Desflurane

Desflurane is a highly fluorinated methyl ethyl ether used for maintenance of general anesthesia. Together with sevoflurane, it is gradually replacing isoflurane for human use, except in the third world where its high cost precludes its use. It has the most rapid onset and offset of the volatile anesthetic drugs used for general anesthesia due to its low solubility in blood.

Nalbuphine	Nalbuphine is a synthetic opioid used commercially as an analgesic under a variety of trade names, including Nubain. It is noteworthy in part for the fact that at low dosages, it is found much more effective by women than by men, and may even increase pain in men, leading to its discontinuation in the UK in 2003.
	Nalbuphine is a semi-synthetic narcotic agonist-antagonist analgesic of the phenanthrene series.
Sufentanil	Sufentanil is a powerful synthetic opioid analgesic drug, approximately 5 to 10 times more potent than its analog, Fentanyl. Sufentanil is marketed for use by specialist centres under different trade names, such as Sufenta and Sufentil (India, by Claris Lifesciences Ltd).. Sufentanil was synthesised at Janssen Pharmaceutica in 1974.
Tramadol	Tramadol is a centrally-acting analgesic, used for treating moderate to moderately severe pain. The drug has a wide range of applications, including treatment for restless leg syndrome, acid reflux, and fibermyosis.
	Tramadol was developed by the German pharmaceutical company Grünenthal GmbH in the late 1970s.
Nalmefene	Nalmefene is an opioid receptor antagonist used primarily in the management of alcohol dependence, and also has been investigated for the treatment of other addictions such as pathological gambling and addiction to shopping.
	Nalmefene is an opiate derivative similar in both structure and activity to the opiate antagonist naltrexone. Advantages of Nalmefene relative to naltrexone include longer half-life, greater oral bioavailability and no observed dose-dependent liver toxicity.
Neurosurgery	Neurosurgery is the surgery discipline focused on treating the central nervous system, peripheral nervous systems and spinal column diseases amenable to surgical intervention.

Chapter 1. PART I: Chapter 1 - Chapter 18

Neurosurgery generally has the longest training period of all the medical specialties; in America, the neurosurgeon must complete the eight years of pre-medical and medical education, a one year-long surgical internship (where this is not a part of the residency), and five to seven years of Neurosurgery residency. Many neurosurgeons pursue an additional one to three years of training in a subspecialty fellowship (like pediatric Neurosurgery, epilepsy, tremor, or stroke (`functional`) Neurosurgery, microNeurosurgery, endovascular or open vascular Neurosurgery, or neuro-oncological surgery).

Fracture	A fracture is the (local) separation of an object or material into two, or more, pieces under the action of stress.
	The word fracture is often applied to bones of living creatures, or to crystals or crystalline materials, such as gemstones or metal. Sometimes, in crystalline materials, individual crystals fracture without the body actually separating into two or more pieces.
Suxamethonium	Suxamethonium, also known as succinylcholine, is a paralytic drug used to induce muscle relaxation and short term paralysis, usually to make endotracheal intubation possible. Suxamethonium is sold under the trade names Anectine and Scoline.
	Suxamethonium acts as a depolarizing neuromuscular blocker.
Cardiac arrest	A Cardiac arrest, also known as cardiopulmonary arrest or circulatory arrest, is the abrupt cessation of normal circulation of the blood due to failure of the heart to contract effectively during systole. A Cardiac arrest is different from (but may be caused by) a heart attack or myocardial infarction, where blood flow to the still-beating heart is interrupted (as in cardiogenic shock).
	`Arrested` blood circulation prevents delivery of oxygen to all parts of the body.
Rhabdomyolysis	Rhabdomyolysis is the rapid breakdown (lysis) of skeletal muscle (rhabdomyo) due to injury to muscle tissue. The muscle damage may be caused by physical (e.g., crush injury), chemical, or biological factors. The destruction of the muscle leads to the release of the breakdown products of damaged muscle cells into the bloodstream; some of these, such as myoglobin (a protein), are harmful to the kidney and may lead to acute kidney failure.

Chapter 1. PART I: Chapter 1 - Chapter 18

Rocuronium	Rocuronium is an aminosteroid non-depolarizing (that is, it does not cause initial stimulation of muscles before weakening them) neuromuscular blocker or muscle relaxant used in modern anaesthesia, to facilitate endotracheal intubation and to provide skeletal muscle relaxation during surgery or mechanical ventilation.

Introduced in 1994, Rocuronium has rapid onset, and intermediate duration of action. It is marketed under the trade name of Zemuron in the United States and Esmeron in most other countries. |
| Atracurium besylate | Atracurium besylate is a neuromuscular-blocking drug or skeletal muscle relaxant in the category of non-depolarizing neuromuscular-blocking drugs, used adjunctively in anesthesia to facilitate endotracheal intubation and to provide skeletal muscle relaxation during surgery or mechanical ventilation. Atracurium is classified as an intermediate-duration non-depolarizing neuromuscular blocking agent.

Atracurium besylate was first synthesized in 1974 by George H. Dewar, a pharmacist and a medicinal chemistry doctoral candidate in John B. Stenlake's medicinal chemistry research group in the Department of Pharmacy at the Strathclyde University, Scotland. |
| Aspirin | Aspirin is a salicylate drug, often used as an analgesic to relieve minor aches and pains, as an antipyretic to reduce fever, and as an anti-inflammatory medication.

Aspirin also has an antiplatelet effect by inhibiting the production of thromboxane, which under normal circumstances binds platelet molecules together to create a patch over damage of the walls within blood vessels. Because the platelet patch can become too large and also block blood flow, locally and downstream, Aspirin is also used long-term, at low doses, to help prevent heart attacks, strokes, and blood clot formation in people at high risk for developing blood clots. |
| Atenolol | Atenolol is a selective β_1 receptor antagonist, a drug belonging to the group of beta blockers (sometimes written β-blockers), a class of drugs used primarily in cardiovascular diseases. Introduced in 1976, Atenolol was developed as a replacement for propranolol in the treatment of hypertension. The chemical works by slowing down the heart and reducing its workload. |

Chapter 1. PART I: Chapter 1 - Chapter 18

Cisatracurium	Cisatracurium is a neuromuscular blocking drug or skeletal muscle relaxant in the category of non-depolarizing neuromuscular-blocking drugs, used adjunctively in anesthesia to facilitate endotracheal intubation and to provide skeletal muscle relaxation during surgery or mechanical ventilation. It is a bisbenzyltetrahydroisoquinolinium agent with an intermediate duration of action. Cisatracurium is one of the ten isomers of the parent molecule, atracurium.
Cimetidine	Cimetidine is a histamine H_2-receptor antagonist that inhibits the production of acid in the stomach. It is largely used in the treatment of heartburn and peptic ulcers. It is marketed by GlaxoSmithKline under the trade name Tagamet .
Edrophonium	Edrophonium is a readily reversible acetylcholinesterase inhibitor. It prevents breakdown of the neurotransmitter acetylcholine and acts by competitively inhibiting the enzyme acetylcholinesterase, mainly at the neuromuscular junction. It is sold under the trade names Tensilon, Enlon and Reversol.
Pyridostigmine	Pyridostigmine is a parasympathomimetic and a reversible cholinesterase inhibitor. Since it is a quaternary amine, it is poorly absorbed in the gut and doesn`t cross the blood-brain barrier, except possibly in stressful conditions. In a synapse, action potentials are conducted along motor nerves to their terminals where they initiate a Ca2+ influx and the release of acetylcholine (ACh).
Sugammadex	Sugammadex (designation Org 25969, tradename Bridion) is a novel agent for reversal of neuromuscular blockade by the agent rocuronium in general anaesthesia. It is the first selective relaxant binding agent (SRBA). On January 3, 2008, Schering-Plough submitted a New Drug Application to the US Food and Drug Administration for Sugammadex, but the FDA rejected the application on August 2008.
Anticholinergic	An Anticholinergic agent is a substance that blocks the neurotransmitter acetylcholine in the central and the peripheral nervous system. An example of an Anticholinergic is dicyclomine, and the classic example is atropine. Anticholinergics are administered to reduce the effects mediated by acetylcholine on acetylcholine receptors in neurons through competitive inhibition.
Muscle	Muscle is the contractile tissue of animals and is derived from the mesodermal layer of embryonic germ cells. Muscle cells contain contractile filaments that move past each other and change the size of the cell. They are classified as skeletal, cardiac, or smooth Muscles.
Paralysis	Paralysis is the complete loss of muscle function for one or more muscle groups. Paralysis can cause loss of feeling or loss of mobility in the affected area.

Chapter 1. PART I: Chapter 1 - Chapter 18

	Paralysis is most often caused by damage to the nervous system, especially the spinal cord.
ACE inhibitors	ACE inhibitors or angiotensin-converting enzyme inhibitors, are a group of pharmaceuticals that are used primarily in treatment of hypertension and congestive heart failure, in some cases as the drugs of first choice.
	ACE inhibitors are used primarily in the treatment of hypertension,though they are also sometimes used in those with cardiac failure,renal disease,or systemic sclerosis
	This system is activated in response to hypotension, decreased sodium concentration in the distal tubule, decreased blood volume and renal sympathetic nerve stimulation. In such a situation, the kidneys release renin which cleaves the liver-derived angiotensinogen into angiotensin I. Angiotensin I is then converted to angiotensin II via the ACE in the pulmonary circulation as well as in the endothelium of blood vessels in many parts of the body.
Catecholamines	Catecholamines are sympathomimetic `fight-or-flight` hormones that are released by the adrenal glands in response to stress. They are part of the sympathetic nervous system.
	They are called Catecholamines because they contain a catechol group, and are derived from the amino acid tyrosine.
Tyrosine	Tyrosine or 4-hydroxyphenylalanine, is one of the 20 amino acids that are used by cells to synthesize proteins. It is a non-essential amino acid with a polar side group. The word `Tyrosine` is from the Greek tyros, meaning cheese, as it was first discovered in 1846 by German chemist Justus von Liebig in the protein casein from cheese.
Dopamine	Dopamine is a neurotransmitter that occurs in a wide variety of animals, including both vertebrates and invertebrates. In the brain, this phenethylamine functions as a neurotransmitter, activating the five types of Dopamine receptors--D_1, D_2, D_3, D_4, and D_5--and their variants. Dopamine is produced in several areas of the brain, including the substantia nigra and the ventral tegmental area.
Humulin	Humulin is the brand name for a group of biosynthetic human insulin products, originally developed by Genentech in 1978 (Generic name insulin isophane) and later acquired by Eli Lilly and Company, the company who arguably facilitated the product`s approval with the U.S. Food and Drug Administration.

Clam101

91

Chapter 1. PART I: Chapter 1 - Chapter 18

	Humulin is synthesized in a laboratory strain of Escherichia coli bacteria which has been genetically altered to produce biosynthetic human insulin. The synthesized insulin is then combined with other compounds or types of insulin which affect its shelf life and absorption.
Dobutamine	Dobutamine is a sympathomimetic drug used in the treatment of heart failure and cardiogenic shock. Its primary mechanism is direct stimulation of β_1 receptors of the sympathetic nervous system. Dobutamine was developed by a laboratory led by Drs.
Norepinephrine	Noradrenaline (BAN) is a catecholamine with dual roles as a hormone and a neurotransmitter. As a stress hormone, Norepinephrine affects parts of the brain where attention and responding actions are controlled. Along with epinephrine, Norepinephrine also underlies the fight-or-flight response, directly increasing heart rate, triggering the release of glucose from energy stores, and increasing blood flow to skeletal muscle.
Dexmedetomidine	Dexmedetomidine is a sedative medication used by intensive care units and anesthesiologists, and is marketed under the brand name Precedex (Hospira, Inc). in the United States. It is relatively unique in its ability to provide sedation without causing respiratory depression.
Ephedrine	Ephedrine is a sympathomimetic amine commonly used as a stimulant, appetite suppressant, concentration aid, decongestant, and to treat hypotension associated with anaesthesia. Ephedrine is similar in structure to the (semi-synthetic) derivatives amphetamine and methamphetamine. Chemically, it is an alkaloid derived from various plants in the genus Ephedra (family Ephedraceae).
Phenylephrine	Phenylephrine or Neo-Synephrine is an α_1-adrenergic receptor agonist used primarily as a decongestant, as an agent to dilate the pupil, and to increase blood pressure. Phenylephrine has recently been marketed as a substitute for pseudoephedrine (e.g., Pfizer`s Sudafed (Original Formulation)), but there are recent claims that oral Phenylephrine may be no more effective as a decongestant than a placebo . Phenylephrine is used as a decongestant sold as an oral medicine, as a nasal spray, or as eye drops.

Chapter 1. PART I: Chapter 1 - Chapter 18

Diclofenac	Diclofenac is a non-steroidal anti-inflammatory drug (NSAID) taken to reduce inflammation and as an analgesic reducing pain in conditions such as arthritis or acute injury. It can also be used to reduce menstrual pain, dysmenorrhea. The name is derived from its chemical name: 2-(2,6-dichloranilino)phenylacetic acid.
Endocarditis	Endocarditis is an inflammation of the inner layer of the heart, the endocardium. It usually involves the heart valves (native or prosthetic valves). Other structures which may be involved include the interventricular septum, the chordae tendinae, the mural endocardium, or even on intracardiac devices.
Infective endocarditis	Infective endocarditis is a form of endocarditis caused by infectious agents. The agents are usually bacterial, but other organisms can also be responsible. The valves of the heart do not receive any dedicated blood supply.
Sodium	Sodium is a metallic element with a symbol Na and atomic number 11. It is a soft, silvery-white, highly reactive metal and is a member of the alkali metals within `group 1` . It has only one stable isotope, ^{23}Na. Elemental Sodium was first isolated by Sir Humphry Davy in 1806 by passing an electric current through molten Sodium hydroxide.
Phenoxybenzamine	Phenoxybenzamine is a non-specific, irreversible alpha blocker. It is used in the treatment of hypertension, and specifically that caused by pheochromocytoma. It has a slower onset and a longer lasting effect compared with other alpha blockers.
Renin	Renin, also known as angiotensinogenase is an enzyme that participates in the body`s Renin-angiotensin system (RAS) that mediates extracellular volume (i.e. that of the blood plasma, lymph and interstitial fluid), and arterial vasoconstriction. Thus it regulates the body`s mean arterial blood pressure. Renin was discovered, characterized and named in 1898 by Robert Tigerstedt, Professor of Physiology at the Karolinska Institute in Stockholm.

Chapter 1. PART I: Chapter 1 - Chapter 18

Renin-angiotensin system	The Renin-angiotensin system or the renin-angiotensin-aldosterone system (RAAS) is a hormone system that regulates blood pressure and water (fluid) balance. When blood volume is low, the kidneys secrete renin. Renin stimulates the production of angiotensin.
Down syndrome	Down syndrome, or Down`s syndrome (primarily in the United Kingdom), trisomy 21, or trisomy G, is a chromosomal disorder caused by the presence of all or part of an extra 21st chromosome. It is named after John Langdon Down, the British physician who described the syndrome in 1866. The disorder was identified as a chromosome 21 trisomy by Jérôme Lejeune in 1959. The condition is characterized by a combination of major and minor differences in structure. Often Down syndrome is associated with some impairment of cognitive ability and physical growth, and a particular set of facial characteristics.
Doxazosin	Doxazosin mesylate, a quinazoline compound sold by Pfizer under the brand names Cardura and Carduran, is an alpha blocker used to treat high blood pressure and benign prostatic hyperplasia. On February 22, 2005, the US FDA approved a sustained release form of Doxazosin, to be marketed as Cardura XL. It is an alpha-1 adrenergic receptor blocker that inhibits the binding of norepinephrine to alpha receptors in the autonomic nervous system. The primary effect of this blockage is relaxed vascular smooth muscle tone (vasodilation), which decreases peripheral vascular resistance, leading to decreased blood pressure.
Phentolamine	Phentolamine is a reversible nonselective alpha-adrenergic antagonist. Its primary action is vasodilation due to α_1 blockade. It also can lead to reflex tachycardia because of hypotension and α_2 inhibition, which increases sympathetic tone.

CExam101

Terazosin	Terazosin is a selective alpha 1 antagonist used for treatment of symptoms of an enlarged prostate (BPH). It also acts to lower the blood pressure, and is therefore a drug of choice for men with hypertension and prostate enlargement.
	It works by blocking the action of adrenaline on smooth muscle of the bladder and the blood vessel walls.
Prazosin	Prazosin, trade names Minipress,Vasoflex and Hypovase, is a sympatholytic drug used to treat high blood pressure (hypertension). It belongs to the class of alpha-adrenergic blockers, which lower blood pressure by relaxing blood vessels. Specifically, Prazosin is selective for the alpha-1 receptors on vascular smooth muscle.
Esmolol	Esmolol is a cardioselective beta$_1$ receptor blocker with rapid onset, a very short duration of action, and no significant intrinsic sympathomimetic or membrane stabilising activity at therapeutic dosages.
	It is a class II antiarrhythmic.
	Esmolol decreases the force and rate of heart contractions by blocking beta-adrenergic receptors of the sympathetic nervous system, which are found in the heart and other organs of the body.
Labetalol	Labetalol is a mixed alpha/beta Adrenergic antagonist, which is used to treat high blood pressure.
	Labetalol has stereoisomers. It is a racemic mixture of four isomers.
Metoprolol	Metoprolol is a selective β_1 receptor blocker used in treatment of several diseases of the cardiovascular system, especially hypertension. It is marketed under the brand name Lopressor by Novartis, and Toprol-XL (in the USA); Selokeen (in the Netherlands); as Minax by Alphapharm (in Australia), Metrol by Arrow Pharmaceuticals (in Australia), as Betaloc by AstraZeneca, as Neobloc by Unipharm (in Israel), Presolol by Hemofarm (in Serbia) and as Corvitol by Berlin-Chemie AG . In India, this drug is available under the brand names of Metolar and Starpress.

Chapter 1. PART I: Chapter 1 - Chapter 18

Propranolol	Propranolol is a non-selective beta blocker mainly used in the treatment of hypertension. It was the first successful beta blocker developed. It is the only drug proven effective for the prophylaxis of migraines in children.
Acetylcholine	The chemical compound Acetylcholine is a neurotransmitter in both the peripheral nervous system (PNS) and central nervous system (CNS) in many organisms including humans. Acetylcholine is one of many neurotransmitters in the autonomic nervous system (ANS) and the only neurotransmitter used in the motor division of the somatic nervous system. (Sensory neurons use glutamate and various peptides at their synapses).
Alkaline phosphatase	Alkaline phosphatase is a hydrolase enzyme responsible for removing phosphate groups from many types of molecules, including nucleotides, proteins, and alkaloids. The process of removing the phosphate group is called dephosphorylation. As the name suggests, Alkaline phosphatases are most effective in an alkaline environment.
Atropine	Atropine is a tropane alkaloid extracted from deadly nightshade (Atropa belladonna), jimsonweed (Datura stramonium), mandrake (Mandragora officinarum) and other plants of the family Solanaceae. It is a secondary metabolite of these plants and serves as a drug with a wide variety of effects. It is a competitive antagonist for the muscarinic acetylcholine receptor.
Hygroma	A Hygroma is a false bursa that occurs over bony prominences and pressure points, especially in large breeds of dogs. Repeated trauma from lying on hard surfaces produces an inflammatory response, which results in a dense-walled, fluid-filled cavity. A soft, fluctuant, painless swelling develops over pressure points, especially the olecranon.
Cyanide	A Cyanide is any chemical compound that contains the cyano group (C≡N), which consists of a carbon atom triple-bonded to a nitrogen atom. Inorganic Cyanides are hydrogen Cyanide salts in which Cyanide is generally the anion CN^-. Organic compounds that have a -C≡N functional group bonded to an alkyl residue are called nitriles in IUPAC nomenclature.
Direct thrombin inhibitors	Direct thrombin inhibitors are a class of medication that act as anticoagulants (delaying blood clotting) by directly inhibiting the enzyme thrombin. Some are in clinical use, while others are undergoing clinical development. Several members of the class are expected to replace heparin (and derivatives) and warfarin in various clinical scenarios.

Chapter 1. PART I: Chapter 1 - Chapter 18

Nitroglycerin	Nitroglycerin belongs to a group of drugs called nitrates, which includes many other nitrates like isosorbide dinitrate and isosorbide mononitrate (Imdur, Ismo, Monoket). In medicine, where it is generally called glyceryl trinitrate, Nitroglycerin is used as a heart medication (under the trade names Nitrospan, Nitrostat, and Tridil, amongst others). It is used as a medicine for angina pectoris (ischaemic heart disease) in tablets, ointment, solution for intravenous use, transdermal patches (Trinipatch, Transderm Nitro, Nitro-Dur), or sprays administered sublingually (Nitrolingual Pump Spray, Natispray).
Vasoconstriction	Vasoconstriction is the narrowing of the blood vessels resulting from contraction of the muscular wall of the vessels, particularly the large arteries, small arterioles and veins. The process is the opposite of vasodilation, the widening of blood vessels. The process is particularly important in staunching hemorrhage and acute blood loss.
Balance disorder	A Balance disorder is a disturbance that causes an individual to feel unsteady, giddy, woozy spinning, or floating. Balance is the result of a number of body systems working together. Specifically, in order to achieve balance, the eyes (visual system), ears (vestibular system) and the body's sense of where it is in space (proprioception) need to be intact.
Glycopyrrolate	Glycopyrrolate is a medication of the muscarinic anticholinergic group. It is a synthetic quaternary amine. It is available in oral and intravenous (i.v).
Thrombin	Thrombin also commonly called pro-Thrombin is a coagulation protein in the blood stream that has many effects in the coagulation cascade. It is a serine protease (EC 3.4.21.5) that converts soluble fibrinogen into insoluble strands of fibrin, as well as catalyzing many other coagulation-related reactions. The Thrombin gene is located on the eleventh chromosome (11p11-q12).
Hydralazine	Hydralazine is a direct-acting smooth muscle relaxant used to treat hypertension by acting as a vasodilator primarily in arteries and arterioles. By relaxing vascular smooth muscle, vasodilators act to decrease peripheral resistance, thereby lowering blood pressure and decreasing afterload. The mechanism of action of Hydralazine is not well known.
Enzyme inhibitors	Enzyme inhibitors are molecules that bind to enzymes and decrease their activity. Since blocking an enzyme's activity can kill a pathogen or correct a metabolic imbalance, many drugs are Enzyme inhibitors. They are also used as herbicides and pesticides.

Chapter 1. PART I: Chapter 1 - Chapter 18

Angiotensin	Angiotensin, a protein, causes blood vessels to constrict, and drives blood pressure up. It is part of the renin-Angiotensin system, which is a major target for drugs that lower blood pressure. Angiotensin also stimulates the release of aldosterone from the adrenal cortex.
Antihypertensive	The antihypertensives are a class of drugs that are used to treat hypertension (high blood pressure). Evidence suggests that reduction of the blood pressure by 5 mmHg can decrease the risk of stroke by 34%, of ischaemic heart disease by 21%, and reduce the likelihood of dementia, heart failure, and mortality from cardiovascular disease. There are many classes of antihypertensives, which lower blood pressure by different means; among the most important and most widely used are the thiazide diuretics, the ACE inhibitors, the calcium channel blockers, the beta blockers, and the angiotensin II receptor antagonists or ARBs.
Cardiac glycosides	Cardiac glycosides are drugs used in the treatment of congestive heart failure and cardiac arrhythmia. These glycosides are found as secondary metabolites in several plants, but also in some animals. Cardiac glycosides are used therapeutically mainly in the treatment of cardiac failure, due to their anti-arrhythmic effects.
Glucagon	Glucagon is an important hormone involved in carbohydrate metabolism. Produced by the pancreas, it is released when blood glucose levels start to fall too low, causing the liver to convert stored glycogen into glucose and release it into the bloodstream, raising blood glucose levels and ultimately preventing the development of hypoglycemia. The action of Glucagon is thus opposite to that of insulin, which instructs the body`s cells to take in glucose from the blood.
Dental	The word Dental is used for things pertaining to teeth and could refer to: · Dentistry, a medical profession · Dental Auxiliary · Dental hygienist, a licensed practitioner · Dental technician

· Any of a variety of other Dental professions, such as `Dental assistant`, someone who works in a dentist`s office, but may not be a licensed medical worker

· The American Dental Association

· Dental amalgam controversy

· Dental brace

· Dental cavities

· Dental consonant (linguistics)

· Dental extraction

· Dental restoration

· Dental implants

· Dental alveolus

· Dental caries

· Dental dam

· Dental drill

· Dental emergency

· Dental fillings

· Dental floss

· Dental fluorosis

· Dental insurance

· Dental implant

· Dental Key

· Dental pellicle

· Dental phobia

· Dental plaque

· Dental porcelain

· Dental restoration

· Dental sealant

· Dental surgery

· Dentalize
Other uses:

· Dental Records, a record label .

Heart	The Heart is a muscular organ found in most vertebrates that is responsible for pumping blood throughout the blood vessels by repeated, rhythmic contractions. The term cardiac (as in cardiology) means `related to the Heart` and comes from the Greek καρδιη, kardia, for `Heart.` The vertebrate Heart is composed of cardiac muscle, an involuntary striated muscle tissue which is found only within this organ. The average human Heart, beating at 72 beats per minute, will beat approximately 2.5 billion times during a lifetime (about 66 years).
Heart failure	Heart failure is a condition in which a problem with the structure or function of the heart impairs its ability to supply sufficient blood flow to meet the body`s needs. It should not be confused with cardiac arrest . Common causes of Heart failure include myocardial infarction and other forms of ischemic heart disease, hypertension, valvular heart disease and cardiomyopathy.

Chapter 1. PART I: Chapter 1 - Chapter 18

Hypertension	Hypertension is a chronic medical condition in which the blood pressure is elevated. It is also referred to as high blood pressure or shortened to HT, HTN or HPN. The word `Hypertension`, by itself, normally refers to systemic, arterial Hypertension. Hypertension can be classified as either essential (primary) or secondary.
Angina pectoris	Angina pectoris, commonly known as angina, is severe chest pain due to ischemia (a lack of blood and hence oxygen supply) of the heart muscle, generally due to obstruction or spasm of the coronary arteries (the heart's blood vessels). Coronary artery disease, the main cause of angina, is due to atherosclerosis of the cardiac arteries. The term derives from the Latin angina from the Greek á¼€γχÏŒvη ankhone ('strangling'), and the Latin pectus , and can therefore be translated as 'a strangling feeling in the chest'.
Antiarrhythmic agents	Antiarrhythmic agents are a group of pharmaceuticals that are used to suppress fast rhythms of the heart (cardiac arrhythmias), such as atrial fibrillation, atrial flutter, ventricular tachycardia, and ventricular fibrillation. While the use of Antiarrhythmic agents to suppress atrial arrhythmias (atrial fibrillation and atrial flutter) is still in practice, it is unclear whether suppression of atrial arrhythmias will prolong life. In the past, it was believed that following myocardial infarction (heart attack), suppression of ventricular arrhythmias would prolong life.
Mediastinum	The Mediastinum is a non-delineated group of structures in the thorax, surrounded by loose connective tissue. It is the central compartment of the thoracic cavity. It contains the heart, the great vessels of the heart, esophagus, trachea, phrenic nerve, cardiac nerve, thoracic duct, thymus, and lymph nodes of the central chest.
Tumor	A tumor or tumour is the name for a swelling or lesion formed by an abnormal growth of cells (termed neoplastic). tumor is not synonymous with cancer. A tumor can be benign, pre-malignant or malignant, whereas cancer is by definition malignant.
Energy	In physics, Energy is a scalar physical quantity that describes the amount of work that can be performed by a force, an attribute of objects and systems that is subject to a conservation law. Different forms of Energy include kinetic, potential, thermal, gravitational, sound, light, elastic, and electromagnetic Energy. The forms of Energy are often named after a related force.

Chapter 1. PART I: Chapter 1 - Chapter 18

Embolization	Embolization is a non-surgical, minimally-invasive procedure performed by an interventional radiologist and interventional neuroradiologists. It involves the selective occlusion of blood vessels by purposely introducing emboli. Embolisation is used to treat a wide variety of conditions affecting different organs of the human body.
Atomic number	In chemistry and physics, the Atomic number is the number of protons found in the nucleus of an atom and therefore identical to the charge number of the nucleus. It is conventionally represented by the symbol Z. The Atomic number uniquely identifies a chemical element. In an atom of neutral charge, the Atomic number is also equal to the number of electrons.
Electron	The Electron is a subatomic particle that carries a negative electric charge. It has no known components or substructure, and therefore is believed to be an elementary particle. An Electron has a mass that is approximately 1/1836 that of the proton.
Proton	The Proton is a subatomic particle with an electric charge of +1 elementary charge. It is found in the nucleus of each atom, along with neutrons, but is also stable by itself and has a second identity as the hydrogen ion, H^+. It is composed of three fundamental particles: two up quarks and one down quark.
Alcohol	In chemistry, an Alcohol is any organic compound in which a hydroxyl group (-OH) is bound to a carbon atom of an alkyl or substituted alkyl group. The general formula for a simple acyclic Alcohol is $C_nH_{2n+1}OH$. In common terms, the word Alcohol refers to ethanol, the type of Alcohol found in Alcoholic beverages. Ethanol is a colorless, volatile liquid with a mild odor which can be obtained by the fermentation of sugars.
Alkyl	In chemistry, an Alkyl group is an alkane missing one hydrogen. It has the general formula C_nH_{2n+1}. Typically an Alkyl is a part of a larger molecule.
Alkynes	Alkynes are hydrocarbons that have a triple bond between two carbon atoms, with the formula C_nH_{2n-2}. Alkynes are traditionally known as acetylenes, although the name acetylene also refers specifically to C_2H_2, known formally as ethyne using IUPAC nomenclature. Like other hydrocarbons, Alkynes are generally hydrophobic but tend to be more reactive.
Hydrocarbon	In organic chemistry, a Hydrocarbon is an organic compound consisting entirely of hydrogen and carbon. Hydrocarbons from which one hydrogen atom has been removed are functional groups, called hydrocarbyls. Aromatic Hydrocarbons (arenes), alkanes, alkenes, cycloalkanes and alkyne-based compounds are different types of Hydrocarbons.

Chapter 1. PART I: Chapter 1 - Chapter 18

Organic compound	An Organic compound is any member of a large class of chemical compounds whose molecules contain carbon. For historical reasons discussed below, a few types of compounds such as carbonates, simple oxides of carbon and cyanides, as well as the allotropes of carbon, are considered inorganic. The distinction between `organic` and `inorganic` carbon compounds while `useful in organizing the vast subject of chemistry...
Ketone	In organic chemistry, a Ketone is a type of compound that features one carbonyl group (C=O) bonded to two other carbon atoms, i.e., $R_3CCO-CR_3$ where R can be a variety of atoms and groups of atoms. With carbonyl carbon bonded to two carbon atoms, Ketones are distinct from many other functional groups, such as carboxylic acids, aldehydes, esters, amides, and other oxygen-containing compounds. The double-bond of the carbonyl group distinguishes Ketones from alcohols and ethers.
Phenol	Phenol, also known as carbolic acid, is a toxic, white crystalline solid. Its chemical formula is C_6H_5OH and its structure is that of a hydroxyl group (-OH) bonded to a phenyl ring, making it an aromatic compound. The word Phenol is also used to refer to any compound that contains a six-membered aromatic ring, bonded directly to a hydroxyl group (-OH).
Carboxylic acid	Carboxylic acids are organic acids characterized by the presence of at least one carboxyl group, which has the formula -C(=O)OH, usually written -COOH or $-CO_2H$. Carboxylic acids are Brønsted-Lowry acids -- they are proton donors. Salts and anions of Carboxylic acids are called carboxylates. The general formula of a Carboxylic acid is therefore R-COOH, where R is some monovalent functional group.
Esters	Esters are chemical compounds derived by reacting an oxoacid (one containing an oxo group, X=O) with a hydroxyl compound such as an alcohol or phenol. Esters are usually derived from an inorganic acid or organic acid in which at least one -OH (hydroxyl) group is replaced by an -O-alkyl (alkoxy) group, and most commonly from carboxylic acids and alcohols. Esters are ubiquitous.
Permeable	Permeability, Permeable and semiPermeable have several meanings:

· Permeability (electromagnetism), the degree of magnetization of a material in response to a magnetic field

· Permeability (earth sciences), a measure of the ability of a material (such as rocks) to transmit fluids

· SemiPermeable membrane, a membrane which will allow certain molecules or ions to pass through it by diffusion

· Permeability (nautical), in ship design, the percentage of empty space in a compartment or tank

· Permeation of a gas or vapor through a solid substance

· Vascular permeability, the movement of fluids and molecules between the vascular and extravascular compartments

· Permeability (spatial and transport planning), the extent to which the layout of urban forms enables people or vehicles to move in different directions

· Permeability (foundry sand), is a test of the venting characteristics of a rammed foundry sand

· Another meaning is the ability to move through matter `

Fluid	A fluid or water deprivation test is a medical test for the purposes of diagnosing the causes of polydipsia, a condition of excessive thirst that causes an excessive intake of water. The patient is required, for a prolonged period, to forgo intake of water completely, to determine the cause of the thirst. This test measures changes in body weight, urine output, and urine composition when fluids are withheld.
Osmotic pressure	Osmotic pressure is the pressure that must be applied to a solution to prevent the inward flow of water across a semipermeable membrane. Jacobus Henricus van `t Hoff first proposed a formula for calculating the Osmotic pressure, but this was later improved upon by Harmon Northrop Morse.

On a related note, osmotic potential is the opposite of water potential, which is the degree to which a solvent tends to stay in a liquid.

Anatomy	Anatomy is a branch of biology and medicine that is the consideration of the structure of living things. It is a general term that includes human Anatomy, animal Anatomy and plant Anatomy (phytotomy). In some of its facets Anatomy is closely related to embryology, comparative Anatomy and comparative embryology, through common roots in evolution.
Desmopressin	Desmopressin is a synthetic replacement for vasopressin, the hormone that reduces urine production. It may be taken nasally, intravenously, or as a pill. Doctors prescribe Desmopressin most frequently for treatment of diabetes insipidus or bedwetting.
Electrocardiography	Electrocardiography (ECG or EKG) is a transthoracic interpretation of the electrical activity of the heart over time captured and externally recorded by skin electrodes. It is a noninvasive recording produced by an electrocardiographic device. The etymology of the word is derived from electro, because it is related to electrical activity, cardio, Greek for heart, and graph, a Greek root meaning `to write`.
Pressure	Example reading: $1\ Pa = 1\ N/m^2 = 10^{-5}\ bar = 10.197 \times 10^{-6}\ at = 9.8692 \times 10^{-6}\ atm$, etc. As an example of varying Pressures, a finger can be pressed against a wall without making any lasting impression; however, the same finger pushing a thumbtack can easily damage the wall. Although the force applied to the surface is the same, the thumbtack applies more Pressure because the point concentrates that force into a smaller area.
Acceleration	In physics, and more specifically kinematics, Acceleration is the change in velocity over time. Because velocity is a vector, it can change in two ways: a change in magnitude and/or a change in direction. In one dimension, i.e. a line, Acceleration is the rate at which something speeds up or slows down.
Vascular resistance	Vascular resistance is a term used to define the resistance to flow that must be overcome to push blood through the circulatory system. The resistance offered by the peripheral circulation is known as the systemic Vascular resistance, while the resistance offered by the vasculature of the lungs is known as the pulmonary Vascular resistance. The systemic Vascular resistance may also be referred to as the total peripheral resistance.

Chapter 1. PART I: Chapter 1 - Chapter 18

Atmospheric pressure	Atmospheric pressure is defined as the force per unit area exerted against a surface by the weight of air above that surface at any given point in the Earth's atmosphere. In most circumstances Atmospheric pressure is closely approximated by the hydrostatic pressure caused by the weight of air above the measurement point. Low pressure areas have less atmospheric mass above their location, whereas high pressure areas have more atmospheric mass above their location.
Lithotomy	Lithotomy from Greek for `lithos` and `tomos` (cut), is a surgical method for removal of calculi, stones formed inside certain hollow organs, such as the bladder and kidneys (urinary calculus) and gallbladder (gallstones), that cannot exit naturally through the urethra, ureter or biliary duct. The procedure, which is usually done by means of a surgical incision (therefore invasive), differs from lithotripsy, wherein the stones are crushed either by a minimally invasive probe inserted through the exit canal, or by ultrasound waves (extracorporeal lithotripsy), which is a non-invasive procedure. Human beings have known of bladder stones (`vesical calculi`) for thousands of years, and have attempted to treat them for almost as long.
Entropy	Entropy is an information theoretical concept applied across physics, information theory, mathematics and other branches of science and engineering. When given a system whose exact description is not precisely known, the Entropy is defined as the expected amount of information needed to exactly specify the state of the system, given what we know about the system. The Entropy (S) can be computed using the following formula: $$S = -k \sum_i P_i \ln(P_i)$$ Here the summation is over the possible precisely defined states i the system can be in, and the P_i are the probabilities for the system to be in these states, given what we know about the system.
Sphygmomanometer	A Sphygmomanometer or blood pressure meter is a device used to measure blood pressure, comprising an inflatable cuff to restrict blood flow, and a mercury or mechanical manometer to measure the pressure. It is always used in conjunction with a means to determine at what pressure blood flow is just starting, and at what pressure it is unimpeded. Manual Sphygmomanometers are used in conjunction with a stethoscope.

Chapter 1. PART I: Chapter 1 - Chapter 18

Intracranial pressure	Intracranial pressure (ICP) is the pressure in the cranium and thus in the brain tissue and cerebrospinal fluid (CSF); this pressure is exerted on the brain`s intracranial blood circulation vessels. ICP is maintained in a tight normal range dynamically, through the production and absorption of CSF and pulsates approximately 1mm Hg in a normal healthy adult. CSF pressure has been shown to be influenced by abrupt changes in intrathorasic pressure during coughing (intraabdominal pressure), valsalva (Queckenstedt`s maneuver), and communication with the vasculature (venous and arterial systems).
Cellulitis	Cellulitis is a diffuse inflammation of connective tissue with severe inflammation of dermal and subcutaneous layers of the skin. Cellulitis can be caused by normal skin flora or by exogenous bacteria, and often occurs where the skin has previously been broken: cracks in the skin, cuts, blisters, burns, insect bites, surgical wounds, or sites of intravenous catheter insertion. Skin on the face or lower legs is most commonly affected by this infection, though Cellulitis can occur on any part of the body.
Heat	In physics and thermodynamics, Heat is the process of energy transfer from one body or system due to thermal contact, which in turn is defined as an energy transfer to a body in any other way than due to work performed on the body.
	When an infinitesimal amount of Heat δQ is transferred to a body in thermal equilibrium at absolute temperature T in a reversible way, then it is given by the quantity TdS, where S is the entropy of the body.
	A related term is thermal energy, loosely defined as the energy of a body that increases with its temperature.
Latent heat	The expression Latent heat refers to the amount of energy released or absorbed by a chemical substance during a change of state that occurs without changing its temperature, meaning a phase transition such as the melting of ice or the boiling of water. The term was introduced around 1750 by Joseph Black as derived from the Latin latere, to lie hidden.
	Two of the more common forms of Latent heat encountered are Latent heat of fusion and Latent heat of vaporization (boiling).
CHARGE syndrome	CHARGE syndrome (formerly known as CHARGE association), is a syndrome caused by a genetic disorder. It was first described in 1979.

Chapter 1. PART I: Chapter 1 - Chapter 18

	In 1981, the term `CHARGE` came into use as an acronym for the set of unusual congenital features seen in a number of newborn children.
Partial pressure	In a mixture of ideal gases, each gas has a Partial pressure which is the pressure which the gas would have if it alone occupied the volume. The total pressure of a gas mixture is the sum of the Partial pressures of each individual gas in the mixture. In chemistry, the Partial pressure of a gas in a mixture of gases is defined as above.
Heparin	Heparin, a highly-sulfated glycosaminoglycan, is widely used as an injectable anticoagulant, and has the highest negative charge density of any known biological molecule. It can also be used to form an inner anticoagulant surface on various experimental and medical devices such as test tubes and renal dialysis machines. Pharmaceutical grade Heparin is derived from mucosal tissues of slaughtered meat animals such as porcine (pig) intestine or bovine (cow) lung.
Dilantin	Dilantin is the brand name of the drug phenytoin sodium in the United States, commonly used in the treatment of epilepsy. About one third of children whose mothers are taking this drug during pregnancy develop minor face and limb birth defects. A smaller population will have growth problems and developmental delay, or mental retardation.
Viscosity	Viscosity is a measure of the resistance of a fluid which is being deformed by either shear stress or tensional stress. In everyday terms (and for fluids only), Viscosity is `thickness`. Thus, water is `thin`, having a lower Viscosity, while honey is `thick`, having a higher Viscosity.
Magnetic resonance imaging	Magnetic resonance imaging ,), is primarily a medical imaging technique most commonly used in radiology to visualize the internal structure and function of the body. Magnetic resonance imaging provides much greater contrast between the different soft tissues of the body than computed tomography (CT) does, making it especially useful in neurological (brain), musculoskeletal, cardiovascular, and oncological (cancer) imaging. Unlike CT, it uses no ionizing radiation, but uses a powerful magnetic field to align the nuclear magnetization of (usually) hydrogen atoms in water in the body.

Chapter 1. PART I: Chapter 1 - Chapter 18

Refraction	Refraction is the change in direction of a wave due to a change in its speed. This is most commonly observed when a wave passes from one medium to another at an angle. Refraction of light is the most commonly observed phenomenon, but any type of wave can refract when it interacts with a medium, for example when sound waves pass from one medium into another or when water waves move into water of a different depth.
Transverse	The transverse or costal processes of a vertebra, two in number, project one at either side from the point where the lamina joins the pedicle, between the superior and inferior articular processes. They serve for the attachment of muscles and ligaments.
Ultrasound	Ultrasound is cyclic sound pressure with a frequency greater than the upper limit of human hearing. Although this limit varies from person to person, it is approximately 20 kilohertz (20,000 hertz) in healthy, young adults and thus, 20 kHz serves as a useful lower limit in describing Ultrasound. The production of Ultrasound is used in many different fields, typically to penetrate a medium and measure the reflection signature or supply focused energy.
Electromagnetic spectrum	The Electromagnetic spectrum is the range of all possible frequencies of electromagnetic radiation. The `Electromagnetic spectrum` of an object is the characteristic distribution of electromagnetic radiation emitted or absorbed by that particular object. The Electromagnetic spectrum extends from below frequencies used for modern radio to gamma radiation at the short-wavelength end, covering wavelengths from thousands of kilometers down to a fraction of the size of an atom.
Magnesium	Magnesium is a chemical element with the symbol Mg, atomic number 12 and common oxidation number +2. It is an alkaline earth metal and the eighth most abundant element in the Earth`s crust by mass, although ninth in the known Universe as a whole. This preponderance of Magnesium is related to the fact that it is easily built up in supernova stars from a sequential addition of three helium nuclei to carbon . Magnesium constitutes about 2% of the Earth`s crust by mass, which makes it the eighth most abundant element in the crust.
Magnetism	In physics, the term Magnetism is used to describe how materials respond on the microscopic level to an applied magnetic field; to categorize the magnetic phase of a material. For example, the most well known form of Magnetism is ferroMagnetism such that some ferromagnetic materials produce their own persistent magnetic field. Some well-known ferromagnetic materials that exhibit easily detectable magnetic properties (to form magnets) are nickel, iron, cobalt, gadolinium and their alloys.

Chapter 1. PART I: Chapter 1 - Chapter 18

Microshock	Microshock is a risk in patients with intracardiac conductors, such as external pacemaker electrodes, saline filled catheters, or weak or old heart tissue within the heart. A current as low as 10uAmps directly through the heart, may send a patient directly into ventricular fibrillation.
Electrolyte	In chemistry, an Electrolyte is any substance containing free ions that make the substance electrically conductive. The most typical Electrolyte is an ionic solution, but molten Electrolytes and solid Electrolytes are also possible. Electrolytes commonly exist as solutions of acids, bases or salts.
Shock	· Shock (circulatory), a circulatory medical emergency · Acute stress reaction, often termed `Shock` by laypersons, a psychological condition in response to terrifying events · Post-traumatic stress disorder, a long-term complication of acute stress reaction · Shock (economics), an unexpected or unpredictable event that affects an economy · Shocks (Image Processing) · Electric Shock · Shock (mechanics) · short for `Shock absorber` · Shock wave, one example being a sonic boom · Shock site, a website that is intended to be offensive or Shocking to most viewers

· Shock tactics, a close quarter battle tactic, usually done by specially trained Shock troops.

· Shock troops, troops trained for Shock tactics, usually heavy cavalry or infantry

· The Detroit Shock, a professional women's basketball team

· Shock (Cooking Technique), to quickly stop the cooking process of blanched items by plunging them in ice water.

· Aaron Schock, member of the U.S. House of Representatives representing the 18th district of Illinois.

Radiography

Radiography is the use of ionizing electromagnetic radiation such as X-rays to view objects. Although not technically radiographic techniques, imaging modalities such as PET and MRI are sometimes grouped in Radiography because the radiology department of hospitals handle all forms of imaging. Treatment using radiation is known as radiotherapy.

Scattering

Scattering is a general physical process where some forms of radiation, such as light, sound, or moving particles, are forced to deviate from a straight trajectory by one or more localized non-uniformities in the medium through which they pass. In conventional use, this also includes deviation of reflected radiation from the angle predicted by the law of reflection. Reflections that undergo Scattering are often called diffuse reflections and unscattered reflections are called specular (mirror-like) reflections.

Clark electrode

The Clark electrode is an electrode that measures oxygen on a catalytic platinum surface using the net reaction:

$$O_2 + 4\,e^- + 2\,H_2O \rightarrow 4\,OH^-$$

Leland Clark had developed the first bubble oxygenator for use in cardiac surgery Necessity is the mother of invention, and after a couple of trials, Clark presented his Oxygen Electrode.

Chapter 1. PART I: Chapter 1 - Chapter 18

Pulse	In medicine, a person's Pulse is the arterial palpation of a heartbeat. It can be palpated in any place that allows for an artery to be compressed against a bone, such as at the neck (carotid artery), at the wrist (radial artery), behind the knee (popliteal artery), on the inside of the elbow (brachial artery), and near the ankle joint (posterior tibial artery). The Pulse rate can also be measured by measuring the heart beats directly (the apical Pulse).
Pulse oximetry	Pulse oximetry is a non-invasive method allowing the monitoring of the oxygenation of a patient's hemoglobin. A sensor is placed on a thin part of the patient's anatomy, usually a fingertip or earlobe, or in the case of a neonate, across a foot, and a light containing both red and infrared wavelengths is passed from one side to the other. Changing absorbance of each of the two wavelengths is measured, allowing determination of the absorbances due to the pulsing arteria blood alone, excluding venous blood, skin, bone, muscle, fat, and (in most cases) fingernail polish.
Arterial blood gas	An Arterial blood gas is a blood test that is performed using blood from an artery. It involves puncturing an artery with a thin needle and syringe and drawing a small volume of blood. The most common puncture site is the radial artery at the wrist, but sometimes the femoral artery in the groin or other sites are used.
Pin Index Safety System	The Pin Index Safety System is a safety system that uses geometric features on the yoke to ensure that pneumatic connections between a gas cylinder and a machine that uses pressurized gases are not connected to the wrong gas yoke. This system can be seen on an anesthesia machine. Each gas cylinder has a pin configuration to fit its respective gas yoke.
Fresh gas flow	Fresh gas flow refers to the mixture of medical gases and volatile anaesthetic agents which is produced by an anaesthetic machine. The flow rate and composition of the Fresh gas flow is determined by the anaesthetist. Typically the Fresh gas flow emerges from the common gas outlet, a specific outlet on the anaesthetic machine to which the breathing attachment is then connected.
Orifice	An Orifice is any opening, mouth, hole or vent, as of a pipe, plate, or a body. · Body Orifice · Orifice plate · calibrated Orifice

· Nozzle

· Back Orifice .

Reflex	A Reflex action, also known as a Reflex, is an involuntary and nearly instantaneous movement in response to a stimulus. In most contexts, in particular those involving humans, Reflex actions are mediated via the Reflex arc; this is not always true in other animals, nor does it apply to casual uses of the term `Reflex`. For a Reflex, reaction time or latency is the time from the onset of a stimulus until the organism responds.
Hysterectomy	A Hysterectomy is the surgical removal of the uterus, usually performed by a gynecologist. Hysterectomy may be total ` href=`/wiki/Fundus_(uterus)`>fundus, and cervix of the uterus; often called `complete`) or partial (removal of the uterine body but leaving the cervical stump, also called `supracervical`). It is the most commonly performed gynecological surgical procedure.
Airway management	In cardiopulmonary resuscitation, anaesthesia, emergency medicine, intensive care medicine and first aid, Airway management is the process of ensuring that: · there is an open pathway between a patient's lungs and the outside world, and · the lungs are safe from aspiration. In nearly all circumstances Airway management is the highest priority for clinical care. This is because if there is no airway, there can be no breathing, hence no oxygenation of blood and therefore circulation (and hence all the other vital body processes) will soon cease.
Axon	An Axon or nerve fiber is a long, slender projection of a nerve cell, or neuron, that conducts electrical impulses away from the neuron's cell body or soma. An Axon is one of two types of protoplasmic protrusions that extrude from the cell body of a neuron, the other type being dendrites. Axons are distinguished from dendrites by several features, including shape (dendrites often taper while Axons usually maintain a constant radius), length (dendrites are restricted to a small region around the cell body while Axons can be much longer), and function (dendrites usually receive signals while Axons usually transmit them).

Chapter 1. PART I: Chapter 1 - Chapter 18

Infection	An Infection is the detrimental colonization of a host organism by a foreign species. In an Infection, the infecting organism seeks to utilize the host`s resources to multiply, usually at the expense of the host. The infecting organism, or pathogen, interferes with the normal functioning of the host and can lead to chronic wounds, gangrene, loss of an infected limb, and even death.
Infection Control	Infection control and health care epidemiology is the discipline concerned with preventing the spread of infections within the health-care setting. As such, it is a practical (rather than an academic) sub-discipline of epidemiology. It is an essential (though often underrecognized and undersupported) part of the infrastructure of health care.
Replacement	Replacement means: · Replacements, Tuttle, Lisa · Axiom schema of Replacement · Text Replacement, a feature of word processors correcting automatically common misspellings and typos · Replacement rate · Sampling (statistics) with Replacement .
Cycling	Cycling, also called biCycling or biking, is the use of bicycles for transport, recreation, or for sport. Persons engaged in Cycling are cyclists or bicyclists. Apart from ordinary two-wheeled bicycles, Cycling also includes riding a unicycle, tricycle, quadracycle, and other similar human-powered vehicles (HPVs).
Positive End-expiratory pressure	Positive end-expiratory pressure (PEEP) is a term used in mechanical ventilation to denote the amount of pressure above atmospheric pressure present in the airway at the end of the expiratory cycle. The equivalent in a spontaneously breathing patient is CPAP. PEEP is set on the ventilator. PEEP improves gas exchange by preventing alveolar collapse, recruiting more lung units, increasing functional residual capacity, and redistributing fluid in the alveoli.

Chapter 1. PART I: Chapter 1 - Chapter 18

Tourniquet	A Tourniquet is a constricting or compressing device used to control venous and arterial circulation to an extremity for a period of time. Pressure is applied circumferentially upon the skin and underlying tissues of a limb; this pressure is transferred to the walls of vessels, causing them to become temporarily occluded. It is generally used as a tool for a medical professional in applications such as cannulation or to stem the flow of traumatic bleeding, especially by military medics.
Tidal volume	Tidal volume is the lung volume representing the normal volume of air displaced between normal inspiration and expiration when extra effort is not applied. Typical values are around 500ml or 7ml/kg bodyweight. The volume of gas moved during the respiratory cycle in mechanical ventilation where control (or at least appreciation) of Tidal volume is necessary to ensure adequate ventilation without causing barotrauma.
Barotrauma	Barotrauma is physical damage to body tissues caused by a difference in pressure between an air space inside or beside the body and the surrounding fluid. Barotrauma typically occurs to air spaces within a body when that body moves to or from a higher pressure environment, such as when a SCUBA diver, a free-diving diver or an airplane passenger ascends or descends, or during uncontrolled decompression of a pressure vessel. Boyle's law defines the relationship between the volume of the air space and the ambient pressure.
Health Administration	Health administration or healthcare administration is the field relating to leadership, management, and administration of hospitals, hospital networks, and health care systems. Health care administrators are considered health care professionals. The discipline is known by many names, including health management, healthcare management, health systems management, health care systems management, and medical and health services management.
Occupational Safety and Health Administration	The United States Occupational Safety and Health Administration is an agency of the United States Department of Labor. It was created by Congress of the United States under the Occupational Safety and Health Act, signed by President Richard M Nixon, on December 29, 1970. Its mission is to prevent work-related injuries, illnesses, and occupational fatality by issuing and enforcing rules called standards for workplace safety and health. The agency is headed by a Deputy Assistant Secretary of Labor.

Chapter 1. PART I: Chapter 1 - Chapter 18

Pulmonary trunk	The pulmonary arteries carry blood from the heart to the lungs. They are the only arteries (other than umbilical arteries in the fetus) that carry deoxygenated blood. In the human heart, the pulmonary trunk begins at the base of the right ventricle.
Coronary artery disease	Coronary artery disease is the end result of the accumulation of atheromatous plaques within the walls of the coronary arteries that supply the myocardium (the muscle of the heart) with oxygen and nutrients. It is sometimes also called coronary heart disease (CHD), but although Coronary artery disease is the most common cause of CHD, it is not the only cause. Coronary artery disease is the leading cause of death worldwide.
Myocardial infarction	Myocardial infarction or acute Myocardial infarction (AMyocardial infarction), commonly known as a heart attack, is the interruption of blood supply to part of the heart, causing some heart cells to die. This is most commonly due to occlusion (blockage) of a coronary artery following the rupture of a vulnerable atherosclerotic plaque, which is an unstable collection of lipids (like cholesterol) and white blood cells (especially macrophages) in the wall of an artery. The resulting ischemia (restriction in blood supply) and oxygen shortage, if left untreated for a sufficient period of time, can cause damage or death (infarction) of heart muscle tissue (myocardium).
QT interval	In medicine, specifically cardiology, the QT interval is a measure of the time between the start of the Q wave and the end of the T wave in the heart`s electrical cycle. A prolonged QT interval is a risk factor for ventricular tachyarrhythmias and sudden death. QT interval can be measured by different methods such as the threshold method in which the end of the T wave is determined by the point at which the component of the T wave merges with the isoelectric baseline or the tangent method in which the end of the T wave is determined by the intersection of a line extrapolated from the isoelectric baseline and the tangent line which touches the terminal part of the T wave at the point of maximum downslope.
Ischemia	In medicine, Ischemia is a restriction in blood supply, generally due to factors in the blood vessels, with resultant damage or dysfunction of tissue. It may also be spelled ischaemia or ischæmia. Rather than hypoxia , Ischemia is an absolute or relative shortage of the blood supply to an organ, i.e. a shortage of oxygen, glucose and other blood-borne fuels.

Chapter 1. PART I: Chapter 1 - Chapter 18

Cardiac cycle	Cardiac cycle is the term referring to all or any of the events related to the flow or pressure of blood that occurs from the beginning of one heartbeat to the beginning of the next. The frequency of the Cardiac cycle is the heart rate. Every single `beat` of the heart involves five major stages: First, `Late diastole` which is when the semilunar valves close, the Av valves open and the whole heart is relaxed.
Lead	Lead is a main-group element with symbol Pb and atomic number 82. Lead is a soft, malleable poor metal, also considered to be one of the heavy metals. Lead has a bluish-white color when freshly cut, but tarnishes to a dull grayish color when exposed to air.
G-suit	A G-suit is worn by aviators and astronauts who are subject to high levels of acceleration force (`Gs`). It is designed to prevent a black-out and G-LOC (G-induced Loss Of Consciousness), due to the blood pooling in the lower part of the body when under acceleration, thus depriving the brain of blood. A G-suit does not so much increase the G-threshold, but makes it possible to sustain high G longer without excessive physical fatigue.
Korotkoff	Korotkoff are the sounds that medical personnel listen for when they are taking blood pressure using a non-invasive procedure. They are named after Dr. Nikolai Korotkoff, a Russian physician who described them in 1905, when he was working at the Imperial Medical Academy in St. Petersburg. The sounds heard during measurement of blood pressure are not the same as the heart sounds `lub` and `dub` that are due to the closing of the hearts valves.
Mean arterial pressure	The Mean arterial pressure is a term used in medicine to describe an average blood pressure in an individual. It is defined as the average arterial pressure during a single cardiac cycle. Mean arterial pressure can be determined from: $$MAP = (CO \times SVR) + CVP$$ where: · CO is cardiac output

Chapter 1. PART I: Chapter 1 - Chapter 18

· SVR is systemic vascular resistance

· CVP is central venous pressure and usually small enough to be neglected in this formula.

Ejection fraction	In cardiovascular physiology, Ejection fraction (E_f) is the fraction of blood pumped out of a ventricle with each heart beat. The term Ejection fraction applies to both the right and left ventricles; one can speak equally of the left ventricular Ejection fraction (LVEjection fraction) and the right ventricular Ejection fraction (RVEjection fraction). Without a qualifier, the term Ejection fraction refers specifically to that of the left ventricle.
Echocardiogram	An echocardiogram, often referred to in the medical community as a cardiac ECHO or simply an ECHO, is a sonogram of the heart. Also known as a cardiac ultrasound, it uses standard ultrasound techniques to image two-dimensional slices of the heart. The latest ultrasound systems now employ 3D real-time imaging.
Dyskinesia	Dyskinesia is a movement disorder which consists of effects including diminished voluntary movements and the presence of involuntary movements, similar to tics or chorea. Dyskinesia is a symptom of several medical disorders and is distinguished by the underlying cause. When a Dyskinesia presents after treatment with an antipsychotic drug such as haloperidol (Haldol), it is known as tardive Dyskinesia, and is commonly seen in the face and mouth in the form of `tongue rolling`.
Hypokinesia	Hypokinesia refers to slow or diminished movement of body musculature. It may be associated with basal ganglia diseases; mental disorders; prolonged inactivity due to illness; experimental protocols used to evaluate the physiologic effects of immobility; and other conditions. There are 4 types of this disorder: · Bradykinesia: characterized by slowness of movement and has been linked to Parkinson`s Disease · Freezing: characterized by an inability to move muscles in any desired direction.
Crisis	A Crisis may occur on a personal or societal level. It may be an unstable and dangerous social situation, in political, social, economic, military affairs, or a large-scale environmental event, especially one involving an impending abrupt change. More loosely, it is a term meaning `a testing time` or `emergency event`.

Cram101

Chapter 1. PART I: Chapter 1 - Chapter 18

Cyanosis	Cyanosis is a blue coloration of the skin and mucous membranes due to the presence of > 5g/dl deoxygenated hemoglobin in blood vessels near the skin surface. Although human blood is always a shade of red (except in rare cases of hemoglobin-related disease), the optical properties of skin distort the dark red color of deoxygenated blood to make it appear bluish. The elementary principle behind Cyanosis is that deoxygenated hemoglobin is more prone to the optical bluish discoloration, and also produces vasoconstriction that makes it more evident.
Skin	The skin is a soft outer covering of an animal, in particular a vertebrate. Other animal coverings such the arthropod exoskeleton or the seashell has different developmental origin, structure and chemical composition. The adjective cutaneous literally means `of the skin`.
Hyperthermia	Hyperthermia is an elevated body temperature due to failed thermoregulation. Hyperthermia occurs when the body produces or absorbs more heat than it can dissipate. When the elevated body temperatures are sufficiently high, Hyperthermia is a medical emergency and requires immediate treatment to prevent disability and death.

Chapter 2. PART II: Chapter 19 - Chapter 36

Anesthesia	Anesthesia has traditionally meant the condition of having sensation blocked or temporarily taken away. This allows patients to undergo surgery and other procedures without the distress and pain they would otherwise experience. The word was coined by Oliver Wendell Holmes, Sr.
Histamine	Histamine is a biogenic amine involved in local immune responses as well as regulating physiological function in the gut and acting as a neurotransmitter. Histamine triggers the inflammatory response. As part of an immune response to foreign pathogens, Histamine is produced by basophils and by mast cells found in nearby connective tissues.
Alpha waves	Alpha waves are electromagnetic oscillations in the frequency range of 8-12 Hz arising from synchronous and coherent (in phase / constructive) electrical activity of thalamic pacemaker cells. They are also called Berger's wave in memory of the founder of EEG. Alpha waves are one type of brain waves detected either by electroencephalography (EEG) or magnetoencephalography (MEG) and predominantly originate from the occipital lobe during wakeful relaxation with closed eyes. Alpha waves are reduced with open eyes and drowsiness and sleep.
General anaesthetic	A General anaesthetic drug is an anaesthetic drug that brings about a reversible loss of consciousness. These drugs are generally administered by an anesthesia provider in order to induce or maintain general anaesthesia to facilitate surgery. Drugs given to induce or maintain general anaesthesia are either given as: · Gases or vapors (inhalational anaesthetics) · Injections (intravenous anaesthetics) Most commonly these two forms are combined, with an injection given to induce anaesthesia and a gas used to maintain it, although it is possible to deliver anaesthesia solely by inhalation or injection.
Clinical	Clinical can refer to:

· clinical medical practice

· Clinic

· Illness

· clinical waste, segregated for safety or security

· clinical medical professions

· clinical psychology

· clinical examination; see Physical examination

· clinical conditions, diagnosed from clinical examination alone

· clinical death

· clinical research

· clinical governance of patient care within a health system

· clinical trial, research involving patients

· clinical linguistics, linguistics applied to speech therapy .

Clinical monitoring	Clinical monitoring - Oversight and administrative efforts that monitor a participant`s health during a clinical trial. The government and other clinical trial funding agencies require data and safety monitoring boards to oversee clinical trials. They want to be certain that safety measures are in place to protect participants.
Perspective	Perspective erspective in the graphic arts, such as drawing, is an approximate representation, on a flat surface , of an image as it is seen by the eye. The two most characteristic features of perspective are that objects are drawn: · Smaller as their distance from the observer increases · Foreshortened: the size of an object`s dimensions along the line of sight are relatively shorter than dimensions across the line of sight . Linear perspective works by representing the light that passes from a scene through an imaginary rectangle (the painting), to the viewer`s eye. It is similar to a viewer looking through a window and painting what is seen directly onto the windowpane.
Electromyography	Electromyography (EMG) is a technique for evaluating and recording the activation signal of muscles. EMG is performed using an instrument called an electromyograph, to produce a record called an electromyogram. An electromyograph detects the electrical potential generated by muscle cells when these cells are both mechanically active and at rest.
Trauma	Trauma can represent:

· Physical Trauma, an often serious and body-altering physical injury, such as the removal of a limb

· Blunt Trauma, a type of physical Trauma caused by impact or other force applied from or with a blunt object

· Penetrating Trauma, a type of physical Trauma in which the skin or tissues are pierced by an object

· Psychological Trauma, an emotional or psychological injury, usually resulting from an extremely stressful or life-threatening situation

· Post-cult Trauma, the intense emotional problems that some members of cults and new religious movements experience upon disaffection and disaffiliation

· Trauma team, a group of healthcare workers who attend to seriously ill or injured casualties who arrive at a hospital emergency department

· Trauma center, a hospital equipped to provide comprehensive emergency medical services to patients suffering Traumatic injuries

· Trauma, a character associated with Avengers: The Initiative in the Marvel Universe

· Trauma a psychological thriller directed by Marc Evans and starring Colin Firth

· Trauma a horror film directed by Dario Argento

· Trauma a medical drama set in San Francisco

· Also see Troma Entertainment, a film company specializing in independent, horror, and exploitation films

· Trauma Studios, an American computer game development company

· Trauma Center (series), a surgical based video game.

· `Day Twelve: Trauma`, a song by Ayreon on the album The Human Equation

· `Trauma` (song) by Ayumi Hamasaki

· Trauma by rapper/producer DJ Quik

· Trauma Records, a record label

· Trauma an American Heavy-metal band

· Trauma Flintstone, drag performer and actress

· Baltimore Trauma, professional paintball team from North Carolina

Barbiturates	Barbiturates are drugs that act as central nervous system depressants, and, by virtue of this, they produce a wide spectrum of effects, from mild sedation to total anesthesia. They are also effective as anxiolytics, hypnotics and as anticonvulsants. They have addiction potential, both physical and psychological.
Ultrasound	Ultrasound is cyclic sound pressure with a frequency greater than the upper limit of human hearing. Although this limit varies from person to person, it is approximately 20 kilohertz (20,000 hertz) in healthy, young adults and thus, 20 kHz serves as a useful lower limit in describing Ultrasound. The production of Ultrasound is used in many different fields, typically to penetrate a medium and measure the reflection signature or supply focused energy.
Mu wave	Mu waves, also known as the comb or wicket rhythm, are electromagnetic oscillations in the frequency range of 8-13 Hz and appear in bursts of at 9 - 11 Hz. Mu wave patterns arise from synchronous and coherent (in phase/constructive) electrical activity of large groups of neurons in the human brain. This wave activity appears to be associated with the motor cortex (central scalp), and is diminished with movement or an intent to move, or when others are observed performing actions.

Chapter 2. PART II: Chapter 19 - Chapter 36

Common disease-common variant	The Common disease-common variant hypothesis predicts that common disease-causing alleles will be found in all human populations which manifest a given disease. Common variants (not necessarily disease-causing) are known to exist in coding and regulatory sequences of genes. According to the CD-CV hypothesis, some of those variants lead to susceptibility to complex polygenic diseases.
Pollutant Standards Index	The Pollutant Standards Index provides a uniform system of measuring pollution levels for the major air pollutants. It is based on a scale devised by the United States Environmental Protection Agency (USEPA) to provide a way for broadcasts and newspapers to report air quality on a daily basis. The Pollutant Standards Index is reported as a number on a scale of 0 to 500 and is the air quality indicator.
Evoked potential	An Evoked potential is an electrical potential recorded from the nervous system of a human or other animal following presentation of a stimulus, as distinct from spontaneous potentials as detected by electroencephalography (EEG) or electromyography (EMG). Evoked potential amplitudes tend to be low, ranging from less than a microvolt to several microvolts, compared to tens of microvolts for EEG, millivolts for EMG, and often close to a volt for ECG. To resolve these low-amplitude potentials against the background of ongoing EEG, ECG, EMG and other biological signals and ambient noise, signal averaging is usually required. The signal is time-locked to the stimulus and most of the noise occurs randomly, allowing the noise to be averaged out with averaging of repeated responses.
Brainstem	The Brainstem is the lower part of the brain, adjoining and structurally continuous with the spinal cord. The Brainstem provides the main motor and sensory innervation to the face and neck via the cranial nerves. Though small, this is an extremely important part of the brain as the nerve connections of the motor and sensory systems from the main part of the brain to the rest of the body pass through the brain stem.
Osteoarthritis	Osteoarthritis (OA, also known as degenerative arthritis, degenerative joint disease), is a group of diseases and mechanical abnormalities entailing degradation of joints, including articular cartilage and the subchondral bone next to it. Clinical symptoms of OA may include joint pain, tenderness, stiffness, inflammation, creaking, and locking of joints. In OA, a variety of potential forces-- hereditary, developmental, metabolic, and mechanical--may initiate processes leading to loss of cartilage -- a strong protein matrix that lubricates and cushions the joints.
Auditory	Auditory means of or relating to the process of hearing:

· Auditory system, the neurological structures and pathways of sound perception.

· Sound, the physical signal perceived by the Auditory system.

· Hearing (sense), is the Auditory sense, the sense by which sound is perceived.

· Ear, the Auditory end organ.

· Cochlea, the Auditory branch of the inner ear.

· Auditory illusion, sound trick analogous to an optical illusion.

· Primary Auditory cortex, the part of the higher-level of the brain that serves hearing.

· External Auditory meatus, the ear canal

· Auditory scene analysis, the process by which a scene containing many sounds is perceived

· Auditory phonetics, the science of the sounds of language

· Auditory imagery, hearing in head in the absence of sound

Clinic

A Clinic is a small private or public health facility that is devoted to the care of outpatients, often in a community, in contrast to larger hospitals, which also treat inpatients. Some grow to be institutions as large as major hospitals, whilst retaining the name Clinic. These are often associated with a hospital or medical school.

Disability

Disability is defined by the Americans with Disabilities Act of 1990 as `a physical or mental impairment that substantially limits one or more major life activities.` An individual may also qualify as disabled if he/she has had an impairment in the past or is seen as disabled based on a personal or group standard or norm. Such impairments may include physical, sensory, and cognitive or intellectual impairments. Mental disorders (also known as psychiatric or psychosocial Disability) and various types of chronic disease may also be considered qualifying disabilities.

Heart

The Heart is a muscular organ found in most vertebrates that is responsible for pumping blood throughout the blood vessels by repeated, rhythmic contractions. The term cardiac (as in cardiology) means `related to the Heart` and comes from the Greek καρδῐῆ, kardia, for `Heart.`

Chapter 2. PART II: Chapter 19 - Chapter 36

	The vertebrate Heart is composed of cardiac muscle, an involuntary striated muscle tissue which is found only within this organ. The average human Heart, beating at 72 beats per minute, will beat approximately 2.5 billion times during a lifetime (about 66 years).
Joint	A Joint is the location at which two or more bones make contact. They are constructed to allow movement and provide mechanical support, and are classified structurally and functionally. Joints are mainly classified structurally and functionally.
Joint Commission	The Joint Commission, formerly the Joint Commission on Accreditation of Healthcare Organizations (Joint CommissionAHO), is a private sector United States-based not-for-profit organization. The Joint Commission operates voluntary accreditation programs for hospitals and other health care organizations. The Joint Commission accredits nearly 16,000 health care organizations and programs in the United States.
Airway management	In cardiopulmonary resuscitation, anaesthesia, emergency medicine, intensive care medicine and first aid, Airway management is the process of ensuring that: · there is an open pathway between a patient's lungs and the outside world, and · the lungs are safe from aspiration. In nearly all circumstances Airway management is the highest priority for clinical care. This is because if there is no airway, there can be no breathing, hence no oxygenation of blood and therefore circulation (and hence all the other vital body processes) will soon cease.
Mnemonic	A Mnemonic device is a mind memory and/or learning aid. Commonly, Mnemonics are verbal--such as a very short poem or a special word used to help a person remember something--but may be visual, kinesthetic or auditory. Mnemonics rely on associations between easy-to-remember constructs which can be related back to the data that is to be remembered.
Regurgitation	Regurgitation, Regurgiate or Regurgitate can refer to: · Regurgitation · Vomiting

· Regurgitation

· Regurgitate (band), a goregrind band `

Risk factor	A Risk factor is a variable associated with an increased risk of disease or infection. Risk factors are correlational and not necessarily causal, because correlation does not imply causation. For example, being young cannot be said to cause measles, but young people are more at risk as they are less likely to have developed immunity during a previous epidemic.
Medical record	A Medical record, health record, or medical chart is a systematic documentation of a patient`s medical history and care. The term `Medical record` is used both for the physical folder for each individual patient and for the body of information which comprises the total of each patient`s health history. Medical records are intensely personal documents and there are many ethical and legal issues surrounding them such as the degree of third-party access and appropriate storage and disposal.
Surgical	Surgery is a medical specialty that uses operative manual and instrumental techniques on a patient to investigate and/or treat a pathological condition such as disease or injury, to help improve bodily function or appearance, or sometimes for some other reason. An act of performing surgery may be called a surgical procedure, operation, or simply surgery. In this context, the verb operating means performing surgery.
Allergy	Allergy is a disorder of the immune system often also referred to as atopy. Allergic reactions occur to normally harmless environmental substances known as allergens; these reactions are acquired, predictable, and rapid. Strictly, Allergy is one of four forms of hypersensitivity and is called type I (or immediate) hypersensitivity.
Adverse effect	In medicine, an Adverse effect is a harmful and undesired effect resulting from a medication or other intervention such as surgery. An Adverse effect may be termed a 'side effect', when judged to be secondary to a main or therapeutic effect, and may result from an unsuitable or incorrect dosage or procedure, which could be due to medical error. Adverse effects are sometimes referred to as 'iatrogenic' because they are generated by a physician/treatment.
Adverse effects	In medicine, an adverse effect is a harmful and undesired effect resulting from a medication or other intervention such as surgery. An adverse effect may be termed a 'side effect', when judged to be secondary to a main or therapeutic effect, and may result from an unsuitable or incorrect dosage or procedure, which could be due to medical error. Adverse effects are sometimes referred to as 'iatrogenic' because they are generated by a physician/treatment.

Chapter 2. PART II: Chapter 19 - Chapter 36

Leukemia inhibitory factor	Leukemia inhibitory factor an interleukin 6 class cytokine, is a chemical in cells that affects their growth and development. Leukemia inhibitory factor derives its name from its ability to induce the terminal differentiation of myeloid leukaemic cells. Other properties attributed to the cytokine include: the growth promotion and cell differentiation of different types of target cells, influence on bone metabolism, cachexia, neural development, embryogenesis and inflammation.
Life Support	Life support, in medicine is a broad term that applies to any therapy used to sustain a patients life while they are critically ill or injured. There are many therapies and techniques that may be used by clinicians to achieve the goal of sustaining life. Some examples include: · feeding tubes · Inotropes · total parenteral nutrition · mechanical ventilation · heart/lung bypass · urinary catheterization · dialysis · Cardiopulmonary resuscitation · Defibrillation · Artificial pacemaker These techniques are applied most commonly in the Emergency Department, Intensive Care Unit and, Operating Rooms.
Shock	· Shock (circulatory), a circulatory medical emergency · Acute stress reaction, often termed `Shock` by laypersons, a psychological condition in response to terrifying events

· Post-traumatic stress disorder, a long-term complication of acute stress reaction

· Shock (economics), an unexpected or unpredictable event that affects an economy

· Shocks (Image Processing)

· Electric Shock

· Shock (mechanics)

· short for `Shock absorber`

· Shock wave, one example being a sonic boom

· Shock site, a website that is intended to be offensive or Shocking to most viewers

· Shock tactics, a close quarter battle tactic, usually done by specially trained Shock troops.

· Shock troops, troops trained for Shock tactics, usually heavy cavalry or infantry

· The Detroit Shock, a professional women`s basketball team

· Shock (Cooking Technique), to quickly stop the cooking process of blanched items by plunging them in ice water.

· Aaron Schock, member of the U.S. House of Representatives representing the 18th district of Illinois.

Interaction	Interaction is a kind of action that occurs as two or more objects have an effect upon one another. The idea of a two-way effect is essential in the concept of Interaction, as opposed to a one-way causal effect. A closely related term is interconnectivity, which deals with the Interactions of Interactions within systems: combinations of many simple Interactions can lead to surprising emergent phenomena.
Pain management	Pain management is the medical discipline concerned with the relief of pain.

Acute pain, such pain resulting from trauma, often has a reversible cause and may require only transient measures and correction of the underlying problem. In contrast, chronic pain often results from conditions that are difficult to diagnose and treat, and that may take a long time to reverse.

Small intestine

In vertebrates, the small intestine is the part of the gastrointestinal tract (gut) following the stomach and followed by the large intestine, and is where the vast majority of digestion and absorption of food takes place. In invertebrates such as worms, the terms `gastrointestinal tract` and `large intestine` are often used to describe the entire intestine

Spina bifida

Spina bifida is a developmental birth defect caused by the incomplete closure of the embryonic neural tube. Some vertebrae overlying the spinal cord are not fully formed and remain unfused and open. If the opening is large enough, this allows a portion of the spinal cord to stick out through the opening in the bones.

Disease

A Disease or medical condition is an abnormal condition of an organism that impairs bodily functions, associated with specific symptoms and signs. It may be caused by external factors, such as invading organisms, or it may be caused by internal dysfunctions, such as autoimmune Diseases.

In human beings, `Disease` is often used more broadly to refer to any condition that causes pain, dysfunction, distress, social problems, and/or death to the person afflicted, or similar problems for those in contact with the person.

ACE inhibitors

ACE inhibitors or angiotensin-converting enzyme inhibitors, are a group of pharmaceuticals that are used primarily in treatment of hypertension and congestive heart failure, in some cases as the drugs of first choice.

ACE inhibitors are used primarily in the treatment of hypertension,though they are also sometimes used in those with cardiac failure,renal disease,or systemic sclerosis

This system is activated in response to hypotension, decreased sodium concentration in the distal tubule, decreased blood volume and renal sympathetic nerve stimulation. In such a situation, the kidneys release renin which cleaves the liver-derived angiotensinogen into angiotensin I. Angiotensin I is then converted to angiotensin II via the ACE in the pulmonary circulation as well as in the endothelium of blood vessels in many parts of the body.

Chapter 2. PART II: Chapter 19 - Chapter 36

Antidepressant	An Antidepressant is a psychiatric medication used to alleviate mood disorders, such as major depression and dysthymia. Drugs including the monoamine oxidase inhibitors (MAOIs), tricyclic Antidepressants (TCAs), tetracyclic Antidepressants (TeCAs), selective serotonin reuptake inhibitors (SSRIs), and serotonin-norepinephrine reuptake inhibitors (SNRIs) are most commonly associated with the term. These medications are among those most commonly prescribed by psychiatrists and other physicians, and their effectiveness and adverse effects are the subject of many studies and competing claims.
Clopidogrel	Clopidogrel is an oral antiplatelet agent (thienopyridine class) to inhibit blood clots in coronary artery disease, peripheral vascular disease, and cerebrovascular disease. It is marketed by Bristol-Myers Squibb and Sanofi-Aventis under the trade name Plavix. It works by irreversibly inhibiting a receptor called $P2Y_{12}$, an ADP chemoreceptor.
Diuretic	A Diuretic is any drug that elevates the rate of urination and thus provides a means of forced diuresis. There are several categories of Diuretics. All Diuretics increase the excretion of water from bodies, although each class does so in a distinct way.
Enzyme	Enzymes are mainly proteins, that catalyze (i.e., increase the rates of) chemical reactions. In enzymatic reactions, the molecules at the beginning of the process are called substrates, and the Enzyme converts them into different molecules, called the products. Almost all processes in a biological cell need Enzymes to occur at significant rates.
Humulin	Humulin is the brand name for a group of biosynthetic human insulin products, originally developed by Genentech in 1978 (Generic name insulin isophane) and later acquired by Eli Lilly and Company, the company who arguably facilitated the product's approval with the U.S. Food and Drug Administration. Humulin is synthesized in a laboratory strain of Escherichia coli bacteria which has been genetically altered to produce biosynthetic human insulin. The synthesized insulin is then combined with other compounds or types of insulin which affect its shelf life and absorption.
Hyperglycemia	Hyperglycemia, hyperglycaemia, or high blood sugar is a condition in which an excessive amount of glucose circulates in the blood plasma. This is generally a blood glucose level of 10+ mmol/L (180 mg/dl), but symptoms may not start to become noticeable until later numbers such as 15-20+ mmol/L (270-360 mg/dl)or 15.2-32.6 mmol/L. However, chronic levels exceeding 125 mg/dl can produce organ damage.

	The origin of the term is Greek: hyper-, meaning excessive; -glyc-, meaning sweet; and -emia, meaning `of the blood`.
Hypoglycemia	Hypoglycemia or hypoglycaemia is the medical term for a state produced by a lower than normal level of blood glucose. The term literally means `under-sweet blood` . Hypoglycemia can produce a variety of symptoms and effects but the principal problems arise from an inadequate supply of glucose as fuel to the brain, resulting in impairment of function .
Hypokalemia	Hypokalemia Hypokalaemia refers to the condition in which the concentration of potassium in the blood is low. The prefix hypo- means low (contrast with hyper-, meaning high). Kal refers to kalium, the Neo-Latin for potassium, and -emia means `in the blood.` Normal serum potassium levels are between 3.5 to 5.0 mEq/L; at least 95% of the body`s potassium is found inside cells, with the remainder in the blood.
Hypovolemia	In physiology and medicine, Hypovolemia is a state of decreased blood volume; more specifically, decrease in volume of blood plasma. It is thus the intravascular component of volume contraction (or loss of blood volume due to things such as hemorrhaging or dehydration), but, as it also is the most essential one, Hypovolemia and volume contraction are sometimes used synonymously. It differs from dehydration, which is defined as excessive loss of body water.
Tissue plasminogen activator	Tissue plasminogen activator is a protein involved in the breakdown of blood clots. Specifically, it is a serine protease found on endothelial cells, the cells that line the blood vessels. As an enzyme, it catalyzes the conversion of plasminogen to plasmin, the major enzyme responsible for clot breakdown.
Cimetidine	Cimetidine is a histamine H_2-receptor antagonist that inhibits the production of acid in the stomach. It is largely used in the treatment of heartburn and peptic ulcers. It is marketed by GlaxoSmithKline under the trade name Tagamet .
Desflurane	Desflurane is a highly fluorinated methyl ethyl ether used for maintenance of general anesthesia. Together with sevoflurane, it is gradually replacing isoflurane for human use, except in the third world where its high cost precludes its use. It has the most rapid onset and offset of the volatile anesthetic drugs used for general anesthesia due to its low solubility in blood.

Chapter 2. PART II: Chapter 19 - Chapter 36

Enzyme inhibitors	Enzyme inhibitors are molecules that bind to enzymes and decrease their activity. Since blocking an enzyme`s activity can kill a pathogen or correct a metabolic imbalance, many drugs are Enzyme inhibitors. They are also used as herbicides and pesticides.
Mediastinum	The Mediastinum is a non-delineated group of structures in the thorax, surrounded by loose connective tissue. It is the central compartment of the thoracic cavity. It contains the heart, the great vessels of the heart, esophagus, trachea, phrenic nerve, cardiac nerve, thoracic duct, thymus, and lymph nodes of the central chest.
Streptokinase	Streptokinase(SK), a protein secreted by several species of streptococci can bind and activate human plasminogen. SK is used as an effective and inexpensive clot-dissolving medication in some cases of myocardial infarction (heart attack) and pulmonary embolism.. Streptokinase belongs to a group of medications known as fibrinolytics, and complexes of Streptokinase with human plasminogen can hydrolytically activate other unbound plasminogen by activating through bond cleavage to produce plasmin.
Tetracaine	Tetracaine is a potent local anesthetic of the ester group. It is mainly used topically in ophthalmology and as an antipruritic, and it has been used in spinal anesthesia. In biomedical research, Tetracaine is used to alter the function of calcium release channels (ryanodine receptors) that control the release of calcium from intracellular stores.
Timing	Timing is the spacing of events in time. Some typical uses are: · The act of measuring the elapsed time of something or someone, often at athletic events such as swimming or running, where participants are timed with a device such as a stopwatch. · Engine Timing, for various functions such as ignition, cam Timing to control poppet valve Timing and overlap, and fuel injection Timing. · see ignition Timing · Timing light, · Timing mark

· Comic Timing by a comedian or actor, an element of humor.

· In phonology, the rhythm of a spoken language.

Tumor	A tumor or tumour is the name for a swelling or lesion formed by an abnormal growth of cells (termed neoplastic). tumor is not synonymous with cancer. A tumor can be benign, pre-malignant or malignant, whereas cancer is by definition malignant.
Alcohol	In chemistry, an Alcohol is any organic compound in which a hydroxyl group (-OH) is bound to a carbon atom of an alkyl or substituted alkyl group. The general formula for a simple acyclic Alcohol is $C_nH_{2n+1}OH$. In common terms, the word Alcohol refers to ethanol, the type of Alcohol found in Alcoholic beverages. Ethanol is a colorless, volatile liquid with a mild odor which can be obtained by the fermentation of sugars.
Pelvic inflammatory disease	Pelvic inflammatory disease is a generic term for inflammation of the female uterus, fallopian tubes, and/or ovaries as it progresses to scar formation with adhesions to nearby tissues and organs. This may lead to tissue necrosis and sometimes abscess formation whereby pus can be released into the peritoneum. Pelvic inflammatory disease is often associated with sexually transmitted infections, as it is a common result of such infections.
Androgen	Androgen, also called Androgenic hormones or testoids, is the generic term for any natural or synthetic compound, usually a steroid hormone, that stimulates or controls the development and maintenance of male characteristics in vertebrates by binding to Androgen receptors. This includes the activity of the accessory male sex organs and development of male secondary sex characteristics. Androgens were first discovered in 1936. Androgens are also the original anabolic steroids and the precursor of all estrogens, the female sex hormones.
Burn	A burn is a type of skin injury that may be caused by heat, electricity, chemicals, light, radiation, or friction. Most burns only affect the skin (epidermal tissue and dermis). Rarely deeper tissues, such as muscle, bone, and blood vessel can also be injured.
Malignant hyperthermia	Malignant hyperthermia (Malignant hyperthermia , or `malignant hyperpyrexia due to anaesthesia`) is a rare life-threatening condition that is triggered by exposure to certain drugs used for general anesthesia (specifically all volatile anesthetics), nearly all gas anesthetics, and the neuromuscular blocking agent succinylcholine. In susceptible individuals, these drugs can induce a drastic and uncontrolled increase in skeletal muscle oxidative metabolism, which overwhelms the body`s capacity to supply oxygen, remove carbon dioxide, and regulate body temperature, eventually leading to circulatory collapse and death if not treated quickly.

Susceptibility to Malignant hyperthermia is often inherited as an autosomal dominant disorder, for which there are at least 6 genetic loci of interest, most prominently the ryanodine receptor gene (RYR1).

Steroid	A Steroid is a type of organic compound that contains a specific arrangement of four rings that are joined to each other. Examples of Steroids include cholesterol, the sex hormones estradiol and testosterone, and the anti-inflammatory drug dexamethasone.
	The sterane core of Steroids is composed of seventeen carbon atoms bonded together to form four fused rings: three cyclohexane rings (designated as rings A, B, and C in the figure to the right) and one cyclopentane ring (the D ring).
Sugammadex	Sugammadex (designation Org 25969, tradename Bridion) is a novel agent for reversal of neuromuscular blockade by the agent rocuronium in general anaesthesia. It is the first selective relaxant binding agent (SRBA). On January 3, 2008, Schering-Plough submitted a New Drug Application to the US Food and Drug Administration for Sugammadex, but the FDA rejected the application on August 2008.
Syndrome	In medicine and psychology, the term syndrome refers to the association of several clinically recognizable features, signs (observed by a physician), symptoms (reported by the patient), phenomena or characteristics that often occur together, so that the presence of one feature alerts the physician to the presence of the others. In recent decades the term has been used outside of medicine to refer to a combination of phenomena seen in association. The term syndrome derives from its Greek roots and means literally `run together`, as the features do.
Airway obstruction	Airway obstruction is a respiratory problem caused by increased resistance in the bronchioles that reduces the amount of air inhaled in each breath and the oxygen that reaches the pulmonary arteries. It is different from airway restriction .
	Obstruction can be measured using spirometry.
Awake	Awake refers to the state of being conscious and can be understood in biological terms as the behavioral manifestation of the metabolic state of catabolism. It is the daily recurring period in an organism's life during which consciousness, awareness and all behaviors necessary for survival, i.e., success in (Communication, ambulation, nutritional ingestion and procreation), are conducted. Being Awake is the opposite of being asleep a behavioral manifestation of the daily recurring metabolic state of anabolism.

Chapter 2. PART II: Chapter 19 - Chapter 36

Chapter 2. PART II: Chapter 19 - Chapter 36

Procedures	An ASC is a health care facility that specializes in providing surgery, including certain pain management and diagnostic (e.g., colonoscopy) services in an outpatient setting. Overall, the services provided can be generally called procedures. In simple terms, ASC-qualified procedures can be considered procedures that are more intensive than those done in the average doctor`s office but not so intensive as to require a hospital stay.
Atenolol	Atenolol is a selective β_1 receptor antagonist, a drug belonging to the group of beta blockers (sometimes written β-blockers), a class of drugs used primarily in cardiovascular diseases. Introduced in 1976, Atenolol was developed as a replacement for propranolol in the treatment of hypertension. The chemical works by slowing down the heart and reducing its workload.
Blood	Blood is a specialized bodily fluid that delivers necessary substances to the body's cells -- such as nutrients and oxygen -- and transports waste products away from those same cells. In vertebrates, it is composed of Blood cells suspended in a liquid called Blood plasma. Plasma, which comprises 55% of Blood fluid, is mostly water (90% by volume), and contains dissolved proteins, glucose, mineral ions, hormones, carbon dioxide (plasma being the main medium for excretory product transportation), platelets and Blood cells themselves.
Cardiac surgery	Cardiac surgery is surgery on the heart and/or great vessels performed by a cardiac surgeon. Frequently, it is done to treat complications of ischemic heart disease (for example, coronary artery bypass grafting), correct congenital heart disease, or treat valvular heart disease created by various causes including endocarditis. It also includes heart transplantation.
Cardiovascular system	The circulatory system is an organ system that passes nutrients (such as amino acids and electrolytes), gases, hormones, blood cells, etc. to and from cells in the body to help fight diseases and help stabilize body temperature and pH to maintain homeostasis. This system may be seen strictly as a blood distribution network, but some consider the circulatory system as composed of the Cardiovascular system, which distributes blood, and the lymphatic system, which distributes lymph.
Electrolyte	In chemistry, an Electrolyte is any substance containing free ions that make the substance electrically conductive. The most typical Electrolyte is an ionic solution, but molten Electrolytes and solid Electrolytes are also possible. Electrolytes commonly exist as solutions of acids, bases or salts.

CRam101

Chapter 2. PART II: Chapter 19 - Chapter 36

Endocrine system	The Endocrine system is a system of glands, each of which secretes a type of hormone to regulate the body. The field of study that deals with disorders of endocrine glands is endocrinology, a branch of the wider field of internal medicine. The Endocrine system is an information signal system much like the nervous system.
Epidural	Epidural or extradural hematoma (haematoma) is a type of traumatic brain injury (TBI) in which a buildup of blood occurs between the dura mater (the tough outer membrane of the central nervous system) and the skull. The dura mater also covers the spine, so Epidural bleeds may also occur in the spinal column. Often due to trauma, the condition is potentially deadly because the buildup of blood may increase pressure in the intracranial space and compress delicate brain tissue.
Fluid	A fluid or water deprivation test is a medical test for the purposes of diagnosing the causes of polydipsia, a condition of excessive thirst that causes an excessive intake of water. The patient is required, for a prolonged period, to forgo intake of water completely, to determine the cause of the thirst. This test measures changes in body weight, urine output, and urine composition when fluids are withheld.
Geriatric anesthesia	Geriatric anesthesia is the branch of medicine that studies anesthesia approach in elderly. The perioperative care of elderly patients differs from that of younger patients for a number of reasons. Some of these can be attributed to the changes that occur in the process of aging, but many are also caused by diseases that accompany seniority.
Immune system	An immune system is a system of biological structures and processes within an organism that protects against disease by identifying and killing pathogens and tumour cells. It detects a wide variety of agents, from viruses to parasitic worms, and needs to distinguish them from the organism's own healthy cells and tissues in order to function properly. Detection is complicated as pathogens can evolve rapidly, producing adaptations that avoid the immune system and allow the pathogens to successfully infect their hosts.
Laparoscopic surgery	Laparoscopic surgery, also called minimally invasive surgery (MIS), bandaid surgery, keyhole surgery is a modern surgical technique in which operations in the abdomen are performed through small incisions (usually 0.5-1.5cm) as compared to larger incisions needed in traditional surgical procedures.

Chapter 2. PART II: Chapter 19 - Chapter 36

	Practicioners of `open` surgery sometimes use the misleading defensive term `microscopic` surgery, which implies a small incision. However, open surgery typically requires an incision large enough for the surgeon's hands to enter the patient, while the term microscopic refers to various magnifying devices used during open surgery.
Laser surgery	Laser surgery is surgery using a laser to cut tissue instead of a scalpel. Examples include the use of a laser scalpel in otherwise conventional surgery, and soft tissue Laser surgery, in which the laser beam vaporizes soft tissue with high water content. Laser resurfacing is a technique in which molecular bonds of a material are dissolved by a laser.
Musculoskeletal system	A Musculoskeletal system is an organ system that gives animals (including humans) the ability to move using the muscular and skeletal systems. The Musculoskeletal system provides form, stability, and movement to the body. It is made up of the body's bones (the skeleton), muscles, cartilage, tendons, ligaments, joints, and other connective tissue (the tissue that supports and binds tissues and organs together).
Obstetric	Obstetrics is the surgical specialty dealing with the care of women and their children during pregnancy, childbirth and postnatal. Midwifery is the non-medical equivalent. Veterinary Obstetrics is the same concept for veterinary medicine.
Orthopedic	Orthopedic surgery or Orthopedics (also spelled orthopaedics) is the branch of surgery concerned with conditions involving the musculoskeletal system. Orthopedic surgeons use both surgical and non-surgical means to treat musculoskeletal trauma, sports injuries, degenerative diseases, infections, tumors, and congenital conditions. Nicholas Andry coined the word `orthopaedics`, derived from Greek words for orthos and paideion (`child`), when he published Orthopaedia: or the Art of Correcting and Preventing Deformities in Children in 1741.
Podiatry	Podiatry is a branch of medicine devoted to the study, diagnosis and treatment of disorders of the foot, ankle and lower leg. A podiatrist treats the foot of a patient at a homeless shelter in Homestead, Florida. Within the United Kingdom, the titles `podiatrist` and `chiropodist` are to some extent interchangeable. Although the UK government-appointed regulator acknowledges both titles and makes no distinction between them, they are used differently within the occupation.

Chapter 2. PART II: Chapter 19 - Chapter 36

Respiratory system	The respiratory system`s function is to allow gas exchange to all parts of the body. The space between the alveoli and the capillaries, the anatomy or structure of the exchange system, and the precise physiological uses of the exchanged gases vary depending on the organism. In humans and other mammals, for example, the anatomical features of the respiratory system include airways, lungs, and the respiratory muscles.
Appetite	The Appetite is the desire to eat food, felt as hunger. Appetite exists in all higher life-forms, and serves to regulate adequate energy intake to maintain metabolic needs. It is regulated by a close interplay between the digestive tract, adipose tissue and the brain.
Body mass index	The Body mass index is a controversial statistical measurement which compares a person's weight and height. Though it does not actually measure the percentage of body fat, it may be a useful tool to estimate a healthy body weight based on how tall a person is. Due to its ease of measurement and calculation, it is the most widely used diagnostic tool to identify weight problems within a population, usually whether individuals are underweight, overweight or obese.
Adipose tissue	In histology, Adipose tissue or body fat or just fat is loose connective tissue composed of adipocytes. It is technically composed of roughly only 80% fat; fat in its solitary state exists in the liver and muscles. Adipose tissue is derived from lipoblasts.
Amitriptyline	Amitriptyline is a tricyclic antidepressant (TCA). It is the most widely used TCA and is perhaps also the most effective against depression.
Amphetamine	Amphetamine (amfetamine (INN)) is a psychostimulant drug that is known to produce increased wakefulness and focus in association with decreased fatigue and appetite. Amphetamine is related to drugs such as methAmphetamine, dextroAmphetamine, and levoAmphetamine, which are a group of potent drugs that act by increasing levels of dopamine and norepinephrine in the brain, inducing euphoria. The group includes prescription CNS drugs commonly used to treat attention-deficit hyperactivity disorder (ADHD).
Ankylosing spondylitis	Ankylosing spondylitis, previously known as Bechterew's disease, Bechterew syndrome, and Marie Strümpell disease, a form of Spondyloarthritis, is a chronic, inflammatory arthritis and autoimmune disease. It mainly affects joints in the spine and the sacroilium in the pelvis, and can cause eventual fusion of the spine. It is a member of the group of the spondyloarthropathies with a strong genetic predisposition.

Chapter 2. PART II: Chapter 19 - Chapter 36

Glasgow coma scale	Glasgow Coma Scale or Glasgow Coma Scale, is a neurological scale which aims to give a reliable, objective way of recording the conscious state of a person, for initial as well as subsequent assessment. A patient is assessed against the criteria of the scale, and the resulting points give a patient score between 3 (indicating deep unconsciousness) and either 14 (original scale) or 15 (the more widely used modified or revised scale). Glasgow Coma Scale was initially used to assess level of consciousness after head injury, and the scale is now used by first aid, EMS and doctors as being applicable to all acute medical and trauma patients.
Rheumatoid arthritis	Rheumatoid arthritis is a chronic, systemic inflammatory disorder that may affect many tissues and organs, but principally attacks the joints producing an inflammatory synovitis that often progresses to destruction of the articular cartilage and ankylosis of the joints. Rheumatoid arthritis can also produce diffuse inflammation in the lungs, pericardium, pleura, and sclera, and also nodular lesions, most common in subcutaneous tissue under the skin. Although the cause of Rheumatoid arthritis is unknown, autoimmunity plays a pivotal role in its chronicity and progression.
Coma	In medicine, a Coma is a profound state of unconsciousness. A Comatose person cannot be awakened, fails to respond normally to pain or light, does not have sleep-wake cycles, and does not take voluntary actions. Coma may result from a variety of conditions, including intoxication, metabolic abnormalities, central nervous system diseases, acute neurologic injuries such as stroke, and hypoxia.
Cranial nerves	Cranial nerves are nerves that emerge directly from the brain stem, in contrast to spinal nerves which emerge from segments of the spinal cord. Human Cranial nerves are evolutionarily homologous to those found in many other vertebrates. Cranial nerves XI and XII evolved in the common ancestor to amniotes (non-amphibian tetrapods) thus totaling twelve pairs.
Nerve	A Nerve is an enclosed, cable-like bundle of peripheral axons (the long, slender projections of neurons). A Nerve provides a common pathway for the electrochemical Nerve impulses that are transmitted along each of the axons. Nerves are found only in the peripheral nervous system.
Reflex	A Reflex action, also known as a Reflex, is an involuntary and nearly instantaneous movement in response to a stimulus. In most contexts, in particular those involving humans, Reflex actions are mediated via the Reflex arc; this is not always true in other animals, nor does it apply to casual uses of the term `Reflex`.

For a Reflex, reaction time or latency is the time from the onset of a stimulus until the organism responds.

Cardiac index

Cardiac index is a vasodynamic parameter that relates the cardiac output (CO) to body surface area (BSA), thus relating heart performance to the size of the individual. The unit of measurement is litres per minute per square metre ($l/min/m^2$).
The index is usually calculated using the following formula:

$$ CI = \frac{CO}{BSA} = \frac{SV * HR}{BSA} $$

where

Cardiac index=Cardiac index
BSA=Body surface area
SV=Stroke volume
HR=Heart rate
CO=Cardiac output

The normal range of Cardiac index is 2.6 - 4.2 L/min per square meter.

Hypertension

Hypertension is a chronic medical condition in which the blood pressure is elevated. It is also referred to as high blood pressure or shortened to HT, HTN or HPN. The word `Hypertension`, by itself, normally refers to systemic, arterial Hypertension.

Hypertension can be classified as either essential (primary) or secondary.

Hydrocarbon

In organic chemistry, a Hydrocarbon is an organic compound consisting entirely of hydrogen and carbon. Hydrocarbons from which one hydrogen atom has been removed are functional groups, called hydrocarbyls. Aromatic Hydrocarbons (arenes), alkanes, alkenes, cycloalkanes and alkyne-based compounds are different types of Hydrocarbons.

Infarction	In medicine, an infarction is the process of tissue death (necrosis) caused by blockage of the tissue`s blood supply. The supplying artery may be blocked by an obstruction (e.g. an embolus, thrombus, or atherosclerotic plaque), may be mechanically compressed (e.g. tumor, volvulus, or hernia), ruptured by trauma (e.g. atherosclerosis or vasculitides), or vasoconstricted (e.g. cocaine vasoconstriction leading to myocardial infarction).
	infarctions are commonly associated with hypertension or atherosclerosis.
Myocardial Infarction	Myocardial infarction or acute Myocardial infarction (AMyocardial infarction), commonly known as a heart attack, is the interruption of blood supply to part of the heart, causing some heart cells to die. This is most commonly due to occlusion (blockage) of a coronary artery following the rupture of a vulnerable atherosclerotic plaque, which is an unstable collection of lipids (like cholesterol) and white blood cells (especially macrophages) in the wall of an artery. The resulting ischemia (restriction in blood supply) and oxygen shortage, if left untreated for a sufficient period of time, can cause damage or death (infarction) of heart muscle tissue (myocardium).
Unstable angina	Unstable angina is a type of angina pectoris that is irregular. It is a type of acute coronary syndrome.
	It can be difficult to distinguish from non-Q-wave myocardial infarction.
Cardiology	Cardiology is a specialty dealing with disorders of the heart and blood vessels. The field includes diagnosis and treatment of congenital heart defects, coronary artery disease, heart failure, valvular heart disease and electrophysiology. Physicians specializing in this field of medicine are called cardiologists.
Cardiac dysrhythmia	Cardiac dysrhythmia is a term for any of a large and heterogeneous group of conditions in which there is abnormal electrical activity in the heart. The heart beat may be too fast or too slow, and may be regular or irregular.
	Some arrhythmias are life-threatening medical emergencies that can result in cardiac arrest and sudden death.
Diagnostic test	A Diagnostic test is any kind of medical test performed to aid in the diagnosis or detection of disease. For example:

· to diagnose diseases

· to measure the progress or recovery from disease

· to confirm that a person is free from disease
A drug test can be a specific medical test to ascertain the presence of a certain drug in the body (for example, in drug addicts).

Some medical tests are parts of a simple physical examination which require only simple tools in the hands of a skilled practitioner, and can be performed in an office environment.

Guideline	`Guideline` is the NATO reporting name for the Soviet SA-2 surface-to-air missile. A Guideline is any document that aims to streamline particular processes according to a set routine. By definition, following a Guideline is never mandatory (protocol would be a better term for a mandatory procedure).
Pacemaker	A pacemaker (, so as not to be confused with the heart`s natural pacemaker) is a medical device which uses electrical impulses, delivered by electrodes contacting the heart muscles, to regulate the beating of the heart. The primary purpose of a pacemaker is to maintain an adequate heart rate, either because the heart`s native pacemaker is not fast enough, or there is a block in the heart`s electrical conduction system. Modern pacemakers are externally programmable and allow the cardiologist to select the optimum pacing modes for individual patients.
Chronic obstructive pulmonary disease	Chronic obstructive pulmonary disease refers to chronic bronchitis and emphysema, a pair of two commonly co-existing diseases of the lungs in which the airways become narrowed. This leads to a limitation of the flow of air to and from the lungs causing shortness of breath. In contrast to asthma, the limitation of airflow is poorly reversible and usually gets progressively worse over time.
Emphysema	Emphysema is a long-term, progressive disease of the lung that primarily causes shortness of breath. In people with Emphysema, the lung tissues necessary to support the physical shape and function of the lung are destroyed. It is included in a group of diseases called chronic obstructive pulmonary disease or COPD (pulmonary refers to the lungs).

Chapter 2. PART II: Chapter 19 - Chapter 36

Asthma	Asthma is a common chronic inflammatory disease of the airways characterized by variable and recurring symptoms, airflow obstruction, and bronchospasm. Symptoms include wheezing, cough, chest tightness, and shortness of breath. Medicines such as inhaled short-acting beta-2 agonists may be used to treat acute attacks.
Chronic bronchitis	Chronic bronchitis is a chronic inflammation of the bronchi (medium-size airways) in the lungs. It is generally considered one of the two forms of chronic obstructive pulmonary disease (COPD). It is defined clinically as a persistent cough that produces sputum (phlegm) and mucus, for at least three months in two consecutive years.
Local	Local usually refers to something nearby, or in the immediate area. It may be used in many ways, some of which are related to this general meaning, others which are not: .
Local anesthetic	A Local anesthetic is a drug that causes reversible local anesthesia and a loss of nociception. When it is used on specific nerve pathways (nerve block), effects such as analgesia and paralysis can be achieved. Clinical Local anesthetics belong to one of two classes: aminoamide and aminoester Local anesthetics.
Arthroplasty	Joint replacement consists of replacing painful, arthritic, worn or cancerous parts of the joint with artificial surfaces shaped in such a way as to allow joint movement. Arthroplasty [from Greek arthron, joint, limb, articulate, + -plassein, to form, mould, forge, feign, make an image of] is a procedure of orthopedic surgery, in which the arthritic or dysfunctional joint surface is replaced with something better or by remodelling or realigning the joint by osteotomy or some other procedure.

Previously, a popular form of Arthroplasty was interpositional Arthroplasty with interposition of some other tissue like skin, muscle or tendon to keep inflammatory surfaces apart or excisional Arthroplasty in which the joint surface and bone was removed leaving scar tissue to fill in the gap.

Infection

An Infection is the detrimental colonization of a host organism by a foreign species. In an Infection, the infecting organism seeks to utilize the host`s resources to multiply, usually at the expense of the host. The infecting organism, or pathogen, interferes with the normal functioning of the host and can lead to chronic wounds, gangrene, loss of an infected limb, and even death.

Screening

One meaning of Screening is the investigation of a great number of something (for instance, people) looking for those with a particular problem or feature. For example at an airport many bags are screened by x-ray to try to detect any which may contain weapons or explosives, and people are screened by passing through a metal detector. If only part of a population is screened, Screening is equivalent to sampling in statistics.

Important cases of Screening include:

· Screening

· Screening
Screening can also mean preventing access of something by some sort of barrier. Particular cases:

· Electromagnetic shielding in physics, the exclusion of electric, magnetic, or electromagnetic fields by a metallic screen or shield

· In atomic physics and chemistry, the Screening effect or atomic shielding is the reduction of effective nuclear charge by intervening electron shells

· Screening a process that represents lighter shades as tiny dots, rather than solid areas, of ink by passing ink through a perforated screen

· The investigation of a large population is related; the members of a population are filtered by a metaphorical, rather than physical, screen

· Screening is a process stage when cleaning paper pulp
Other uses:

· Film Screening, showing a film by projection onto a screen

Hyperthermia	Hyperthermia is an elevated body temperature due to failed thermoregulation. Hyperthermia occurs when the body produces or absorbs more heat than it can dissipate. When the elevated body temperatures are sufficiently high, Hyperthermia is a medical emergency and requires immediate treatment to prevent disability and death.
Hyperthyroidism	Hyperthyroidism is the term for overactive tissue within the thyroid gland causing an overproduction of thyroid hormones (thyroxine or `T4` and/or triiodothyronine or `T3`). Hyperthyroidism is thus a cause of thyrotoxicosis, the clinical condition of increased thyroid hormones in the blood. It is important to note that Hyperthyroidism and thyrotoxicosis are not synonymous.
Thyroid	The thyroid is one of the largest endocrine glands in the body. This gland is found in the neck inferior to (below) the thyroid cartilage (also known as the Adam`s apple in men) and at approximately the same level as the cricoid cartilage. The thyroid controls how quickly the body uses energy, makes proteins, and controls how sensitive the body should be to other hormones.
Hypothyroidism	Hypothyroidism is the disease state in humans and in animals caused by insufficient production of thyroid hormone by the thyroid gland. Cretinism is a form of Hypothyroidism found in infants. About three percent of the general population is hypothyroidic.
Chest radiograph	In medicine, a Chest radiograph, commonly called a chest x-ray (CXR), is a projection radiograph of the chest used to diagnose conditions affecting the chest, its contents, and nearby structures. Chest radiographs are among the most common films taken, being diagnostic of many conditions.

Chapter 2. PART II: Chapter 19 - Chapter 36

	Like all methods of radiography, Chest radiography employs ionizing radiation in the form of x-rays to generate images of the chest.
Fasting	Fasting is primarily the act of willingly abstaining from some or all food, drink, or both, for a period of time. An absolute fast is normally defined as abstinence from all food and liquid for a defined period, usually a single day (24 hours), or several daytime periods. Other fasts may be only partially restrictive, limiting particular foods or substance.
Pregnancy	Pregnancy is the carrying of one or more offspring, known as a fetus or embryo, inside the uterus of a female. In a pregnancy, there can be multiple gestations, as in the case of twins or triplets. Human pregnancy is the most studied of all mammalian pregnancies.
TIC	A Tic is a sudden, repetitive, nonrhythmic, stereotyped motor movement or vocalization involving discrete muscle groups. Tics can be invisible to the observer, such as abdominal tensing or toe crunching. Common motor and phonic Tics are, respectively, eye blinking and throat clearing.
Fluid balance	Fluid balance is the concept of human homeostasis that the amount of fluid lost from the body is equal to the amount of fluid taken in. Euvolemia is the state of normal body fluid volume. Water is necessary for all life on Earth.
Sodium	Sodium is a metallic element with a symbol Na and atomic number 11. It is a soft, silvery-white, highly reactive metal and is a member of the alkali metals within `group 1`. It has only one stable isotope, ^{23}Na. Elemental Sodium was first isolated by Sir Humphry Davy in 1806 by passing an electric current through molten Sodium hydroxide.
Balance disorder	A Balance disorder is a disturbance that causes an individual to feel unsteady, giddy, woozy spinning, or floating. Balance is the result of a number of body systems working together. Specifically, in order to achieve balance, the eyes (visual system), ears (vestibular system) and the body's sense of where it is in space (proprioception) need to be intact.
Hyponatremia	Hyponatremia is an electrolyte disturbance in which the sodium concentration in the plasma is lower than normal.

Severe or rapidly progressing Hyponatremia can result in swelling of the brain , and the symptoms of Hyponatremia are mainly neurological. Hyponatremia is most often a complication of other medical illnesses in which either fluids rich in sodium are lost (for example because of diarrhea or vomiting), or excess water accumulates in the body at a higher rate than it can be excreted (for example in polydipsia or syndrome of inappropriate antidiuretic hormone, SIADH).

Nerve block

Regional Nerve blockade, or more commonly Nerve block, is a general term used to refer to the injection of local anesthetic onto or near nerves for temporary control of pain. It can also be used as a diagnostic tool to identify specific nerves as pain generators. Permanent Nerve block can be produced by destruction of nerve tissue.

Peripheral

A Peripheral is a device attached to a host computer but not part of it whose primary functionality is dependent upon the host, and can therefore be considered as expanding the host`s capabilities, while not forming part of the system`s core architecture.

Examples are printers, scanners, tape drives, microphones, speakers, webcams, and cameras.

Whether something is a Peripheral or part of a computer is not always clearly demarcated; a video capture card inside a computer case is not part of the core computer but is contained in the case.

Pharmacokinetics

Pharmacokinetics is a branch of pharmacology dedicated to the determination of the fate of substances administered externally to a living organism. In practice, this discipline is applied mainly to drug substances, though in principle it concerns itself with all manner of compounds ingested or otherwise delivered externally to an organism, such as nutrients, metabolites, hormones, toxins, etc.

Pharmacokinetics is often studied in conjunction with pharmacodynamics.

Central pontine myelinolysis

Central pontine myelinolysis is a neurologic disease caused by severe damage of the myelin sheath of nerve cells in the brainstem, more precisely in the area termed the pons.
It can also occur outside the pons. The term `osmotic demyelinization syndrome` is similar to `Central pontine myelinolysis`, but also includes areas outside the pons.

Chapter 2. PART II: Chapter 19 - Chapter 36

Magnesium	Magnesium is a chemical element with the symbol Mg, atomic number 12 and common oxidation number +2. It is an alkaline earth metal and the eighth most abundant element in the Earth`s crust by mass, although ninth in the known Universe as a whole. This preponderance of Magnesium is related to the fact that it is easily built up in supernova stars from a sequential addition of three helium nuclei to carbon . Magnesium constitutes about 2% of the Earth`s crust by mass, which makes it the eighth most abundant element in the crust.
Blood volume	Blood volume is the volume of blood (both red blood cells and plasma) in a person's circulatory system. A typical adult has a Blood volume of approximately between 4.7 and 5 liters, with females generally having less Blood volume than males.
Transfusion	Blood Transfusion is the process of transferring blood or blood-based products from one person into the circulatory system of another. Blood Transfusions can be life-saving in some situations, such as massive blood loss due to trauma, or can be used to replace blood lost during surgery. Blood Transfusions may also be used to treat a severe anaemia or thrombocytopenia caused by a blood disease.
Cryoprecipitate	Cryoprecipitate is a frozen blood product prepared from plasma. It is often transfused as a four to six unit pool instead of as a single product. Many uses of the product have been replaced by factor concentrates, but it is still routinely stocked by many hospital blood banks.
Fresh frozen plasma	The term Fresh frozen plasma refers to the liquid portion of human blood that has been frozen and preserved quickly after a blood donation and will be used for blood transfusion. The capitalized term Fresh frozen plasma is the proper name in the United States for the fluid portion of one unit of human blood that has been centrifuged, separated, and frozen solid at −18 °C (−0.4 °F) (or colder) within 8 hours of collection. Other single-donor plasma units, either frozen or liquid, are substituted for Fresh frozen plasma. Indications for these products are similar to those for Fresh frozen plasma with the exception heat-sensitive proteins in the plasma, such as factor V, and the term is often used to mean any transfused plasma product.
Blood substitutes	Blood substitutes are used to fill fluid volume and/or carry oxygen and other blood gases in the cardiovascular system. Although commonly used, the term is not accurate since human blood performs many important functions which Blood substitutes may not. Red blood cells transport oxygen, white blood cells defend against disease, platelets promote clotting, and plasma proteins perform various functions.

Red blood cells	Red blood cells are the most common type of blood cell and the vertebrate organism`s principal means of delivering oxygen ($O_2$) to the body tissues via the blood flow through the circulatory system. They take up oxygen in the lungs or gills and release it while squeezing through the body`s capillaries. These cells` cytoplasm is rich in hemoglobin, an iron-containing biomolecule that can bind oxygen and is responsible for the blood`s red color.
Polymerase chain reaction	In molecular biology, the Polymerase chain reaction is a technique to amplify a single or few copies of a piece of DNA across several orders of magnitude, generating thousands to millions of copies of a particular DNA sequence. The method relies on thermal cycling, consisting of cycles of repeated heating and cooling of the reaction for DNA melting and enzymatic replication of the DNA. Primers (short DNA fragments) containing sequences complementary to the target region along with a DNA polymerase (after which the method is named) are key components to enable selective and repeated amplification. As Polymerase chain reaction progresses, the DNA generated is itself used as a template for replication, setting in motion a chain reaction in which the DNA template is exponentially amplified.
Graft-versus-host disease	Graft-versus-host disease (GVHD) is a common complication of allogeneic bone marrow transplantation in which functional immune cells in the transplanted marrow recognize the recipient as `foreign` and mount an immunologic attack. It can also take place in a blood transfusion under certain circumstances. According to the 1959 Billingham Criteria, 3 criteria must be met in order for GVHD to occur.
Assertive community treatment	Assertive community treatment is a highly intensive and integrated approach for community mental health service delivery. Assertive community treatment programs serve people whose symptoms of mental illness result in severe functional difficulties that interfere with their ability to achieve personally meaningful recovery goals in several major areas of life: working, having friends, living independently, and so forth. The defining characteristics of Assertive community treatment include: · a clear focus on those participants (clients) who require the most help from the service delivery system; · an explicit mission to promote the participants' independence, rehabilitation, and recovery, and in so doing to prevent homelessness and unnecessary hospitalization; · a primary emphasis on home visits and other in vivo (out-of-the-office) interventions, eliminating the need to transfer learned behaviors from an artificial rehabilitation or treatment setting to the 'real world';

· a participant-to-staff ratio that is low enough to allow the Assertive community treatment 'core services team' to perform virtually all of the necessary rehabilitation, treatment, and community support tasks themselves in a coordinated and efficient manner -- unlike traditional case managers, who broker or 'farm out' most of the work to other professionals;

· a 'total team approach' in which all of the staff work with all of the participants;

· an interdisciplinary assessment and service planning process that typically involves a psychiatrist and one or more nurses, social workers, substance abuse specialists, vocational rehabilitation specialists, and peer recovery specialists (individuals who have had personal, successful experience with the recovery process);

· a willingness on the part of the team to take ultimate professional responsibility for the participants' well-being in all areas of community functioning, including most especially the 'nitty-gritty' aspects of everyday life;

· a conscious effort to help people avoid crisis situations in the first place or, if that proves impossible, to intervene at any time of the day or night to keep crises from turning into unnecessary hospitalizations; and

· a promise to work with people on a time-unlimited basis, as long as they demonstrate a continuing need for this highly intensive and integrated form of professional help.

Anesthesiologist	An anaesthetist also 'anaesthesiologist,' is a medical doctor trained to administer anesthesia (e.g. a drug) and manage the medical care of patients before, during, and after surgery. According to Mosby's Medical Dictionary, 8th edition, 2009, anesthetist is a general term used to describe a health care professional trained to administer anesthesia to their patients. In addition, the source defines an Anesthesiologist is a physician who completes an accredited residency program in anesthesiology.
Nurse Anesthetist	A Nurse anesthetist is a registered nurse and advanced practice nurse who has acquired additional education to administer anesthesia. In the United States, education is overseen by the American Association of Nurse anesthetists AANurse anesthetist Council on Accreditation of Nurse Anesthesia Educational Programs. The Nurse anesthetist`s education and official title vary in different nations.

Chapter 2. PART II: Chapter 19 - Chapter 36

Schwann cell	Schwann cells are glia of the peripheral nervous system (PNS). They are involved in many important aspects of peripheral nerve biology; the conduction of nervous impulses along axons, nerve development and regeneration, trophic support for neurons, production of the nerve extracellular matrix and presentation of antigens to T-lymphocytes. Charcot-Marie-Tooth disease (CMT), Guillain-Barré syndrome (GBS), schwannomatosis and chronic inflammatory demyelinating polyneuropathy (CIDP) are all neuropathies involving Schwann cells.
Schwann cells	Schwann cells are glia of the peripheral nervous system (PNS). They are involved in many important aspects of peripheral nerve biology; the conduction of nervous impulses along axons, nerve development and regeneration, trophic support for neurons, production of the nerve extracellular matrix and presentation of antigens to T-lymphocytes. Charcot-Marie-Tooth disease (CMT), Guillain-Barré syndrome (GBS), schwannomatosis and chronic inflammatory demyelinating polyneuropathy (CIDP) are all neuropathies involving Schwann cells.
Anatomy	Anatomy is a branch of biology and medicine that is the consideration of the structure of living things. It is a general term that includes human Anatomy, animal Anatomy and plant Anatomy (phytotomy). In some of its facets Anatomy is closely related to embryology, comparative Anatomy and comparative embryology, through common roots in evolution.
Blood pressure	Blood pressure is the pressure (force per unit area) exerted by circulating blood on the walls of blood vessels, and constitutes one of the principal vital signs. The pressure of the circulating blood decreases as it moves away from the heart through arteries and capillaries, and toward the heart through veins. When unqualified, the term Blood pressure usually refers to brachial arterial pressure: that is, in the major blood vessel of the upper left or right arm that takes blood away from the heart.
Brachial plexus	The Brachial plexus is an arrangement of nerve fibers, running from the spine, formed by the ventral rami of the lower four cervical and first thoracic nerve roots (C5-T1). It proceeds through the neck, the axilla (armpit region), and into the arm. The Brachial plexus is responsible for cutaneous and muscular innervation of the entire upper limb, with two exceptions: the trapezius muscle innervated by the spinal accessory nerve (CN XI) and an area of skin near the axilla innervated by the intercostobrachial nerve.
Physiology	Physiology is the study of the mechanical, physical, and biochemical functions of living organisms. Physiology has traditionally been divided between plant Physiology and animal and all living things Physiology but the principles of Physiology are universal, no matter what particular organism is being studied. For example, what is learned about the Physiology of yeast cells may also apply to human cells that one may be studying.

Chapter 2. PART II: Chapter 19 - Chapter 36

Ischemia	In medicine, Ischemia is a restriction in blood supply, generally due to factors in the blood vessels, with resultant damage or dysfunction of tissue. It may also be spelled ischaemia or ischæmia.
	Rather than hypoxia , Ischemia is an absolute or relative shortage of the blood supply to an organ, i.e. a shortage of oxygen, glucose and other blood-borne fuels.
Neurolemma	Neurolemma is the outermost nucleated cytoplasmic layer of Schwann cells that surrounds the axon of the neuron. It forms the outermost layer of the nerve fiber in the peripheral nervous system.
	The Neurolemma is underlain by the basal lamina (referred to as the medullary sheath in the included illustrations.
Posttraumatic stress disorder	Posttraumatic stress disorder is an anxiety disorder that can develop after exposure to one or more traumatic events that threatened or caused great physical harm. It is a severe and ongoing emotional reaction to an extreme psychological trauma. This stressor may involve someone`s actual death, a threat to the patient`s or someone else`s life, serious physical injury, an unwanted sexual act, or a threat to physical or psychological integrity, overwhelming psychological defenses.
Blood flow	Blood flow is the flow of blood in the cardiovascular system. It can be calculated by dividing the vascular resistance into the pressure gradient.
	Mathematically, Blood flow is described by Darcy's law (which can be viewed as the fluid equivalent of Ohm's law) and approximately by Hagen-Poiseuille equation.
Metabolism	Metabolism is the set of chemical reactions that happen in living organisms to maintain life. These processes allow organisms to grow and reproduce, maintain their structures, and respond to their environments. Metabolism is usually divided into two categories.
Pathology	Pathology is the study and diagnosis of disease through examination of organs, tissues, bodily fluids, and whole bodies (autopsies). The term also encompasses the related scientific study of disease processes, called General Pathology. Medical Pathology is divided in two main branches, Anatomical Pathology and Clinical Pathology.

Supine position	The Supine position is a position of the body: lying down with the face up, as opposed to the prone position, which is face down, sometimes with the hands behind the head or neck. When used in surgical procedures, it allows access to the peritoneal, thoracic and pericardial regions; as well as the head, neck and extremities.
	Using terms defined in the anatomical position, the dorsal side is down, and the ventral side is up.
Portal hypertension	In medicine, Portal hypertension is hypertension (high blood pressure) in the portal vein and its tributaries.
	It is often defined as a portal pressure gradient (the difference in pressure between the portal vein and the hepatic veins) of 5 mm Hg or greater.
	Causes can be divided into prehepatic, intrahepatic, and posthepatic.
Rhabdomyolysis	Rhabdomyolysis is the rapid breakdown (lysis) of skeletal muscle (rhabdomyo) due to injury to muscle tissue. The muscle damage may be caused by physical (e.g., crush injury), chemical, or biological factors. The destruction of the muscle leads to the release of the breakdown products of damaged muscle cells into the bloodstream; some of these, such as myoglobin (a protein), are harmful to the kidney and may lead to acute kidney failure.
Median sternotomy	Median sternotomy is a type of surgical procedure in which a vertical inline incision is made along the sternum, after which the sternum itself is divided, or `cracked`. This procedure provides access to the heart and lungs for surgical procedures such as heart transplant, corrective surgery for congenital heart defects (CHDs), or coronary artery bypass surgery.
	Median sternotomy is often mistakenly referred to as open heart surgery; however, open heart involves incision of the pericardium, and many Median sternotomy procedures do not require this.

Chapter 2. PART II: Chapter 19 - Chapter 36

Tourniquet	A Tourniquet is a constricting or compressing device used to control venous and arterial circulation to an extremity for a period of time. Pressure is applied circumferentially upon the skin and underlying tissues of a limb; this pressure is transferred to the walls of vessels, causing them to become temporarily occluded. It is generally used as a tool for a medical professional in applications such as cannulation or to stem the flow of traumatic bleeding, especially by military medics.
Ulnar nerve	In human anatomy, the Ulnar nerve is a nerve which runs near the ulna bone. The Ulnar nerve is the largest unprotected nerve in the human body (meaning, unprotected by muscle or bone), and the only unprotected nerve that does not serve a purely sensory function (those nerves specifically meant to perceive changes in the environment, such as nerves in the skin). This nerve is directly connected to the little finger, and the adjacent half of the ring finger, supplying the palmar side of these fingers, including both front and back of the tips, perhaps as far back as the fingernail beds.
Asymptomatic	In medicine, a disease is Asymptomatic if a patient carries a disease or infection but experiences no symptoms. A condition might be Asymptomatic if it fails to show the noticeable symptoms with which it is usually associated. Asymptomatic infections are also called subclinical infections.
Neuropathy	Neuropathy is a medical term referring to disorders of the nerves of the peripheral nervous system (specifically excluding encephalopathy and myelopathy, which pertain to the central nervous system). It is usually considered equivalent to peripheral Neuropathy, which is defined as deranged function and structure of peripheral motor, sensory, and autonomic neurons, involving either the entire neuron or selected levels. According to some sources, a disorder of the cranial nerves can be considered a Neuropathy.
Abdominal aorta	The Abdominal aorta is the largest artery in the abdominal cavity. As part of the aorta, it is a direct continuation of the descending aorta (of the thorax). It begins at the level of the diaphragm, crossing it via the aortic hiatus, technically behind the diaphragm, at the vertebral level of T12. It travels down the posterior wall of the abdomen in front of the vertebral column.
Nerve root	A Nerve root is the initial segment of a nerve leaving the central nervous system. Types include: · A cranial Nerve root, the beginning of one of the twelve pairs leaving the central nervous system from the brain stem or the highest levels of the spinal cord;

· A spinal Nerve root, the beginning of one of the thirty-one pairs leaving the central nervous system from the spinal cord. Each spinal Nerve root consists of the union of a sensory dorsal root and a motor ventral root.

Hemiparesis	Hemiparesis is weakness on one side of the body. Contrast with Hemiplegia, which is total paralysis of the arm, leg, and trunk on the same side of the body. Hemiparesis is generally caused by lesions of the corticospinal tract, which runs down from the cortical neurons of the frontal lobe to the motor neurons of the spinal cord and is responsible for the movements of the muscles of the body and its limbs.
Lithotomy	Lithotomy from Greek for `lithos` and `tomos` (cut), is a surgical method for removal of calculi, stones formed inside certain hollow organs, such as the bladder and kidneys (urinary calculus) and gallbladder (gallstones), that cannot exit naturally through the urethra, ureter or biliary duct. The procedure, which is usually done by means of a surgical incision (therefore invasive), differs from lithotripsy, wherein the stones are crushed either by a minimally invasive probe inserted through the exit canal, or by ultrasound waves (extracorporeal lithotripsy), which is a non-invasive procedure. Human beings have known of bladder stones (`vesical calculi`) for thousands of years, and have attempted to treat them for almost as long.
Paraplegia	Paraplegia is an impairment in motor and/or sensory function of the lower extremities. It is usually the result of spinal cord injury or a congenital condition such as spina bifida which affects the neural elements of the spinal canal. The area of the spinal canal which is affected in Paraplegia is either the thoracic, lumbar, or sacral regions.
Quadriplegia	Quadriplegia, also known as tetraplegia, is paralysis caused by illness or injury to a human that results in the partial or total loss of use of all of their limbs and torso; paraplegia is similar but does not affect the arms. The loss is usually sensory and motor, which means both sensation and control are lost. It is caused by damage to the brain or the spinal cord at a high level C1 - C8 - in particular, spinal cord injuries secondary to an injury to the cervical spine.

Chapter 2. PART II: Chapter 19 - Chapter 36

Spinal cord	The Spinal cord is a long, thin, tubular bundle of nervous tissue and support cells that extends from the brain. The brain and Spinal cord together make up the central nervous system. The Spinal cord extends down to the space in between the first and second lumbar vertebrae.
Anterior ischemic optic neuropathy	Anterior ischemic optic neuropathy is a medical condition involving loss of vision due to damage to the optic nerve from insufficient blood supply. Anterior ischemic optic neuropathy is generally divided into two types: arteritic Anterior ischemic optic neuropathy (or AAnterior ischemic optic neuropathy) and non-arteritic Anterior ischemic optic neuropathy (NAnterior ischemic optic neuropathy or simply Anterior ischemic optic neuropathy The distinction between AAnterior ischemic optic neuropathy and NAnterior ischemic optic neuropathy was made to highlight the different etiologies of Anterior ischemic optic neuropathy.
Retina	The vertebrate Retina is a light sensitive tissue lining the inner surface of the eye. The optics of the eye create an image of the visual world on the Retina, which serves much the same function as the film in a camera. Light striking the Retina initiates a cascade of chemical and electrical events that ultimately trigger nerve impulses.
Arteries	Arteries are blood vessels that carry blood away from the heart. All Arteries, with the exception of the pulmonary and umbilical Arteries, carry oxygenated blood. The circulatory system is extremely important for sustaining life.
Artery	The arterial system is the higher-pressure portion of the circulatory system. Arterial pressure varies between the peak pressure during heart contraction, called the systolic pressure, and the minimum, or diastolic pressure between contractions, when the heart expands and refills. This pressure variation within the Artery produces the pulse which is observable in any Artery, and reflects heart activity.
Vein	In the circulatory system, Veins are blood vessels that carry blood towards the heart. Most Veins carry deoxygenated blood from the tissues back to the lungs; exceptions are the pulmonary and umbilical Veins, both of which carry oxygenated blood. They differ from arteries in structure and function; for example, arteries are more muscular than Veins and they carry blood away from the heart.

Chapter 2. PART II: Chapter 19 - Chapter 36

Compartment syndrome	Compartment syndrome is an acute medical problem following injury, surgery or in most cases repetitive and extensive muscle use, in which increased pressure (usually caused by inflammation) within a confined space (fascial compartment) in the body impairs blood supply. Without prompt surgical treatment, it may lead to nerve damage and muscle death. This condition is most commonly seen in the anterior compartment and posterior compartment of the leg.
Mean arterial pressure	The Mean arterial pressure is a term used in medicine to describe an average blood pressure in an individual. It is defined as the average arterial pressure during a single cardiac cycle. Mean arterial pressure can be determined from: $$MAP = (CO \times SVR) + CVP$$ where: · CO is cardiac output · SVR is systemic vascular resistance · CVP is central venous pressure and usually small enough to be neglected in this formula.
Stent	In medicine, a Stent is a man-made `tube` inserted into a natural passage/conduit in the body to prevent a disease-induced, localized flow constriction. The term may also refer to a tube used to temporarily hold such a natural conduit open to allow access for surgery. The origin of the word Stent remains unsettled.
Perfusion	In physiology, Perfusion is the process of nutritive delivery of arterial blood to a capillary bed in the biological tissue.` Tests of adequate Perfusion are a part of patient triage performed by medical or emergency personnel in a mass casualty incident.

Perfusion can be calculated with the following formula, where Pa is mean arterial pressure, Pv is mean venous pressure, and R is vascular resistance:

$$F = \frac{P_A - P_V}{R}$$

The term `Pa - Pv` is sometimes presented as `ΔP`, for the change in pressure.

The terms `Perfusion` and `Perfusion pressure` are sometimes used interchangeably, but the equation should make clear that resistance can have an effect on the Perfusion, but not on the Perfusion pressure.

Carbon dioxide	Carbon dioxide is a chemical compound composed of two oxygen atoms covalently bonded to a single carbon atom. It is a gas at standard temperature and pressure and exists in Earth`s atmosphere in this state. CO_2 is a trace gas being only 0.038% of the atmosphere.
Crush syndrome	Crush syndrome (also traumatic rhabdomyolysis or Bywaters` syndrome) is a serious medical condition characterized by major shock and renal failure following a crushing injury to skeletal muscle. Cases commonly occur in catastrophes such as earthquakes or war, where victims have been trapped under fallen masonry. The syndrome was discovered by British physician Eric Bywaters in patients during the 1941 London Blitz.
Positive airway pressure	Positive airway pressure is a method of respiratory ventilation used primarily in the treatment of sleep apnea, for which it was first developed. Positive airway pressure ventilation is also commonly used for critically ill patients in hospital with respiratory failure, and in newborn infants (neonates). In these patients, Positive airway pressure ventilation can prevent the need for endotracheal intubation, or allow earlier extubation.
Pulmonary trunk	The pulmonary arteries carry blood from the heart to the lungs. They are the only arteries (other than umbilical arteries in the fetus) that carry deoxygenated blood.
	In the human heart, the pulmonary trunk begins at the base of the right ventricle.

Chapter 2. PART II: Chapter 19 - Chapter 36

Air embolism	An Air embolism is a pathological condition caused by gas bubbles in a vascular system. The most common context is a human body, in which case it refers to gas bubbles in the bloodstream (embolism in a medical context refers to any large moving mass or defect in the blood stream). However Air embolisms may also occur in the xylem of vascular plants, especially when suffering from water stress.
Capnography	Capnography is the monitoring of the concentration or partial pressure of carbon dioxide (CO_2) in the respiratory gases. Its main development has been as a monitoring tool for use during anaesthesia and intensive care. It is usually presented as a graph of expiratory CO_2 plotted against time, or, less commonly, but more usefully, expired volume.
Endotracheal tube	An Endotracheal tube is used in general anaesthesia, intensive care and emergency medicine for airway management and mechanical ventilation. The tube is inserted into a patient`s trachea in order to ensure that the airway is not closed off and that air is able to reach the lungs. The Endotracheal tube is regarded as the most reliable available method for protecting a patient`s airway.
Foramen	In anatomy, a Foramen is any opening. Many foramina transmit muscle or a nerve.

. |
Capacitance	In electromagnetism and electronics, Capacitance is the ability of a body to hold an electrical charge. Capacitance is also a measure of the amount of electric charge stored (or separated) for a given electric potential. A common form of charge storage device is a parallel-plate capacitor.
Fluoxetine	Fluoxetine is an antidepressant of the selective serotonin reuptake inhibitor (SSRI) class. Fluoxetine is approved for the treatment of major depression (including pediatric depression), obsessive-compulsive disorder (in both adult and pediatric populations), bulimia nervosa, panic disorder and premenstrual dysphoric disorder. Despite the availability of newer agents, it remains extremely popular.
Inferior vena cava	The Inferior vena cava is the large vein that carries de-oxygenated blood from the lower half of the body into the right atrium of the heart.

	It is posterior to the abdominal cavity and runs alongside of the vertebral column on its right side (i.e. it is a retroperitoneal structure). It enters the right atrium at the lower right, back side of the heart.
Insulin	Insulin is a hormone that is central to regulating the energy and glucose metabolism in the body. Insulin causes cells in the liver, muscle, and fat tissue to take up glucose from the blood, storing it as glycogen in the liver and muscle. Insulin stops the use of fat as an energy source.
Laryngospasm	In medicine, Laryngospasm is an uncontrolled/involuntary muscular contraction (spasm) of the laryngeal cords. The condition typically lasts less than 30 or 60 seconds, and causes a partial blocking of breathing in, while breathing out remains easier. It may be triggered when the vocal cords or the area of the trachea below the cords detects the entry of water, mucus, blood, or other substance.
Leg	A Leg is a limb on an organism`s body that supports the rest of the animal above the ground between the ankle and the hip and the groin. and is used for locomotion. The end of the Leg farthest from the animal`s body is often either modified or attached to another structure that is modified to disperse the animal`s weight on the ground .
Stethoscope	The Stethoscope is an acoustic medical device for auscultation, or listening to the internal sounds of an animal body. It is often used to listen to heart sounds. It is also used to listen to intestines and blood flow in arteries and veins.
Transducer	Acoustic waves emitted by ultrasonics transducer crystals exhibit a property known as self-focusing . Note that this is distinct from the electronically controlled focusing employed in diagnostic ultrasound devices which employ arrays of transducers. The self-focusing effect exists even for a single crystal.
Catheter	In medicine a Catheter is a tube that can be inserted into a body cavity, duct or vessel. Catheters thereby allow drainage, injection of fluids or access by surgical instruments. The process of inserting a Catheter is Catheterization.
Chemosis	Chemosis is the swelling of the conjunctiva. It is usually caused by allergies or viral infections, as well as eye rubbing. Chemosis is also included in the Chandler Classification system of orbital infections.

Chapter 2. PART II: Chapter 19 - Chapter 36

Infusion	An Infusion is the outcome of steeping plants with a desired flavour in water or oil.
	The first recorded use of essential oils was in the 10th or 11th century by the Persian polymath Avicenna, possibly in the Canon of Medicine.
	An Infusion is very similar to a decoction but is used with herbs that are more volatile or dissolve readily in water, or release their active ingredients easily in oil.
Liver	The liver is a vital organ present in vertebrates and some other animals. It has a wide range of functions, including detoxification, protein synthesis, and production of biochemicals necessary for digestion. The liver is necessary for survival; there is currently no way to compensate for the absence of liver function.
Liver disease	Liver disease is a broad term describing any single number of diseases affecting the liver. Many are accompanied by jaundice caused by increased levels of bilirubin in the system. The bilirubin results from the breakup of the hemoglobin of dead red blood cells; normally, the liver removes bilirubin from the blood and excretes it through bile.
Skull	The skull is a bony structure found in the head of many animals. The skull supports the structures of the face and protects the head against injury.
	The skull can be divided into two parts: the cranium and the mandible.
Pneumocephalus	Pneumocephalus is the presence of air or gas within the cranial cavity. It is usually associated with disruption of the skull: after head and facial trauma, tumors of the skull base, after neurosurgery or otorhinolaryngology, and rarely, spontaneously. Pneumocephalus can occur in scuba diving, but is very rare in this context.
Brace	
	· Brace (orthopaedic), a device used to restrict or assist body movement
	· Back Brace, a device limiting motion of the spine
	· Milwaukee Brace, a kind of back Brace used in the treatment of spinal curvatures

· Cervical collar, also called a neck Brace, used to restrict neck movement

· Dental Braces, a device used to reposition teeth

· Brace (tool), a hand tool

· Brace (theatre), a stabilizer for a piece of scenery

· A reinforcement used in architecture, such as in timber framing

· Brace position, a body stance used to prepare for a crash

· The { and } symbols, also known as Braces

· Curly bracket programming language, a programming language that uses Braces.

· Military Brace, a body posture primarily used in military schools

· Braces (clothing), known in American English as suspenders, elastic fabric straps used to support trousers

· Brace (singer) , a Dutch singer

· Braces (sailing), the lines used to rotate the yards around the mast .

Vascular resistance	Vascular resistance is a term used to define the resistance to flow that must be overcome to push blood through the circulatory system. The resistance offered by the peripheral circulation is known as the systemic Vascular resistance, while the resistance offered by the vasculature of the lungs is known as the pulmonary Vascular resistance. The systemic Vascular resistance may also be referred to as the total peripheral resistance.
Central venous pressure	Central venous pressure describes the pressure of blood in the thoracic vena cava, near the right atrium of the heart. Central venous pressure reflects the amount of blood returning to the heart and the ability of the heart to pump the blood into the arterial system. It is a good approximation of right atrial pressure, which is a major determinant of right ventricular end diastolic volume.

Chapter 2. PART II: Chapter 19 - Chapter 36

Vasoconstriction	Vasoconstriction is the narrowing of the blood vessels resulting from contraction of the muscular wall of the vessels, particularly the large arteries, small arterioles and veins. The process is the opposite of vasodilation, the widening of blood vessels. The process is particularly important in staunching hemorrhage and acute blood loss.
Barotrauma	Barotrauma is physical damage to body tissues caused by a difference in pressure between an air space inside or beside the body and the surrounding fluid. Barotrauma typically occurs to air spaces within a body when that body moves to or from a higher pressure environment, such as when a SCUBA diver, a free-diving diver or an airplane passenger ascends or descends, or during uncontrolled decompression of a pressure vessel. Boyle's law defines the relationship between the volume of the air space and the ambient pressure.
Peptide	Peptides are short polymers formed from the linking, in a defined order, of α-amino acids. The link between one amino acid residue and the next is called an amide bond or a Peptide bond.

Proteins are polyPeptide molecules (or consist of multiple polyPeptide subunits). |
Pneumoperitoneum	Pneumoperitoneum is air or gas in the abdominal (peritoneal) cavity. It is often seen on X-ray, but small amounts are often missed, and CT is nowadays regarded as a criterion standard in the assessment of a Pneumoperitoneum. CT can visualize quantities as small as 5 cm³ of air or gas.
Heparin	Heparin, a highly-sulfated glycosaminoglycan, is widely used as an injectable anticoagulant, and has the highest negative charge density of any known biological molecule. It can also be used to form an inner anticoagulant surface on various experimental and medical devices such as test tubes and renal dialysis machines. Pharmaceutical grade Heparin is derived from mucosal tissues of slaughtered meat animals such as porcine (pig) intestine or bovine (cow) lung.
Nortriptyline	Nortriptyline is a second-generation tricyclic antidepressant marketed as the hydrochloride under the trade names Sensoval, Aventyl, Pamelor, Norpress, Allegron and Nortrilen. It is used in the treatment of major depression and childhood nocturnal enuresis (bedwetting). In addition, it is sometimes used for chronic illnesses such as chronic fatigue syndrome, chronic pain and migraines, and labile affect in some neurological conditions.
Respiratory tract	In humans the Respiratory tract is the part of the anatomy that has to do with the process of respiration.

The Respiratory tract is divided into 3 segments:

· Upper Respiratory tract: nose and nasal passages, paranasal sinuses, and throat or pharynx

· Respiratory airways: voice box or larynx, trachea, bronchi, and bronchioles

· Lungs: respiratory bronchioles, alveolar ducts, alveolar sacs, and alveoli
The Respiratory tract is a common site for infections. Upper Respiratory tract infections are probably the most common infections in the world.

Most of the Respiratory tract exists merely as a piping system for air to travel in the lungs; alveoli are the only part of the lung that exchanges oxygen and carbon dioxide with the blood.

Upper respiratory tract	The upper respiratory tract refers to the following parts of the respiratory system: · nose and paranasal sinuses · oral cavity (also part of the digestive system) · throat · pharynx · nasopharynx · oropharynx · laryngopharynx

241

· larynx (The larynx can be considered part of the upper respiratory tract or the lower respiratory tract depending on the source. Some specify that the glottis (vocal cords) is the defining line between the upper and lower respiratory tracts; others make the line at the cricoid cartilage). upper respiratory tract infections are amongst the most common infections in the world.

Pharynx	The pharynx is the part of the neck and throat situated immediately posterior to the mouth and nasal cavity, and cranial, or superior, to the esophagus, larynx, and trachea.
	The pharynx is part of the digestive system and respiratory system of many organisms.
	Because both food and air pass through the pharynx, a flap of connective tissue called the epiglottis closes over the trachea when food is swallowed to prevent choking or aspiration.
Fibroblast	A Fibroblast is a type of cell that synthesizes the extracellular matrix and collagen, the structural framework (stroma) for animal tissues, and plays a critical role in wound healing. Fibroblasts are the most common cells of connective tissue in animals.
Larynx	The Larynx , colloquially known as the `voice box`, is an organ in the neck of mammals involved in protection of the trachea and sound production. It manipulates pitch and volume. The Larynx houses the vocal folds, which are an essential component of phonation.
Vallecula	Vallecula is an anatomic term for a crevice, depression, or furrow in something.
	There are a variety of Valleculae in the human body, including one between the hemispheres of the brain, on the inferior surface of the cerebellum, in which the medulla oblongata is located (Vallecula of cerebellum). Other common Valleculae are: in the nail matrix, and in the throat.
Vascular endothelial growth factor	Vascular endothelial growth factor is a chemical signal produced by cells that stimulates the growth of new blood vessels. It is part of the system that restores the oxygen supply to tissues when blood circulation is inadequate. Vascular endothelial growth factor`s normal function is to create new blood vessels during embryonic development, new blood vessels after injury, and new vessels (collateral circulation) to bypass blocked vessels.

Chapter 2. PART II: Chapter 19 - Chapter 36

Muscle	Muscle is the contractile tissue of animals and is derived from the mesodermal layer of embryonic germ cells. Muscle cells contain contractile filaments that move past each other and change the size of the cell. They are classified as skeletal, cardiac, or smooth Muscles.
Bronchioles	The Bronchioles or bronchioli are the first airway branches that no longer contain cartilage. They are branches of the bronchi. The Bronchioles terminate by entering the circular sacs called alveoli.
Cricothyrotomy	A Cricothyrotomy is an emergency incision through the skin and cricothyroid membrane to secure a patient's airway during certain emergency situations, such as an airway obstructed by a foreign object or swelling, a patient who is not able to breathe adequately on their own, or in cases of major facial trauma which prevent the insertion of an endotracheal tube through the mouth. A Cricothyrotomy is usually performed by emergency physicians, surgeons, field medics, or paramedics. Usually it is performed as a last resort when control of the airway by usual means (an endotracheal tube through the mouth) have failed or are not feasible.
Blade	A Blade is the flat part of a tool, weapon, or machine that normally has a cutting edge and/or pointed end typically made of a flaking stone, such as flint, or metal, most recently steel. A Blade is used to cut, stab, slash, chop, slice, throw, thrust, position and/or place (an example of this is razor wire), shoot (an example of this is the ballistic knife) or scrape (an example of this is an ink eraser). Blades are used for utility purposes (food, craft, and outdoors, primarily) and for combat.
Laryngoscope	A Laryngoscope (larynx+scope) is a medical instrument that is used to obtain a view of the vocal folds and the glottis, which is the space between the cords. The first Laryngoscope was invented in 1854 by Manuel Patricio Rodríguez García. There are many types of Laryngoscopes.
Anxiolytics	An anxiolytic is a drug used for the treatment of symptoms of anxiety. Anxiolytics have been shown to be useful in the treatment of anxiety disorders. Though not Anxiolytics, beta-receptor blockers such as propranolol and oxprenolol can be used to combat the somatic symptoms of anxiety.
Large intestine	The large intestine is the second to last part of the digestive system--the final stage of the alimentary canal is the anus --in vertebrate animals. Its function is to absorb water from the remaining indigestible food matter, and then to pass useless waste material from the body

CLAM101

Chapter 2. PART II: Chapter 19 - Chapter 36

Jet ventilation	Jet ventilation is a special type of mechanical ventilation for surgical operations in the airway. Jet ventilation is characterized by the insufflation of gas portions with high velocity into the airway. The latter has to be open to the atmosphere in order to allow an unhindered gas egress and therefore to avoid overdistention (barotrauma) of the lungs.
Ventilation	Ventilation is the intentional movement of air from outside a building to the inside. It is the V in HVAC. With clothes dryers, and combustion equipment such as water heaters, boilers, fireplaces, and wood stoves, their exhausts are often called vents or flues -- this should not be confused with Ventilation. The vents or flues carry the products of combustion which have to be expelled from the building in a way which does not cause harm to the occupants of the building.
Percutaneous	In surgery, Percutaneous pertains to any medical procedure where access to inner organs or other tissue is done via needle-puncture of the skin, rather than by using an `open` approach where inner organs or tissue are exposed (typically with the use of a scalpel). The Percutaneous approach is commonly used in vascular procedures. This involves a needle catheter getting access to a blood vessel, followed by the introduction of a wire through the lumen of the needle.
Tracheotomy	Tracheotomy and tracheostomy are surgical procedures on the neck to open a direct airway through an incision in the trachea (the windpipe). They are performed by paramedics, veterinarians, emergency physicians and surgeons. Both surgical and percutaneous techniques are now widely used.
Pulmonary edema	Pulmonary edema is fluid accumulation in the lungs. It leads to impaired gas exchange and may cause respiratory failure. It is due to either failure of the heart to remove fluid from the lung circulation (`cardiogenic Pulmonary edema`) or a direct injury to the lung parenchyma (`noncardiogenic Pulmonary edema`).
AIDS	AIDS: Acquired immune deficiency syndrome
	HIV: Human immunodeficiency virus
	CD4+: CD4+ T helper cells
	CCR5: Chemokine (C-C motif) receptor 5
	CDC: Centers for Disease Control and Prevention
	WHO: World Health Organization

PCP: Pneumocystis pneumonia

TB: Tuberculosis

MTCT: Mother-to-child transmission

HAART: Highly active antiretroviral therapy

Acquired immune deficiency syndrome or acquired immunodeficiency syndrome (AIDS) is a disease of the human immune system caused by the human immunodeficiency virus (HIV).

STI/STD: Sexually transmitted infection/disease
This condition progressively reduces the effectiveness of the immune system and leaves individuals susceptible to opportunistic infections and tumors. HIV is transmitted through direct contact of a mucous membrane or the bloodstream with a bodily fluid containing HIV, such as blood, semen, vaginal fluid, preseminal fluid, and breast milk.

Croup	Croup is a group of respiratory diseases that often affects infants and children under age 6. It is characterized by a barking cough; a whistling, obstructive sound (stridor) as the child breathes in; and hoarseness due to obstruction in the region of the larynx. It may be mild, moderate or severe, and severe cases, with breathing difficulty, can be fatal if not treated in a hospital.
Metoclopramide	Metoclopramide is an antiemetic and gastroprokinetic agent. Thus it is primarily used to treat nausea and vomiting, and to facilitate gastric emptying in patients with gastroparesis. It is also a primary treatment for migraine headaches.
Bainbridge reflex	The Bainbridge reflex is an increase in heart rate due to an increase in central venous pressure. Increased blood volume is detected by stretch receptors located in both atria at the venoatrial junctions. A scientist by the name of Francis Arthur Bainbridge reported this reflex in 1915 when he was experimenting on dogs.
Gross anatomy	Gross anatomy is the study of anatomy at the macroscopic level. The term gross distinguishes it from other areas of anatomical study, including microscopic anatomy, which must be studied with the aid of a microscope.

Gross anatomy is studied using both invasive and noninvasive methods with the goal of obtaining information about the macroscopic structure and organization of organs and organ systems.

Impulse

In classical mechanics, an Impulse is defined as the integral of a force with respect to time. When a force is applied to a rigid body it changes the momentum of that body. A small force applied for a long time can produce the same momentum change as a large force applied briefly, because it is the product of the force and the time for which it is applied that is important.

Pericardium

The Pericardium is a double-walled sac that contains the heart and the roots of the great vessels.

There are two layers to the pericardial sac: the fibrous Pericardium and the serous Pericardium. The serous Pericardium, in turn, is divided into two layers, the parietal Pericardium, which is fused to and inseparable from the fibrous Pericardium, and the visceral Pericardium, which is part of the epicardium.

Right atrium

The Right atrium is one of four chambers (two atria and two ventricles) in the hearts of mammals (including humans) and archosaurs (which include birds and crocodilians). It receives deoxygenated blood from the superior and inferior vena cava and the coronary sinus, and pumps it into the right ventricle through the tricuspid valve. Attached to the Right atrium is the right auricular appendix.

End-diastolic volume

In cardiovascular physiology, End-diastolic volume (EDV) is the volume of blood in a ventricle at the end of filling (diastole). Because greater EDVs cause greater distention of the ventricle, EDV is often used synonymously with preload, which refers to the length of the sarcomeres in cardiac muscle prior to contraction (systole). An increase in EDV increases the preload on the heart and, through the Frank-Starling mechanism of the heart, increases the amount of blood ejected from the ventricle during systole (stroke volume).

Left ventricle

The Left ventricle is one of four chambers (two atria and two ventricles) in the human heart. It receives oxygenated blood from the left atrium via the mitral valve, and pumps it into the aorta via the aortic valve.

The Left ventricle is longer and more conical in shape than the right, and on transverse section its concavity presents an oval or nearly circular outline.

Chapter 2. PART II: Chapter 19 - Chapter 36

Myocardium	Cardiac muscle is a type of involuntary striated muscle found in the walls of the heart, specifically the Myocardium. Cardiac muscle cells are known as cardiac myocytes (or cardiomyocytes). Cardiac muscle is one of three major types of muscle, the others being skeletal and smooth muscle.
Right ventricle	The Right ventricle is one of four chambers (two atria and two ventricles) in the human heart. It receives deoxygenated blood from the right atrium via the tricuspid valve, and pumps it into the pulmonary artery via the pulmonary valve and pulmonary trunk. It is triangular in form, and extends from the right atrium to near the apex of the heart.
Chemosensor	A Chemosensor is a sensory receptor that transduces a chemical signal into an action potential. Or, more generally, a Chemosensor detects certain chemical stimuli in the environment. There are two main classes of the Chemosensor: direct and distance. · Examples of distance chemoreceptors are: · olfactory receptor neurons in the olfactory system · neurons in the vomeronasal organ that detect pheromones · Examples of direct chemoreceptors include · taste buds in the gustatory system · carotid bodies and aortic bodies detect changes primarily in pH and CO_2 inside the body.

Chapter 2. PART II: Chapter 19 - Chapter 36

Coronary circulation	Coronary circulation is the circulation of blood in the blood vessels of the heart muscle. Although blood fills the chambers of the heart, the muscle tissue of the heart (the myocardium) is so thick that it requires coronary blood vessels to deliver blood deep into it. The vessels that deliver oxygen-rich blood to the myocardium are known as coronary arteries.
Mitral valve	The Mitral valve is a dual-flap valve in the heart that lies between the left atrium and the left ventricle (LV). The Mitral valve and the tricuspid valve are known collectively as the atrioventricular valves because they lie between the atria and the ventricles of the heart and control the flow of blood.
	A normally-functioning Mitral valve opens secondary to increased pressure from the left atrium as it fills with blood.
Bundle of His	The Bundle of His, also known as the AV bundle or atrioventricular bundle, is a collection of heart muscle cells specialized for electrical conduction that transmits the electrical impulses from the AV node (located between the atria and the ventricles) to the point of the apex of the fascicular branches. The fascicular branches then lead to the Purkinje fibers which innervate the ventricles, causing the cardiac muscle of the ventricles to contract at a paced interval.
	These specialized muscle fibres in the heart were named after the Swiss cardiologist Wilhelm His, Jr., who discovered them in 1893.
Atrioventricular node	The Atrioventricular node is a part of electrical control system of the heart that co-ordinates heart rate. It electrically connects atrial and ventricular chambers. The Atrioventricular node is an area of specialized tissue between the atria and the ventricles of the heart, specifically in the posteroinferior region of the interatrial septum near the opening of the coronary sinus, which conducts the normal electrical impulse from the atria to the ventricles.
Sinoatrial node	The Sinoatrial node is the impulse-generating (pacemaker) tissue located in the right atrium of the heart, and thus the generator of sinus rhythm. It is a group of cells positioned on the wall of the right atrium, near the entrance of the superior vena cava. These cells are modified cardiac myocytes.
Excimer laser	An Excimer laser is a form of ultraviolet laser which is commonly used in eye surgery and semiconductor manufacturing. The term excimer is short for `excited dimer`, while exciplex is short for `excited complex`. An Excimer laser typically uses a combination of an inert gas (argon, krypton, or xenon) and a reactive gas (fluorine or chlorine).

Chapter 2. PART II: Chapter 19 - Chapter 36

Excitation-contraction coupling	Excitation-contraction coupling is a term coined in 1952 to describe the physiological process of converting an electrical stimulus to mechanical response . This process is fundamental to muscle physiology, whereby the electrical stimulus is usually an action potential and the mechanical response is contraction. Excitation-contraction coupling coupling can be dysregulated in many disease conditions.
Membrane	A Membrane is a layer of material which serves as a selective barrier between two phases and remains impermeable to specific particles, molecules, or substances when exposed to the action of a driving force. Some components are allowed passage by the Membrane into a permeate stream, whereas others are retained by it and accumulate in the retentate stream. Membranes can be of various thickness, with homogeneous or heterogeneous structure.
Membrane potential	Membrane potential is the voltage difference (or electrical potential difference) between the interior and exterior of a cell. All animal cells are surrounded by a plasma membrane composed of a lipid bilayer with many diverse protein assemblages embedded in it. The fluid on both sides of the membrane contains high concentrations of mobile ions, of which sodium (Na^+), potassium (K^+), chloride (Cl^-), and calcium (Ca^{2+}) are the most important.
QRS complex	The QRS complex is a recording of a single heartbeat on the ECG that corresponds to the depolarization of the right and left ventricles. Ventricles contain more muscle mass than the atria, therefore the QRS complex is considerably larger than the P wave. The His/Purkinje specialised muscle cells coordinate the depolarization of both ventricles, the QRS complex is 80 to 120 ms in duration represented by three small squares or less, but any abnormality of conduction takes longer and causes widened QRS complexes.
Cardiac cycle	Cardiac cycle is the term referring to all or any of the events related to the flow or pressure of blood that occurs from the beginning of one heartbeat to the beginning of the next. The frequency of the Cardiac cycle is the heart rate. Every single `beat` of the heart involves five major stages: First, `Late diastole` which is when the semilunar valves close, the Av valves open and the whole heart is relaxed.
Diastole	Diastole is the period of time when the heart fills with blood after systole (contraction). Ballistics accurately describes Diastole as recoil opposed to coil or Systole. Ventricular Diastole is the period during which the ventricles are relaxing, while atrial Diastole is the period during which the atria are relaxing.
End-systolic volume	End-systolic volume (ESV) is the volume of blood in the left ventricle at the end of contraction and the beginning of filling, or diastole.

ESV is the lowest volume of blood in the ventricle at any point in the cardiac cycle.

End systolic volume can be used clinically as a measurement of the adequacy of cardiac emptying, related to systolic function.

Cardiac output

Cardiac output (Q) is the volume of blood being pumped by the heart, in particular by a ventricle in a minute. This is measured in dm^3 min^{-1} (1 dm^3 equals 1000 cm^3 or 1 litre). An average Cardiac output would be 5L.min^{-1} for a human male and 4.5L.min^{-1} for a female.

Baroreceptors

Baroreceptors are sensors located in the blood vessels of several mammals. They are a type of mechanoreceptor that detects the pressure of blood flowing through them, and can send messages to the central nervous system to increase or decrease total peripheral resistance and cardiac output. Baroreceptors act immediately as part of a negative feedback system called the baroreflex, as soon as there is a change from the usual blood pressure mean arterial blood pressure, returning the pressure to a normal level.

Baroreflex

The Baroreflex or baroreceptor reflex is one of the body's homeostatic mechanisms for maintaining blood pressure. It provides a negative feedback loop in which an elevated blood pressure reflexively causes heart rate and thus blood pressure to decrease; similarly, decreased blood pressure depresses the Baroreflex, causing heart rate and thus blood pressure to rise.

The system relies on specialized neurons, known as baroreceptors, in the aortic arch, carotid sinuses, and elsewhere to monitor changes in blood pressure and relay them to the brainstem.

Arteriole

An Arteriole is a small diameter blood vessel in the microcirculation that extends and branches out from an artery and leads to capillaries.

Arterioles have thin muscular walls (usually only one to two layers of smooth muscle) and are the primary site of vascular resistance. Arterioles receive autonomic nervous system innervation and respond to various circulating hormones in order to regulate their diameter.

Capillaries

Capillaries are the smallest of a body's blood vessels and are part of the microcirculation. They are only 1 cell thick. These microvessels, measuring 5-10 μm in diameter, connect arterioles and venules, and enable the exchange of water, oxygen, carbon dioxide, and many other nutrient and waste chemical substances between blood and surrounding tissues.

259

Chapter 2. PART II: Chapter 19 - Chapter 36

Oculocardiac reflex	The Oculocardiac reflex, Aschner phenomenon, Aschner reflex, or Aschner-Dagnini reflex, is a decrease in pulse rate associated with traction applied to extraocular muscles and/or compression of the eyeball. The reflex is mediated by nerve connections between the trigeminal cranial nerve and the vagus nerve of the parasympathetic nervous system. The afferent tracts are derived mainly from the ophthalmic division of the trigeminal nerve, although tracts from the maxillary and mandibular division have also been documented.
Venule	A Venule is a small blood vessel in the microcirculation that allows deoxygenated blood to return from the capillary beds to the larger blood vessels called veins.
	Venules are blood vessels that drain blood directly from the capillary beds. Many Venules unite to form a vein.
Aorta	The Aorta is the largest artery in the body, originating from the left ventricle of the heart and extends down to the abdomen, where it branches off into two smaller arteries. The Aorta brings oxygenated blood to all parts of the body in the systemic circulation.
	The Aorta is usually divided into five segments/sections:
	· Ascending Aorta--the section between the heart and the arch of Aorta
	· Arch of Aorta--the peak part that looks somewhat like an inverted 'U'
	· Descending Aorta--the section from the arch of Aorta to the point where it divides into the common iliac arteries
	· Thoracic Aorta--the half of the descending Aorta above the diaphragm
	· Abdominal Aorta--the half of the descending Aorta below the diaphragm
	All amniotes have a broadly similar arrangement to that of humans, albeit with a number of individual variations. In fish, however, there are two separate vessels referred to as Aortas.

Chapter 2. PART II: Chapter 19 - Chapter 36

Hyperpyrexia	In medicine, Hyperpyrexia is an excessive and unusual elevation of set body temperature greater than or equal to 41 °C (105.8 °F). It is an extremely high fever. Such a high temperature is considered a medical emergency as it may indicate a serious underlying condition such as sepsis or Kawasaki syndrome.
Hypersensitivity	Hypersensitivity refers to undesirable (damaging, discomfort-producing and sometimes fatal) reactions produced by the normal immune system. Hypersensitivity reactions require a pre-sensitized (immune) state of the host. The four-group classification was expounded by P. H. G. Gell and Robin Coombs in 1963.
Etiology	Etiology (alternatively aEtiology, aitiology) is the study of causation, or origination. The word is most commonly used in medical and philosophical theories, where it is used to refer to the study of why things occur, or even the reasons behind the way that things act, and is used in philosophy, physics, psychology, government, medicine, theology and biology in reference to the causes of various phenomena. An etiological myth is a myth intended to explain a name or create a mythic history for a place or family.
Hepatitis	Hepatitis (plural hepatitides) implies injury to the liver characterized by the presence of inflammatory cells in the tissue of the organ. The name is from ancient Greek hepar , the root being hepat- (á¼¡πατ-), meaning liver, and suffix -itis, meaning `inflammation` (c. 1727).
Pericarditis	Pericarditis is an inflammation (-itis) of the pericardium (the fibrous sac surrounding the heart). Pericarditis can be classified according to the composition of the inflammatory exudate. Types include: · serous · purulent · fibrinous · caseous · hemorrhagic · Post infarction

Pericardiocentesis can be performed to permit analysis of the pericardial fluid.

Acute Pericarditis is more common than chronic Pericarditis, and can occur as a complication of infections, immunologic conditions, or heart attack.

Acute pericarditis

Acute pericarditis is an inflammation of the sac surrounding the heart --- the pericardium --- usually lasting < 6 weeks. It is by far the most common condition affecting the pericardium. According to a recent article, the most common causes of Acute pericarditis include:

· (35%) Neoplastic

· (23%) Autoimmune

· (21%) Viral - adenovirus, enterovirus, cytomegalovirus, influenza virus, hepatitis B virus, and herpes simplex virus, etc

· (6%) Bacterial (other than tuberculosis)

· (6%) Uremia

· (4%) Tuberculosis

· (4%) Idiopathic

· (remaining) trauma, drugs, post-AMI, myocarditis, dissecting aortic aneurysm, radiation
Chest pain is one of the common symptoms of Acute pericarditis.

Cardiac tamponade

Cardiac tamponade, also known as pericardial tamponade, is an emergency condition in which fluid accumulates in the pericardium (the sac in which the heart is enclosed). If the fluid significantly elevates the pressure on the heart it will prevent the heart's ventricles from filling properly. This in turn leads to a low stroke volume.

Constrictive Pericarditis

In many cases, Constrictive pericarditis is a late sequela of an inflammatory condition of the pericardium. The inflammatory condition is usually an infection that involves the pericardium, but it may be after a heart attack or after heart surgery.

Chapter 2. PART II: Chapter 19 - Chapter 36

	Almost half the cases of Constrictive pericarditis in the developing world are idiopathic in origin.
Mitral stenosis	Mitral stenosis is a valvular heart disease characterized by the narrowing of the orifice of the mitral valve of the heart.
	In normal cardiac physiology, the mitral valve opens during left ventricular diastole, to allow blood to flow from the left atrium to the left ventricle. Blood flows in the proper direction because during this phase of the cardiac cycle the pressure in the left ventricle is lower than the pressure in the left atrium, and the blood flows down the pressure gradient.
Mitral regurgitation	Mitral regurgitation, mitral insufficiency or mitral incompetence is a disorder of the heart in which the mitral valve does not close properly when the heart pumps out blood. It is the abnormal leaking of blood from the left ventricle, through the mitral valve, and into the left atrium, when the left ventricle contracts, i.e. there is regurgitation of blood back into the left atrium. Mitral regurgitation is the most common form of valvular heart disease.
Aortic insufficiency	Aortic insufficiency is the leaking of the aortic valve of the heart that causes blood to flow in the reverse direction during ventricular diastole, from the aorta into the left ventricle.
	Aortic insufficiency can be due to abnormalities of either the aortic valve or the aortic root (the beginning of the aorta).
	About half of the cases of Aortic insufficiency are due to the aortic root dilatation (annuloaortic ectasia), which is idiopathic in over 80% of cases, but otherwise occurs with aging and hypertension, Marfan syndrome, aortic dissection, and syphilis.
Hypertriglyceridemia	In medicine, Hypertriglyceridemia denotes high (hyper-) blood levels (-emia) of triglycerides, the most abundant fatty molecule in most organisms. It has been associated with atherosclerosis, even in the absence of hypercholesterolemia (high cholesterol levels). It can also lead to pancreatitis in excessive concentrations.
Hypertrophic cardiomyopathy	Hypertrophic cardiomyopathy is the leading cause of sudden cardiac death (SCD) in young athletes. Hypertrophic cardiomyopathyM is a genetic disorder that causes the muscle of the heart (the myocardium) to thicken (or hypertrophy) without any apparent reason. When the heart thickens and becomes enlarged, particularly at the septum and left ventricle, it can cause dangerous arrhythmias (abnormal heart rhythms).

Chapter 2. PART II: Chapter 19 - Chapter 36

Mitral valve prolapse	Mitral valve prolapse is a valvular heart disease characterized by the displacement of an abnormally thickened mitral valve leaflet into the left atrium during systole. There are various types of Mitral valve prolapse, broadly classified as classic and nonclassic. In its nonclassic form, Mitral valve prolapse carries a low risk of complications.
Cardiopulmonary bypass	Cardiopulmonary bypass (CPB) is a technique that temporarily takes over the function of the heart and lungs during surgery, maintaining the circulation of blood and the oxygen content of the body. The CPB pump itself is often referred to as a Heart-Lung Machine or the Pump. Cardiopulmonary bypass pumps are operated by allied health professionals known as perfusionists in association with surgeons who connect the pump to the patient's body.
Coronary artery disease	Coronary artery disease is the end result of the accumulation of atheromatous plaques within the walls of the coronary arteries that supply the myocardium (the muscle of the heart) with oxygen and nutrients. It is sometimes also called coronary heart disease (CHD), but although Coronary artery disease is the most common cause of CHD, it is not the only cause. Coronary artery disease is the leading cause of death worldwide.
Lung	The Lung or pulmonary system is the essential respiration organ in air-breathing animals, including most tetrapods, a few fish and a few snails. In mammals and the more complex life forms, the two Lungs are located in the chest on either side of the heart. Their principal function is to transport oxygen from the atmosphere into the bloodstream, and to release carbon dioxide from the bloodstream into the atmosphere.
Diabetes	Diabetes mellitus --often referred to as diabetes--is a condition in which the body either does not produce enough, or does not properly respond to, insulin, a hormone produced in the pancreas. Insulin enables cells to absorb glucose in order to turn it into energy. This causes glucose to accumulate in the blood , leading to various potential complications. Many types of diabetes are recognized: The principal three are: · Type 1: Results from the body's failure to produce insulin.

Type 1 diabetes:	Diabetes mellitus--often simply referred to as diabetes--is a condition in which a person has a high blood sugar (glucose) level as a result of the body either not producing enough insulin, or because body cells do not properly respond to the insulin that is produced. Insulin is a hormone produced in the pancreas which enables body cells to absorb glucose, to turn into energy. If the body cells do not absorb the glucose, the glucose accumulates in the blood (hyperglycemia), leading to various potential medical complications. There are many types of diabetes, the most common of which are: · Type 1 diabetes: results from the body`s failure to produce insulin, and presently requires the person to inject insulin. · Type 2 diabetes: results from insulin resistance, a condition in which cells fail to use insulin properly, sometimes combined with an absolute insulin deficiency. · Gestational diabetes: is when pregnant women, who have never had diabetes before, have a high blood glucose level during pregnancy.
Partial thromboplastin time	The Partial thromboplastin time or activated Partial thromboplastin time is a performance indicator measuring the efficacy of both the `intrinsic` (now referred to as the contact activation pathway) and the common coagulation pathways. Apart from detecting abnormalities in blood clotting, it is also used to monitor the treatment effects with heparin, a major anticoagulant. It is used in conjunction with the prothrombin time (PT) which measures the extrinsic pathway.
Prothrombin time	The Prothrombin time and its derived measures of prothrombin ratio (PR) and international normalized ratio (INR) are measures of the extrinsic pathway of coagulation. They are used to determine the clotting tendency of blood, in the measure of warfarin dosage, liver damage, and vitamin K status. The reference range f is usually around 12-15 seconds; the normal range for the INR is 0.8-1.2. Prothrombin time measures factors II, V, VII, X and fibrinogen.
Fan death	Fan death is a South Korean urban legend which states that an electric fan, if left running overnight in a closed room, can cause the death of those inside (by suffocation, poisoning,). Fans manufactured and sold in Korea are equipped with a timer switch that turns them off after a set number of minutes, which users are frequently urged to set when going to sleep with a fan on.

The specifics behind belief in the myth of fan-death often offer several explanations for the precise mechanism by which the fan kills.

Pulmonary artery catheter	In medicine Pulmonary artery catheterization is the insertion of a catheter into a pulmonary artery. Its purpose is diagnostic; it is used to detect heart failure or sepsis, monitor therapy, and evaluate the effects of drugs. The Pulmonary artery catheter allows direct, simultaneous measurement of pressures in the right atrium, right ventricle, pulmonary artery, and the filling pressure (`wedge` pressure) of the left atrium.
Extracorporeal	An Extracorporeal medical procedure is a medical procedure which is performed outside the body.
	A procedure in which blood is taken from a patient`s circulation to have a process applied to it before it is returned to the circulation. All of the apparatus carrying the blood outside the body is termed the Extracorporeal circuit.
	· Hemodialysis
	· Hemofiltration
	· Plasmapheresis
	· Apheresis
	· Extracorporeal membrane oxygenation (ECMO)
	· Cardiopulmonary bypass during open heart surgery.
Coagulation	Coagulation is a complex process by which blood forms clots. It is an important part of hemostasis , wherein a damaged blood vessel wall is covered by a platelet and fibrin-containing clot to stop bleeding and begin repair of the damaged vessel. Disorders of Coagulation can lead to an increased risk of bleeding (hemorrhage) or clotting (thrombosis).
Coagulopathy	Coagulopathy, clotting disorder, and bleeding disorder, are a medical terms for a defect in the body`s mechanism for blood clotting.

While there are several possible causes, they generally result in excessive bleeding and a lack of clotting.

Acquired causes of Coagulopathy include anticoagulation with warfarin, liver failure, and disseminated intravascular coagulation.

Fibrinogen

Fibrin (also called Factor Ia) is a fibrous protein involved in the clotting of blood, and is non globular. It is a fibrillar protein that is polymerised to form a `mesh` that forms a hemostatic plug or clot (in conjunction with platelets) over a wound site.

Fibrin is made from Fibrinogen, a soluble plasma glycoprotein that is synthesised by the liver.

Platelet

Platelets, or thrombocytes, are small, irregularly-shaped anuclear cells , 2-3 µm in diameter, which are derived from fragmentation of precursor megakaryocytes. The average lifespan of a Platelet is between 8 and 12 days. Platelets play a fundamental role in hemostasis and are a natural source of growth factors.

Agonist

An Agonist is a chemical that binds to a receptor of a cell and triggers a response by the cell. An Agonist often mimics the action of a naturally occurring substance.

An Agonist produces an action.

Aprotinin

Aprotinin BPTI (Trasylol, Bayer) is a protein, that is used as medication administered by injection to reduce bleeding during complex surgery, such as heart and liver surgery. Its main effect is the slowing down of fibrinolysis, the process that leads to the breakdown of blood clots. The aim in its use is to decrease the need for blood transfusions during surgery, as well as end-organ damage due to hypotension (low blood pressure) as a result of marked blood loss.

Desmopressin

Desmopressin is a synthetic replacement for vasopressin, the hormone that reduces urine production. It may be taken nasally, intravenously, or as a pill. Doctors prescribe Desmopressin most frequently for treatment of diabetes insipidus or bedwetting.

Premedication

Premedication refer to a drug treatment given to a patient before a (surgical or invasive) medical procedure. These drugs are typically sedative or analgesic.

	Premedication before chemotherapy for cancer often refers to special drug regimens (usually 2 or more drugs, eg dexamethasone, diphenhydramine and omeprazole) given to a patient minutes to hours before the chemotherapy to avert side effects or hypersensitivity reactions (i.e. allergic reactions).
Tranexamic acid	Tranexamic acid is often prescribed for excessive bleeding. It is an antifibrinolytic that competitively inhibits the activation of plasminogen to plasmin, a molecule responsible for the degradation of fibrin. Fibrin is the basic framework for the formation of a blood clot in hemostasis.
Ventricular assist device	A Ventricular assist device is a mechanical device that is used to partially or completely replace the function of a failing heart. Some Ventricular assist devices are intended for short term use, typically for patients recovering from heart attacks or heart surgery, while others are intended for long term use (months to years and in some cases for life), typically for patients suffering from congestive heart failure. Ventricular assist devices need to be clearly distinguished from artificial hearts, which are designed to completely take over cardiac function and generally require the removal of the patient's heart.
Off-pump coronary artery bypass	Off-pump coronary artery bypass or 'beating heart' surgery is a form of coronary artery bypass graft (CABG) surgery performed without cardiopulmonary bypass (heart-lung machine) as a treatment for coronary heart disease. During most bypass surgeries, the heart is stopped and a heart-lung machine takes over the work of the heart and lungs. When a cardiac surgeon chooses to perform the CABG procedure off-pump, also known as OPCAB (Off-pump coronary artery bypass), the heart is still beating while the graft attachments are made to bypass a blockage.
Grafting	In medicine, grafting is a surgical procedure to transplant tissue without a blood supply. The implanted tissue must obtain a blood supply from the new vascular bed or otherwise die. The term is most commonly applied to skin grafting, however many tissues can be grafted: skin, bone, nerves, tendons, neurons, and cornea are the tissue commonly grafted today.
Opioid	An Opioid is a chemical that works by binding to Opioid receptors, which are found principally in the central nervous system and the gastrointestinal tract. The receptors in these two organ systems mediate both the beneficial effects and the side effects of Opioids. The analgesic effects of Opioids are due to decreased perception of pain, decreased reaction to pain as well as increased pain tolerance.

277

Chapter 2. PART II: Chapter 19 - Chapter 36

Mitral valve repair	Mitral valve repair is a cardiac surgery procedure performed by cardiac surgeons to treat stenosis (narrowing) or regurgitation (leakage) of the mitral valve. The mitral valve is the `inflow valve` for the left side of the heart. Blood flows from the lungs, where it picks up oxygen, through the pulmonary veins, to the left atrium of the heart.
Atrial fibrillation	Atrial fibrillation is the most common cardiac arrhythmia (abnormal heart rhythm) and involves the two upper chambers (atria) of the heart. Its name comes from the fibrillating of the heart muscles of the atria, instead of a coordinated contraction. It can often be identified by taking a pulse and observing that the heartbeats don't occur at regular intervals.
Catheter ablation	Catheter ablation is an invasive procedure used to remove a faulty electrical pathway from the hearts of those who are prone to developing cardiac arrhythmias such as atrial fibrillation, atrial flutter, supraventricular tachycardias (SVT) and Wolff-Parkinson-White syndrome. It involves advancing several flexible catheters into the patient`s blood vessels, usually either in the femoral vein, internal jugular vein, or subclavian vein. The catheters are then advanced towards the heart and high-frequency electrical impulses are used to induce the arrhythmia, and then ablate (destroy) the abnormal tissue that is causing it.
Peripheral vascular disease	Peripheral vascular disease , also known as peripheral artery disease (PAD) or peripheral artery occlusive disease (PAOD), includes all diseases caused by the obstruction of large arteries in the arms and legs. Peripheral vascular disease can result from atherosclerosis, inflammatory processes leading to stenosis, an embolism or thrombus formation. It causes either acute or chronic ischemia (lack of blood supply), typically of the legs.
Abdominal aortic aneurysm	Abdominal aortic aneurysm is a localized dilatation (ballooning) of the abdominal aorta exceeding the normal diameter by more than 50 percent. Approximately 90 percent of Abdominal aortic aneurysms occur infrarenally (below the kidneys), but they can also occur pararenally (at the level of the kidneys) or suprarenally (above the kidneys). Such aneurysms can extend to include one or both of the iliac arteries in the pelvis.
Retroperitoneal	The retroperitoneum (or extraperitoneum) is the anatomical space in the abdominal cavity behind (retro) the peritoneum. It has no specific delineating anatomical structures. Organs are Retroperitoneal if they only have peritoneum on their anterior side. The retroperitoneam can be further subdivided into the:

· Perirenal space

· Anterior pararenal space

· Posterior pararenal space
Structures that lie behind the peritoneum are termed `Retroperitoneal`.

Aortic dissection	Aortic dissection is a tear in the wall of the aorta that causes blood to flow between the layers of the wall of the aorta and force the layers apart. Aortic dissection is a medical emergency and can quickly lead to death, even with optimal treatment. If the dissection tears the aorta completely open (through all three layers), massive and rapid blood loss occurs.
Endarterectomy	Endarterectomy is a surgical procedure to remove the atheromatous plaque material, or blockage, in the lining of an artery constricted by the buildup of soft/hardening deposits. It is carried out by separating the plaque from the arterial wall.
	It was first performed on a superficial femoral artery in 1946 by the Portuguese surgeon João Cid dos Santos.
Transient ischemic attack	A transient ischemic attack is a change in the blood supply to a particular area of the brain, resulting in brief neurologic dysfunction that persists, by definition, for less than 24 hours. If symptoms persist longer, then it is categorized as a stroke.
	A cerebral infarct that lasts longer than 24 hours, but less than 72 hours is termed a reversible ischemic neurologic deficit or RIND.
	Symptoms vary widely from person to person, depending on the area of the brain involved.
Kidney	The Kidneys are paired organs, which have the production of urine as their primary function. Kidneys are seen in many types of animals, including vertebrates and some invertebrates. They are an essential part of the urinary system, but have several secondary functions concerned with homeostatic functions.

Chapter 2. PART II: Chapter 19 - Chapter 36

Kidneys	The Kidneys are paired organs, which have the production of urine as their primary function. Kidneys are seen in many types of animals, including vertebrates and some invertebrates. They are an essential part of the urinary system, but have several secondary functions concerned with homeostatic functions.
Bronchus	A Bronchus is a passage of airway in the respiratory tract that conducts air into the lungs. No gas exchange takes place in this part of the lungs.
	The trachea divides into two main bronchi (also mainstem bronchi), the left and the right, at the level of the sternal angle at the anatomical point known as the carina. The right main Bronchus is wider, shorter, and more vertical than the left main Bronchus. The right main Bronchus subdivides into three lobar bronchi while the left main Bronchus divides into two.
Pleura	In human anatomy, the Pleural cavity is the body cavity that surrounds the lungs. The Pleura is a serous membrane which folds back upon itself to form a two-layered, membrane structure. The thin space between the two Pleural layers is known as the Pleural cavity; it normally contains a small amount of Pleural fluid.
Elastic recoil	Elastic recoil is the rebound of the lungs after having been stretched by inhalation the ease with which the lung rebounds. With inhalation, the interpleural pressure (the pressure within the pleural cavity) of the lungs decreases. Relaxing the diaphragm during expiration allows the lungs to recoil and regain the interpleural pressure experienced previously at rest.
Tidal volume	Tidal volume is the lung volume representing the normal volume of air displaced between normal inspiration and expiration when extra effort is not applied. Typical values are around 500ml or 7ml/kg bodyweight.
	The volume of gas moved during the respiratory cycle in mechanical ventilation where control (or at least appreciation) of Tidal volume is necessary to ensure adequate ventilation without causing barotrauma.
Vital capacity	Vital capacity is the maximum amount of air a person can expel from the lungs after a maximum inspiration. It is equal to the inspiratory reserve volume plus the tidal volume plus the expiratory reserve volume.
	A person`s Vital capacity can be measured by a spirometer which can be a wet or regular spirometer.

Chapter 2. PART II: Chapter 19 - Chapter 36

Acidosis	Acidosis is an increased acidity (i.e. an increased hydrogen ion concentration). If not further qualified, it usually refers to acidity of the blood plasma. Acidosis is said to occur when arterial pH falls below 7.35, while its counterpart (alkalosis) occurs at a pH over 7.45.
Arterial blood gas	An Arterial blood gas is a blood test that is performed using blood from an artery. It involves puncturing an artery with a thin needle and syringe and drawing a small volume of blood. The most common puncture site is the radial artery at the wrist, but sometimes the femoral artery in the groin or other sites are used.
Cor pulmonale	Cor pulmonale or pulmonary heart disease is a change in structure and function of the right ventricle of the heart as a result of a respiratory disorder. Right ventricular hypertrophy (RVH) is the predominant change in chronic Cor pulmonale, whereas in acute cases, dilation dominates. Both hypertrophy and dilation are the result of increased right ventricular pressure.
Deep vein thrombosis	In medicine, Deep vein thrombosis is the formation of a blood clot (`thrombus`) in a deep vein. It is a form of thrombophlebitis (inflammation of a vein with clot formation). Deep vein thrombosis commonly affects the leg veins (such as the femoral vein or the popliteal vein) or the deep veins of the pelvis.
Pulmonary embolism	Pulmonary embolism is a blockage of the main artery of the lung or one of its branches by a substance that has travelled from elsewhere in the body through the bloodstream (embolism). Usually this is due to embolism of a thrombus (blood clot) from the deep veins in the legs, a process termed venous thromboembolism. A small proportion is due to the embolization of air, fat or amniotic fluid.
Aspiration pneumonia	Aspiration pneumonia is bronchopneumonia that develops due to the entrance of foreign materials that enter the bronchial tree, usually oral or gastric contents (including food, saliva, or nasal secretions). Depending on the acidity of the aspirate, a chemical pneumonitis can develop, and bacterial pathogens (particularly anaerobic bacteria) may add to the inflammation. Aspiration pneumonia is often caused by an incompetent swallowing mechanism, such as occurs in some forms of neurological disease (a common cause being strokes) or while a person is intoxicated.
Atelectasis	Atelectasis is a medical condition in which the lungs are not fully inflated. It may affect part or all of one lung. It is a condition where the alveoli are deflated, as distinct from pulmonary consolidation.

285

Chapter 2. PART II: Chapter 19 - Chapter 36

Flail chest	A Flail chest is a life-threatening medical condition that occurs when a segment of the chest wall bones breaks under extreme stress and becomes detached from the rest of the chest wall. It occurs when multiple adjacent ribs are broken in multiple places, separating a segment, so a part of the chest wall moves independently. The number of ribs that must be broken varies by differing definitions: some sources say at least two adjacent ribs are broken in at least two places, some require three or more ribs in two or more places.
Idiopathic	Idiopathic is an adjective used primarily in medicine meaning arising spontaneously or from an obscure or unknown cause. From Greek á¼´διος, idios + πÎ¬θος, pathos (suffering), it means approximately `a disease of its own kind.` It is technically a term from nosology, the classification of disease. For most medical conditions, one or more causes are somewhat understood, but in a certain percentage of people with the condition, the cause may not be readily apparent or characterized.
Idiopathic pulmonary fibrosis	Idiopathic pulmonary fibrosis (or cryptogenic fibrosing alveolitis (CFA)) is a chronic, progressive form of lung disease characterized by fibrosis of the supporting framework (interstitium) of the lungs. By definition, the term is used only when the cause of the pulmonary fibrosis is unknown (`idiopathic`). When lung tissue from patients with Idiopathic pulmonary fibrosis is examined under a microscope by a pathologist, it shows a characteristic set of histologic/pathologic features known as usual interstitial pneumonia (UIP).
Pleural effusion	Pleural effusion is excess fluid that accumulates in the pleural cavity, the fluid-filled space that surrounds the lungs. Excessive amounts of such fluid can impair breathing by limiting the expansion of the lungs during inhalation. Four types of fluids can accumulate in the pleural space: · Serous fluid (hydrothorax) · Blood (hemothorax) · Chyle (chylothorax) · Pus (pyothorax or empyema)

Pleural effusion is usually diagnosed on the basis of medical history and physical exam, and confirmed by chest x-ray.

Pneumothorax	In medicine (pulmonology), a Pneumothorax is a potential medical emergency wherein air or gas is present in the pleural cavity. A Pneumothorax can occur spontaneously. It can also occur as the result of disease or injury to the lung, or due to a puncture to the chest wall.
Respiratory distress syndrome	There are two forms of Respiratory distress syndrome: · ARDS, which is acute (or adult) Respiratory distress syndrome · Infant Respiratory distress syndrome which is a complication of premature birth, also known as hyaline membrane disease (HMD) Also, respiratory distress can mean: · Shortness of breath · Respiratory failure `
Sarcoidosis	Sarcoidosis is a systemic disease of unknown aetiology that results in the formation of non-caseating granulomas in multiple organs. The prevalence is higher among blacks than whites by a ratio of 20:1. Usually the disease is localized to the chest, but urogenital involvement is found in 0.2% of clinically diagnosed cases and 5% of those diagnosed at necropsy.
Antihypertensive	The antihypertensives are a class of drugs that are used to treat hypertension (high blood pressure). Evidence suggests that reduction of the blood pressure by 5 mmHg can decrease the risk of stroke by 34%, of ischaemic heart disease by 21%, and reduce the likelihood of dementia, heart failure, and mortality from cardiovascular disease. There are many classes of antihypertensives, which lower blood pressure by different means; among the most important and most widely used are the thiazide diuretics, the ACE inhibitors, the calcium channel blockers, the beta blockers, and the angiotensin II receptor antagonists or ARBs.

Chapter 2. PART II: Chapter 19 - Chapter 36

Antihypertensives	The antihypertensives are a class of drugs that are used to treat hypertension (high blood pressure). Evidence suggests that reduction of the blood pressure by 5 mmHg can decrease the risk of stroke by 34%, of ischaemic heart disease by 21%, and reduce the likelihood of dementia, heart failure, and mortality from cardiovascular disease. There are many classes of antihypertensives, which lower blood pressure by different means; among the most important and most widely used are the thiazide diuretics, the ACE inhibitors, the calcium channel blockers, the beta blockers, and the angiotensin II receptor antagonists or ARBs.
Respiratory failure	The term Respiratory failure, in medicine, is used to describe inadequate gas exchange by the respiratory system, with the result that arterial oxygen and/or carbon dioxide levels cannot be maintained within their normal ranges. A drop in blood oxygenation is known as hypoxemia; a rise in arterial carbon dioxide levels is called hypercapnia. The normal reference values are: oxygen PaO_2 > 60 mmHg, and carbon dioxide PaCO2 < 45 mmHg.
Oxygen toxicity	Oxygen toxicity is a condition resulting from the harmful effects of breathing molecular oxygen at elevated partial pressures. It is also known as Oxygen toxicity syndrome, oxygen intoxication, and oxygen poisoning. Historically, the central nervous system condition was called the Paul Bert effect, and the pulmonary condition the Lorrain Smith effect, after the researchers who pioneered its discovery and description in the late 19th century.
Connective	Connective may be referring to: .
Connective tissue	Connective tissue is a form of fibrous tissue.. It is one of the four types of tissue in traditional classifications (the others being epithelial, muscle, and nervous tissue). Collagen is the main protein of Connective tissue in animals and the most abundant protein in mammals, making up about 25% of the total protein content. It is largely a category of exclusion rather than one with a precise defintion, but all or most tissues in this category are similarly: · Involved in structure and support.

· Derived from mesoderm, usually.

· Characterized largely by the traits of non-living tissue.

Heart failure	Heart failure is a condition in which a problem with the structure or function of the heart impairs its ability to supply sufficient blood flow to meet the body`s needs. It should not be confused with cardiac arrest . Common causes of Heart failure include myocardial infarction and other forms of ischemic heart disease, hypertension, valvular heart disease and cardiomyopathy.
Hemothorax	A Hemothorax is a condition that results from blood accumulating in the pleural cavity. Its cause is usually traumatic, from a blunt or penetrating injury to the thorax, resulting in a rupture of the serous membrane either lining the thorax or covering the lungs. This rupture allows blood to spill into the pleural space, equalizing the pressures between it and the lungs.
Tension pneumothorax	A Tension pneumothorax is a life-threatening condition that results from a progressive deterioration and worsening of a simple pneumothorax, associated with the formation of a one-way valve at the point of a rupture in the lung. Air becomes trapped in the pleural cavity between the chest wall and the lung, and builds up, putting pressure on the lung and keeping it from inflating fully. Upon inspiration, when the pressure inside the chest and pleural cavity falls as a result of the respiratory muscles increasing chest dimensions, air is sucked in through the one way valve, into the pleural space.
Kyphoscoliosis	Kyphoscoliosis describes an abnormal curvature of the spine in both a coronal and sagittal plane. It is a combination of kyphosis and scoliosis.
Bronchoscopy	Bronchoscopy is a technique of visualizing the inside of the airways for diagnostic and therapeutic purposes. An instrument (bronchoscope) is inserted into the airways, usually through the nose or mouth, or occasionally through a tracheostomy. This allows the practitioner to examine the patient`s airways for abnormalities such as foreign bodies, bleeding, tumors, or inflammation.

Physical examination	Physical examination or clinical examination is the process by which a health care provider investigates the body of a patient for signs of disease. It generally follows the taking of the medical history -- an account of the symptoms as experienced by the patient. Together with the medical history, the Physical examination aids in determining the correct diagnosis and devising the treatment plan.
Auscultation	Auscultation is the technical term for listening to the internal sounds of the body, usually using a stethoscope; based on the Latin verb auscultare 'to listen'. Auscultation is performed for the purposes of examining the circulatory system and respiratory system , as well as the gastrointestinal system (bowel sounds). The term was introduced by René-Théophile-Hyacinthe Laennec.
Hypoxic pulmonary vasoconstriction	Hypoxic pulmonary vasoconstriction is a physiological phenomenon in which pulmonary arteries constrict in the presence of hypoxia (low oxygen levels) without hypercapnia (high carbon dioxide levels), redirecting blood flow to alveoli with a higher oxygen content. The process might at first seem illogical, as low oxygen levels should theoretically lead to increased blood flow to the lungs to receive increased gaseous exchange. However, it is explained by the fact that constriction leads to redistribution of bloodflow to better-ventilated areas of the lung, which increases the total area involved in gaseous exchange.
Thoracotomy	Thoracotomy is an incision into the pleural space of the chest. It is performed by a surgeon, and, rarely, by emergency physicians, to gain access to the thoracic organs, most commonly the heart, the lungs, the esophagus or thoracic aorta, or for access to the anterior spine such as is necessary for access to tumors in the spine. Thoracotomy is a major surgical maneuver--the first step in many thoracic surgeries including lobectomy or pneumonectomy for lung cancer--and as such requires general anesthesia with endotracheal tube insertion and mechanical ventilation.
Mediastinoscopy	Mediastinoscopy is a surgical procedure that enables visualization of the contents of the mediastinum, usually for the purpose of obtaining a biopsy. Mediastinoscopy is often used for staging of lymph nodes of lung cancer or for diagnosing other conditions effecting structures in the mediastinum such as sarcoidosis or lymphoma. Mediastinoscopy involves making an incision approximately 1 cm above the suprasternal notch of the sternum, or breast bone.

Chapter 2. PART II: Chapter 19 - Chapter 36

Thoracoscopy	Thoracoscopy is a medical procedure involving internal inspection of the pleural cavity. It was developed by Hans Christian Jacobaeus, a Swedish internist in 1910 for the treatment of tuberculous intra-thoracic adhesions. He used a cystoscope to examine the thoracic cavity, developing his technique over the next twenty years.
Bullous keratopathy	Bullous keratopathy is a pathological condition in which small vesicles are formed in the cornea due to endothelial dysfunction. In a healthy cornea, corneal endothelium keeps the tissues from excess fluid absorption, pumping it back into subepithelium. When affected by some reason, such as Fuchs' dystrophy or a trauma during cataract removal, endothelium fails to function, stroma begins to swell.
Central nervous system	The Central nervous system is the part of the nervous system that functions to coordinate the activity of all parts of the bodies of multicellular organisms. In vertebrates, the Central nervous system is enclosed in the meninges. It contains the majority of the nervous system and consists of the brain and the spinal cord.
Microglia	Microglia are a type of glial cells that are the resident macrophages of the brain and spinal cord, and thus act as the first and main form of active immune defense in the central nervous system (CNS). Microglia constitute 20% of the total glial cell population within the brain. Microglia are distributed in large non-overlapping regions throughout the brain and spinal cord.
Neuron	A neuron is an electrically excitable cell that processes and transmits information by electrochemical signaling, via connections with other cells called synapses. neurons are the core components of the nervous system, which includes the brain, spinal cord, and peripheral ganglia. A number of specialized types of neurons exist: sensory neurons respond to touch, sound, light and numerous other stimuli affecting cells of the sensory organs that then send signals to the spinal cord and brain.
Nitric oxide	Nitric oxide or nitrogen monoxide (systematic name) is a chemical compound with chemical formula Nitric oxide. This gas is an important signaling molecule in the body of mammals, including humans, and is an extremely important intermediate in the chemical industry. It is also an air pollutant produced by cigarette smoke, automobile engines and power plants. Nitric oxide is an important messenger molecule involved in many physiological and pathological processes within the mammalian body both beneficial and detrimental.

Chapter 2. PART II: Chapter 19 - Chapter 36

Blood-brain barrier	The Blood-brain barrier (Blood-brain barrierB) is a separation of circulating blood and cerebrospinal fluid maintained by the choroid plexus in the central nervous system (CNS). Endothelial cells restrict the diffusion of microscopic objects (e.g. bacteria) and large or hydrophillic molecules into the CSF, while allowing the diffusion of small hydrophobic molecules (O_2, hormones, CO_2). Cells of the barrier actively transport metabolic products such as glucose across the barrier with specific proteins.
Cerebrospinal fluid	Cerebrospinal fluid (CSF), Liquor cerebrospinalis, is a clear bodily fluid that occupies the subarachnoid space and the ventricular system around and inside the brain. In essence, the brain `floats` in it. The CSF occupies the space between the arachnoid mater (the middle layer of the brain cover, meninges), and the pia mater (the layer of the meninges closest to the brain).
Aseptic meningitis	Aseptic meningitis is a condition in which the layers lining of the brain become inflamed and a pyogenic bacterial source is not to blame. Meningitis is diagnosed on a history of characteristic symptoms and certain examination findings (e.g., Kernig's sign). Investigations should show an increase in the number of leukocytes present in the cerebrospinal fluid (CSF), obtained via lumbar puncture, (normal being fewer than five visible per microscopic High Power Field).
Peripheral nervous system	The peripheral nervous system resides or extends outside the central nervous system (CNS), which consists of the brain and spinal cord. The main function of the peripheral nervous system is to connect the CNS to the limbs and organs. Unlike the central nervous system, the peripheral nervous system is not protected by bone or by the blood-brain barrier, leaving it exposed to toxins and mechanical injuries.
Efferent	Efferent is an anatomical term with the following meanings: · Conveying away from a center, for example the Efferent arterioles conveying blood away from the Bowman`s capsule in the Kidney. Opposite to Afferent. · Something that so conducts, see Efferent nerve fiber · Efferent lymph vessel ·

Chapter 2. PART II: Chapter 19 - Chapter 36

Electrophysiology	Electrophysiology is the study of the electrical properties of biological cells and tissues. It involves measurements of voltage change or electric current on a wide variety of scales from single ion channel proteins to whole organs like the heart. In neuroscience, it includes measurements of the electrical activity of neurons, and particularly action potential activity.
Excitatory postsynaptic potential	In neuroscience, an Excitatory postsynaptic potential (EPSP) is a temporary depolarization of postsynaptic membrane potential caused by the flow of positively charged ions into the postsynaptic cell as a result of opening of ligand-sensitive channels. They are the opposite of inhibitory postsynaptic potentials (IPSPs), which usually result from the flow of negative ions into the cell or positive ions out of the cell. A postsynaptic potential is defined as excitatory if it makes it easier for the neuron to fire an action potential.
Neurotransmitter	Neurotransmitters are endogenous chemicals which relay, amplify, and modulate signals between a neuron and another cell. Neurotransmitters are packaged into synaptic vesicles that cluster beneath the membrane on the presynaptic side of a synapse, and are released into the synaptic cleft, where they bind to receptors in the membrane on the postsynaptic side of the synapse. Release of Neurotransmitters usually follows arrival of an action potential at the synapse, but may follow graded electrical potentials.
Neurotransmitters	Neurotransmitters are endogenous chemicals which relay, amplify, and modulate signals between a neuron and another cell. Neurotransmitters are packaged into synaptic vesicles that cluster beneath the membrane on the presynaptic side of a synapse, and are released into the synaptic cleft, where they bind to receptors in the membrane on the postsynaptic side of the synapse. Release of Neurotransmitters usually follows arrival of an action potential at the synapse, but may follow graded electrical potentials.
Acetylcholine	The chemical compound Acetylcholine is a neurotransmitter in both the peripheral nervous system (PNS) and central nervous system (CNS) in many organisms including humans. Acetylcholine is one of many neurotransmitters in the autonomic nervous system (ANS) and the only neurotransmitter used in the motor division of the somatic nervous system. (Sensory neurons use glutamate and various peptides at their synapses).
Bioequivalence	Bioequivalence is a term in pharmacokinetics used to assess the expected in vivo biological equivalence of two proprietary preparations of a drug. If two products are said to be bioequivalent it means that they would be expected to be, for all intents and purposes, the same.

	Birkett (2003) defined Bioequivalence by stating that, 'two pharmaceutical products are bioequivalent if they are pharmaceutically equivalent and their bioavailabilities (rate and extent of availability) after administration in the same molar dose are similar to such a degree that their effects, with respect to both efficacy and safety, can be expected to be essentially the same.
Monoamine oxidase inhibitors	Monoamine oxidase inhibitors are a class of powerful antidepressant drugs prescribed for the treatment of depression. They are particularly effective in treating atypical depression, and have also shown efficacy in smoking cessation.
	Due to potentially lethal dietary and drug interactions, MAOIs had been reserved as a last line of defense, used only when other classes of antidepressant drugs (for example selective serotonin reuptake inhibitors and tricyclic antidepressants) have failed.
Corticospinal tract	The corticospinal or pyramidal tract is a collection of axons that travel between the cerebral cortex of the brain and the spinal cord.
	The Corticospinal tract mostly contains motor axons. It actually consists of two separate tracts in the spinal cord: the lateral Corticospinal tract and the medial Corticospinal tract.
Isoflurane	Isoflurane (2-chloro-2-(difluoromethoxy)-1,1,1-trifluoro-ethane) is a halogenated ether used for inhalational anesthesia. Together with enflurane and halothane, it replaced the flammable ethers used in the pioneer days of surgery. Its use in human medicine is now starting to decline, being replaced with sevoflurane, desflurane and the intravenous anaesthetic propofol.
Nitrous oxide	Nitrous oxide, commonly known as laughing gas, is a chemical compound with the formula N_2O. It is an oxide of nitrogen. At room temperature, it is a colorless non-flammable gas, with a pleasant, slightly sweet odor and taste.
Rocuronium	Rocuronium is an aminosteroid non-depolarizing (that is, it does not cause initial stimulation of muscles before weakening them) neuromuscular blocker or muscle relaxant used in modern anaesthesia, to facilitate endotracheal intubation and to provide skeletal muscle relaxation during surgery or mechanical ventilation.
	Introduced in 1994, Rocuronium has rapid onset, and intermediate duration of action. It is marketed under the trade name of Zemuron in the United States and Esmeron in most other countries.

Chapter 2. PART II: Chapter 19 - Chapter 36

Sevoflurane	Sevoflurane is a sweet-smelling, non-flammable, highly fluorinated methyl isopropyl ether used for induction and maintenance of general anesthesia. Together with desflurane, it is replacing isoflurane and halothane in modern anesthesiology. It is often administered in a mixture of nitrous oxide and oxygen.
Etidocaine	Etidocaine, marketed under the trade name Duranest, is a local anesthetic given by injection during surgical procedures and labor and delivery.
Etodolac	Etodolac: Etodolac belongs to a class of drugs called nonsteroidal anti-inflammatory drugs (NSAIDs). Other members of this class include aspirin, ibuprofen (Motrin, Advil, Nuprin, etc.), naproxen (Aleve, Naprosyn), indomethacin (Indocin), nabumetone (Relafen) and numerous others. These drugs are used for the management of mild to moderate pain, fever, and inflammation.
Etomidate	Etomidate is a short acting intravenous anaesthetic agent used for the induction of general anaesthesia and for sedation for short procedures such as reduction of dislocated joints and cardioversion. It was discovered at Janssen Pharmaceutica in 1964. Etomidate, a hypnotic is a carboxylated imidazole derivative.
Fentanyl	Fentanyl -- brand names include Actiq, Durogesic, Duragesic, Fentora, Onsolis, Sublimaze and Instanyl -- is a synthetic primary μ-opioid agonist commonly used to treat chronic breakthrough pain and is commonly used in pre-procedures. It is approximately 100 times more potent than morphine, with 100 micrograms of Fentanyl approximately equivalent to 10 mg of morphine and 75 mg of pethidine (meperidine) in analgesic activity. It has an LD_{50} of 3.1 milligrams per kilogram in rats, 0.03 milligrams per kilogram in monkeys, and an undetermined LD_{50} in humans.
Propofol	Propofol is a short-acting, intravenously administered hypnotic agent. Its uses include the induction and maintenance of general anesthesia, sedation for mechanically ventilated adults, and procedural sedation. Propofol is also commonly used in veterinary medicine.
Remifentanil	Remifentanil is a potent ultra short-acting synthetic opioid analgesic drug. It is given to patients during surgery to relieve pain and as an adjunct to an anaesthetic. Remifentanil is used for sedation as well as combined with other medications for use in general anesthesia.

Chapter 2. PART II: Chapter 19 - Chapter 36

Alfentanil	Alfentanil is a potent but short-acting synthetic opioid analgesic drug, used for anaesthesia in surgery. It is an analogue of fentanyl with around 1/10 the potency of fentanyl and around 1/3 of the duration of action, but with an onset of effects 4x faster than fentanyl. It is an OP3 mu-agonist.
Sufentanil	Sufentanil is a powerful synthetic opioid analgesic drug, approximately 5 to 10 times more potent than its analog, Fentanyl. Sufentanil is marketed for use by specialist centres under different trade names, such as Sufenta and Sufentil (India, by Claris Lifesciences Ltd).. Sufentanil was synthesised at Janssen Pharmaceutica in 1974.
Intracranial pressure	Intracranial pressure (ICP) is the pressure in the cranium and thus in the brain tissue and cerebrospinal fluid (CSF); this pressure is exerted on the brain`s intracranial blood circulation vessels. ICP is maintained in a tight normal range dynamically, through the production and absorption of CSF and pulsates approximately 1mm Hg in a normal healthy adult. CSF pressure has been shown to be influenced by abrupt changes in intrathorasic pressure during coughing (intraabdominal pressure), valsalva (Queckenstedt`s maneuver), and communication with the vasculature (venous and arterial systems).
Hyperventilation	In medicine, Hyperventilation is the state of breathing faster and/or deeper than necessary, bringing about lightheadedness and other undesirable symptoms often associated with panic attacks. Hyperventilation can also be a response to metabolic acidosis, a condition that causes acidic blood pH levels. Counterintuitively, such side effects are not precipitated by the sufferer`s lack of oxygen or air.
Measurement	In science, Measurement is the process of obtaining the magnitude of a quantity, such as length or mass, relative to a unit of Measurement, such as a meter or a kilogram. The term can also be used to refer to the result obtained after performing the process. The word `Measurement` is derived from the Greek word `metron` which means a limited proportion.
Monitoring	To monitor or Monitoring generally means to be aware of the state of a system. Below are specific examples: · to observe a situation for any changes which may occur over time, using a monitor or measuring device of some sort:

· Baby monitor, medical monitor, Heart rate monitor

· BioMonitoring

· Cure Monitoring for composite materials manufacturing

· Deformation Monitoring

· Election Monitoring

· Mining Monitoring

· Natural hazard Monitoring

· Network Monitoring

· Structural Monitoring

· Website Monitoring

· Futures Monitoring, Media Monitoring service

· to observe the behaviour or communications of individuals or groups

· Monitoring competence at a task.

· Clinical Monitoring for new medical drugs
Monitoring Integration Platform

· Indiktor - Monitoring Integration Platform

Chapter 2. PART II: Chapter 19 - Chapter 36

Craniotomy	A Craniotomy is a surgical operation in which a bone flap is removed from the skull, to access the brain. Craniotomies are often a critical operation performed on patients suffering from brain lesions or traumatic brain injury (TBI), and can also allow doctors to surgically implant deep brain stimulators for the treatment of Parkinson`s disease, epilepsy and cerebellar tremor. The procedure is also widely used in neuroscience for extracellular recording, brain imaging, and for neurological manipulations such as electrical stimulation and chemical titration.
Cerebral aneurysm	A Cerebral aneurysm or brain aneurysm is a cerebrovascular disorder in which weakness in the wall of a cerebral artery or vein causes a localized dilation or ballooning of the blood vessel. A common location of Cerebral aneurysms is on the arteries at the base of the brain, known as the Circle of Willis. Approximately 85% of Cerebral aneurysms develop in the anterior part of the Circle of Willis, and involve the internal carotid arteries and their major branches that supply the anterior and middle sections of the brain.
Subarachnoid hemorrhage	A Subarachnoid hemorrhage is bleeding into the subarachnoid space--the area between the arachnoid membrane and the pia mater surrounding the brain. This may occur spontaneously, usually from a ruptured cerebral aneurysm, or may result from head injury. Symptoms of SAH include a severe headache with a rapid onset (`thunderclap headache`), vomiting, confusion or a lowered level of consciousness, and sometimes seizures.
Vasospasm	Vasospasm refers to a condition in which blood vessels spasm, leading to vasoconstriction. This can lead to tissue ischemia and death (necrosis). Cerebral Vasospasm may arise in the context of subarachnoid hemorrhage.
Arteriovenous malformation	Arteriovenous malformation or AVM is an abnormal connection between veins and arteries, usually congenital. This pathology is widely known because of its occurrence in the central nervous system, but can appear in any location. The genetic transmission patterns of AVM, if any, are unknown. Symptoms of AVM vary according to the location of the malformation. Roughly 88% of people affected with AVM are asymptomatic; often the malformation is discovered as part of an autopsy or during treatment of an unrelated disorder (called in medicine an incidental finding); in rare cases its expansion or a micro-bleed from an AVM in the brain can cause epilepsy, deficit or pain.

Chapter 2. PART II: Chapter 19 - Chapter 36

Subdural hematoma	A Subdural hematoma or subdural haematoma, also known as a subdural hemorrhage, is a type of hematoma, a form of traumatic brain injury in which blood gathers within the outermost meningeal layer, between the dura mater, which adheres to the skull, and the arachnoid mater. Usually resulting from tears in veins that cross the subdural space, subdural hemorrhages may cause an increase in intracranial pressure (ICP), which can cause compression of and damage to delicate brain tissue. Subdural hematomas are often life-threatening when acute, but chronic Subdural hematomas are usually not deadly if treated.
Nephron	Nephron is the basic structural and functional unit of the kidney. Its chief function is to regulate the concentration of water and soluble substances like sodium salts by filtering the blood, reabsorbing what is needed and excreting the rest as urine. A nephron eliminates wastes from the body, regulates blood volume and blood pressure, controls levels of electrolytes and metabolites, and regulates blood pH. Its functions are vital to life and are regulated by the endocrine system by hormones such as antidiuretic hormone, aldosterone, and parathyroid hormone.
Renal blood flow	In the physiology of the kidney, Renal blood flow is the volume of blood delivered to the kidneys per unit time. In humans, the kidneys together receive roughly 25% of cardiac output, amounting to 1.5 L/min in a 70-kg adult male. Renal blood flow is closely related to renal plasma flow (RPF), which is the volume of blood plasma delivered to the kidneys per unit time.
Proximal tubule	The proximal tubule is the portion of the duct system of the nephron leading from Bowman`s capsule to the loop of Henle.  The most distinctive characteristic of the proximal tubule is its brush border (or `striated border`). The luminal surface of the epithelial cells of this segment of the nephron is covered with densely packed microvilli forming a border readily visible under the light microscope giving the brush border cell its name.
Loop of Henle	In the kidney, the Loop of Henle is the portion of the nephron that leads from the proximal convoluted tubule to the distal convoluted tubule. The loop has a hairpin bend in the renal medulla. The main function of this structure is to create a concentration gradient in the medulla of the kidney.

313

Chapter 2. PART II: Chapter 19 - Chapter 36

Secretion	Secretion is the process of elaborating, releasing, and oozing chemicals, or a secreted chemical substance from a cell or gland. In contrast to excretion, the substance may have a certain function, rather than being a waste product.
	Secretion in bacterial species means the transport or translocation of effector molecules for example proteins, enzymes or toxins (such as cholera toxin in pathogenic bacteria for example Vibrio cholerae) from across the interior (cytoplasm or cytosol) of a bacterial cell to its exterior.
Antidiuretic	An Antidiuretic is an agent or drug that, administered to an organism, helps control body water balance by reducing urination, opposing diuresis.
	Antidiuretics are the drugs that reduce urine volume, particularly in diabetes insipidus (DI) which is their primary indication.
	These are classified as:
	· Antidiuretic hormones: ADH/Vasopressin, Desmopressin, Lypressin, Terlipressin
	· Miscellaneous: Chlorpropamide, Carbamazepine
Distal tubule	The distal convoluted tubule (DCT) is a portion of kidney nephron between the loop of Henle and the collecting duct system.
	It is partly responsible for the regulation of potassium, sodium, calcium, and pH.
	· It regulates pH by absorbing bicarbonate and secreting protons (H^+) into the filtrate, or by absorbing protons and secreting bicarbonate into the filtrate.
	· Sodium and potassium levels are controlled by secreting K^+ and absorbing Na^+. Sodium absorption by the Distal tubule is mediated by the hormone aldosterone. Aldosterone increases sodium reabsorption.

Hormone	A Hormone is a chemical released by one or more cells that affects cells in other parts of the organism. Only a small amount of Hormone is required to alter cell metabolism. It is essentially a chemical messenger that transports a signal from one cell to another.
Aldosterone	Aldosterone is a hormone that increases the reabsorption of sodium and water and the release (secretion) of potassium in the kidneys. This increases blood volume and, therefore, increases blood pressure. Conversely, drugs that interfere with the secretion or action of Aldosterone are in use as antihypertensives.
Dilantin	Dilantin is the brand name of the drug phenytoin sodium in the United States, commonly used in the treatment of epilepsy. About one third of children whose mothers are taking this drug during pregnancy develop minor face and limb birth defects. A smaller population will have growth problems and developmental delay, or mental retardation.
Vitamin	A Vitamin is an organic compound required as a nutrient in tiny amounts by an organism. The term Vitamin was derived from `Vitamine,` a combination word from vital and amine, because it was suggested that the organic micronutrient food factors which prevented beriberi and perhaps other similar dietary-deficiency diseases, might be chemical amines. This proved incorrect for the micronutrient class, and the word was shortened.
Angiotensin	Angiotensin, a protein, causes blood vessels to constrict, and drives blood pressure up. It is part of the renin-Angiotensin system, which is a major target for drugs that lower blood pressure. Angiotensin also stimulates the release of aldosterone from the adrenal cortex.
Prostaglandin	A prostaglandin is any member of a group of lipid compounds that are derived enzymatically from fatty acids and have important functions in the animal body. Every prostaglandin contains 20 carbon atoms, including a 5-carbon ring. They are mediators and have a variety of strong physiological effects, such as regulating the contraction and relaxation of smooth muscle tissue.
Vitamin D	Vitamin D is a group of fat-soluble prohormones, the two major forms of which are Vitamin D_2 (or ergocalciferol) and Vitamin D_3 (or cholecalciferol). Vitamin D obtained from sun exposure, food, and supplements, is biologically inert and must undergo two hydroxylation reactions to be activated in the body. Calcitriol (1,25-Dihydroxycholecalciferol) is the active form of Vitamin D found in the body.
Nephrotoxicity	Nephrotoxicity is a poisonous effect of some substances, both toxic chemicals and medication, on the kidney. There are various forms of toxicity. Nephrotoxicity should not be confused with the fact that some medications have a predominantly renal excretion and need their dose adjusted for the decreased renal function .

CRAM101

Chapter 2. PART II: Chapter 19 - Chapter 36

Necrosis	Necrosis is the premature death of cells and living tissue. Necrosis is caused by external factors, such as infection, toxins or trauma. This is in contrast to apoptosis, which is a naturally occurring cause of cellular death.
Fracture	A fracture is the (local) separation of an object or material into two, or more, pieces under the action of stress. The word fracture is often applied to bones of living creatures, or to crystals or crystalline materials, such as gemstones or metal. Sometimes, in crystalline materials, individual crystals fracture without the body actually separating into two or more pieces.
Renal failure	Renal failure or kidney failure is a situation in which the kidneys fail to function adequately. It is divided into acute and chronic forms; either form may be due to a large number of other medical problems. Biochemically, it is typically detected by an elevated serum creatinine.
Dialysis	In medicine, Dialysis is primarily used to provide an artificial replacement for lost kidney function due to renal failure. Dialysis may be used for very sick patients who have suddenly but temporarily, lost their kidney function (acute renal failure) or for quite stable patients who have permanently lost their kidney function (stage 5 chronic kidney disease). When healthy, the kidneys maintain the body's internal equilibrium of water and minerals (sodium, potassium, chloride, calcium, phosphorus, magnesium, sulfate) and the kidneys remove from the blood the daily metabolic load of fixed hydrogen ions.
Hemodialysis	In medicine, Hemodialysis is a method for removing waste products such as creatinine and urea, as well as free water from the blood when the kidneys are in renal failure. Hemodialysis is one of three renal replacement therapies (the other two being renal transplant; peritoneal dialysis). Hemodialysis can be an outpatient or inpatient therapy.
Hypoxemia	Hypoxemia is generally defined as decreased partial pressure of oxygen in blood, sometimes specifically as less than 60 mmHg (8.0 kPa) or causing hemoglobin oxygen saturation of less than 90%.

	The Hypoxemia definition as decreased partial pressure of oxygen excludes decreased oxygen content caused by anemia (decreased content of oxygen binding protein hemoglobin) or other primary hemoglobin deficiency, because they don`t decrease the partial pressure of oxygen in blood. Still, some simply define it as insufficient oxygenation or total oxygen content of (arterial) blood, which, without further specification, would include both concentration of dissolved oxygen and oxygen bound to hemoglobin.
Urinalysis	A Urinalysis is an array of tests performed on urine and one of the most common methods of medical diagnosis. A part of a Urinalysis can be performed by using urine dipsticks, in which the test results can be read as color changes. A typical medical Urinalysis usually includes: · a description of color and appearance.
Blood urea nitrogen	The Blood urea nitrogen test is a measure of the amount of nitrogen in the blood in the form of urea, and a measurement of renal function. Urea is a substance secreted by the liver, and removed from the blood by the kidneys. The liver produces urea in the urea cycle as a waste product of the digestion of protein.
Proteinuria	Proteinuria (/prÉ™ÊŠtiË ˈn(j)ÊŠÉ™riÉ™/, from protein and urine) means the presence of an excess of serum proteins in the urine. The protein in the urine often causes the urine to become foamy, although foamy urine may also be caused by bilirubin in the urine (bilirubinuria), retrograde ejaculation, pneumaturia (air bubbles in the urine) due to a fistula, or drugs such as pyridium. Proteinuria is often diagnosed by a simple dipstick test although it is possible for the test to give a false negative even with nephrotic range Proteinuria if the urine is dilute.
Creatine	Creatine is a nitrogenous organic acid that occurs naturally in vertebrates and helps to supply energy to muscle. Creatine was identified in 1832 when Michel Eugène Chevreul discovered it as a component of skeletal muscle, which he later named Creatine after the Greek word for flesh, κρîας .

	Creatine is naturally produced in the human body from amino acids primarily in the kidney and liver.
Serum	In blood, the serum is the component that is neither a blood cell nor a clotting factor; it is the blood plasma with the fibrinogens removed. serum includes all proteins not used in blood clotting and all the electrolytes, antibodies, antigens, hormones, and any exogenous substances (e.g., drugs and microorganisms). The study of serum is serology.
Oliguria	Oliguria is the decreased production of urine. The decreased production of urine may be a sign of dehydration, renal failure, hypovolemic shock or urinary obstruction/urinary retention. It can be contrasted with anuria, which represents a more complete suppression of urination.
Neuromuscular blocking drugs	Neuromuscular blocking drugs block neuromuscular transmission at the neuromuscular junction, causing paralysis of the affected skeletal muscles. This is accomplished either by acting presynaptically via the inhibition of acetylcholine (ACh) synthesis or release, or by acting postsynaptically at the acetylcholine receptors of the motor nerve end-plate. While there are drugs that act presynaptically (such as botulinum toxin and tetrodotoxin), the clinically-relevant drugs work postsynaptically.
Suxamethonium	Suxamethonium, also known as succinylcholine, is a paralytic drug used to induce muscle relaxation and short term paralysis, usually to make endotracheal intubation possible. Suxamethonium is sold under the trade names Anectine and Scoline. Suxamethonium acts as a depolarizing neuromuscular blocker.
Aspirin	Aspirin is a salicylate drug, often used as an analgesic to relieve minor aches and pains, as an antipyretic to reduce fever, and as an anti-inflammatory medication. Aspirin also has an antiplatelet effect by inhibiting the production of thromboxane, which under normal circumstances binds platelet molecules together to create a patch over damage of the walls within blood vessels. Because the platelet patch can become too large and also block blood flow, locally and downstream, Aspirin is also used long-term, at low doses, to help prevent heart attacks, strokes, and blood clot formation in people at high risk for developing blood clots.

CRAM101

Chapter 2. PART II: Chapter 19 - Chapter 36

Atracurium besylate	Atracurium besylate is a neuromuscular-blocking drug or skeletal muscle relaxant in the category of non-depolarizing neuromuscular-blocking drugs, used adjunctively in anesthesia to facilitate endotracheal intubation and to provide skeletal muscle relaxation during surgery or mechanical ventilation. Atracurium is classified as an intermediate-duration non-depolarizing neuromuscular blocking agent. Atracurium besylate was first synthesized in 1974 by George H. Dewar, a pharmacist and a medicinal chemistry doctoral candidate in John B. Stenlake's medicinal chemistry research group in the Department of Pharmacy at the Strathclyde University, Scotland.
Cisatracurium	Cisatracurium is a neuromuscular blocking drug or skeletal muscle relaxant in the category of non-depolarizing neuromuscular-blocking drugs, used adjunctively in anesthesia to facilitate endotracheal intubation and to provide skeletal muscle relaxation during surgery or mechanical ventilation. It is a bisbenzyltetrahydroisoquinolinium agent with an intermediate duration of action. Cisatracurium is one of the ten isomers of the parent molecule, atracurium.
Azathioprine	Azathioprine is a drug that suppresses the immune system. Azathioprine is used in organ transplantation and autoimmune disease. Some of the autoimmune diseases are rheumatoid arthritis, pemphigus, Inflammatory Bowel Disease (such as Crohn's disease and Ulcerative Colitis), multiple sclerosis, autoimmune hepatitis and restrictive lung disease.
Sirolimus	Sirolimus is an immunosuppressant drug used to prevent rejection in organ transplantation; it is especially useful in kidney transplants. A macrolide, Sirolimus was first discovered as a product of the bacterium Streptomyces hygroscopicus in a soil sample from Easter Island -- an island also known as `Rapa Nui`, hence the name. It is marketed under the trade name Rapamune by Wyeth.
Tachycardia	Tachycardia comes from the Greek words tachys and kardia (of the heart). Tachycardia typically refers to a heart rate that exceeds the normal range for a resting heartrate (heartrate in an inactive or sleeping individual). In humans, the upper threshold of a normal heart rate is usually based upon age, sometimes it can be very dangerous depending on how hard the heart is working and the activity: · 1-2 days: >159 beats per minute (bpm)

· 3-6 days: >166 bpm

· 1-3 weeks: >182 bpm

· 1-2 months: >179 bpm

· 3-5 months: >186 bpm

· 6-11 months: >169 bpm

· 1-2 years: >151 bpm

· 3-4 years: >137 bpm

· 5-7 years: >133 bpm

· 8-11 years: >130 bpm

· 12-15 years: >119 bpm

· >15 years - adult: >100 bpm

When the heart beats rapidly, the heart pumps less efficiently and provides less blood flow to the rest of the body, including the heart itself. The increased heart rate also leads to increased work and oxygen demand for the heart (myocardium), which can cause a heart attack (myocardial infarction) if it persists.

| Tachypnea | Tachypnea is characterized by rapid breathing. |

Tachypnea is characterized by rapid breathing.
It is not identical with hyperventilation - Tachypnea may be necessary for a sufficient gas-exchange of the body, for example after exercise, in which case it is not hyperventilation.

Tachypnea differs from hyperpnea in that Tachypnea is rapid shallow breaths, while hyperpnea is rapid deep breaths.

Chapter 2. PART II: Chapter 19 - Chapter 36

Tacrolimus	Tacrolimus is an immunosuppressive drug whose main use is after allogeneic organ transplant to reduce the activity of the patient`s immune system and so lower the risk of organ rejection. It reduces interleukin-2 (IL-2) production by T-cells. It is also used in a topical preparation in the treatment of severe atopic dermatitis (eczema), severe refractory uveitis after bone marrow transplants, and the skin condition vitiligo.
Lithotripsy	Extracorporeal Shock Wave Lithotripsy is the non-invasive treatment of kidney stones (urinary calculosis) and biliary calculi (stones in the gallbladder or in the liver) using an acoustic pulse. Lithotripsy and the lithotriptor were developed in the early 1980s in Germany by Dornier Medizintechnik GmbH , and came into widespread use with the introduction of the HM-3 lithotriptor in 1983. Within a few years, ESWL became a standard treatment of calculosis. It is estimated that more than one million patients are treated annually with ESWL in the USA alone.
Side effects	Side Effects is an anthology of 17 comical short stories written by Woody Allen between 1975 and 1980, all but one of which were previously published in, variously, The New Republic, The New York Times, The New Yorker, and The Kenyon Review. The first story, Remembering Needleman, is a one-liner and non-sequitur filled obituary, four weeks after the fact, of Professor Sandor Needleman. The fifth story, My Apology, is Allen`s tale of a recurring fantasy/dream of his where he imagines himself in the sandals of Socrates during the philosopher`s final days in prison.
Percutaneous nephrolithotomy	Percutaneous nephrolithotomy is a surgical procedure to remove stones from the kidney by a small puncture wound (up to about 1 cm) through the skin. It is most suitable to remove stones of more than 2 cm in size. It is usually done under general anesthesia or spinal anesthesia.
Skin	The skin is a soft outer covering of an animal, in particular a vertebrate. Other animal coverings such the arthropod exoskeleton or the seashell has different developmental origin, structure and chemical composition. The adjective cutaneous literally means `of the skin` .
Pancreatitis	Pancreatitis is inflammation of the pancreas that can occur in two very different forms. Acute Pancreatitis is sudden while chronic Pancreatitis `is characterized by recurring or persistent abdominal pain with or without steatorrhea or diabetes mellitus.`

Excessive alcohol use is often cited as the most common cause of acute Pancreatitis, yet gallstones are actually the most common cause. Less common causes include hypertriglyceridemia (but not hypercholesterolemia) and only when triglyceride values exceed 1500 mg/dl (16 mmol/L), hypercalcemia, viral infection (e.g., mumps), trauma (to the abdomen or elsewhere in the body) including post-ERCP (i.e., Endoscopic Retrograde Cholangiopancreatography), vasculitis (i.e., inflammation of the small blood vessels within the pancreas), and autoimmune Pancreatitis.

Proton pump inhibitors	Proton pump inhibitors are a group of drugs whose main action is a pronounced and long-lasting reduction of gastric acid production. They are the most potent inhibitors of acid secretion available today. The group followed and has largely superseded another group of pharmaceuticals with similar effects, but different mode-of-action, called H_2-receptor antagonists.
Tears	Tears are the liquid product of a process of crying to clean and lubricate the eyes. The word lacrimation (also spelled lachrymation) may also be used in a medical or literary sense to refer to crying. Strong emotions, such as sorrow or elation, may lead to crying.
Insulinoma	An Insulinoma is a tumour of the pancreas that is derived from beta cells and secretes insulin. Beta cells secrete insulin in response to increases in blood glucose. The resulting increase in insulin acts to lower blood glucose back to normal levels at which point further secretion of insulin is stopped.
Chronic Pancreatitis	Chronic pancreatitis is a long-standing inflammation of the pancreas that alters its normal structure and functions. It can present as episodes of acute inflammation in a previously injured pancreas, or as chronic damage with persistent pain or malabsorption.
Budd-Chiari syndrome	In medicine (gastroenterology and hepatology), Budd-Chiari syndrome is the clinical picture caused by occlusion of the hepatic veins. It presents with the classical triad of abdominal pain, ascites and hepatomegaly. Examples of occlusion include thrombosis of hepatic veins.
Schistosomiasis	Schistosomiasis (also known as bilharzia, bilharziosis or snail fever) is a parasitic disease caused by several species of fluke of the genus Schistosoma. Although it has a low mortality rate, Schistosomiasis often is a chronic illness that can damage internal organs and, in children, impair growth and cognitive development. The urinary form of Schistosomiasis is associated with increased risks for bladder cancer in adults.

Chapter 2. PART II: Chapter 19 - Chapter 36

Cirrhosis	Cirrhosis is a consequence of chronic liver disease characterized by replacement of liver tissue by fibrous scar tissue as well as regenerative nodules (lumps that occur as a result of a process in which damaged tissue is regenerated), leading to progressive loss of liver function. Cirrhosis is most commonly caused by alcoholism, hepatitis B and C, and fatty liver disease but has many other possible causes. Some cases are idiopathic, i.e., of unknown cause.
Erythema	Erythema is redness of the skin, which can be caused by several things, including capillary congestion. It can be caused by infection, massage, electrical treatment, acne medication, allergies, exercise, solar radiation (sunburn), cutaneous radiation syndrome, or waxing and plucking of the hairs -- any of which can cause the capillaries to dilate, resulting in redness. Erythema is a common side effect of radiotherapy treatment due to patient exposure to ionizing radiation.
Octreotide	Octreotide is an octapeptide that mimics natural somatostatin pharmacologically, though it is a more potent inhibitor of growth hormone, glucagon, and insulin than the natural hormone. It was first synthesized in 1979 by the chemist Wilfried Bauer. Since Octreotide resembles somatostatin in physiological activities, it can: · Inhibit secretion of many hormones, such as gastrin, cholecystokinin, glucagon, growth hormone, insulin, secretin, pancreatic polypeptide, TSH, and vasoactive intestinal peptide. · Reduce secretion of fluids by the intestine and pancreas. · Reduce gastrointestinal motility and inhibit contraction of the gallbladder. · Inhibit the action of certain hormones from the anterior pituitary. · Cause vasoconstriction in the blood vessels. · Reduce portal vessel pressures in bleeding varices · It has also been shown to produce analgesic effects, most probably acting as a partial agonist at the mu opioid receptor. Most Frequent Adverse Effects: Abdominal pain with cramps, bradycardia, cardiac conduction changes, gastrointestinal reactions (including nausea/vomiting and diarrhea or constipation) and injection site reactions.

Somatostatin	Somatostatin (also known as growth hormone-inhibiting hormone (GHIH) or somatotropin release-inhibiting factor (SRIF)) is a peptide hormone that regulates the endocrine system and affects neurotransmission and cell proliferation via interaction with G-protein-coupled Somatostatin receptors and inhibition of the release of numerous secondary hormones.
	Somatostatin has two active forms produced by alternative cleavage of a single preproprotein: one of 14 amino acids, the other of 28 amino acids.
	Somatostatin is secreted in several locations in the digestive system:
	· stomach
	· intestine
	· delta cells of the pancreas Somatostatin is produced by neuroendocrine neurons of the periventricular nucleus of the hypothalamus. These neurons project to the median eminence, where Somatostatin is released from neurosecretory nerve endings into the hypothalamo-hypophysial portal circulation.
Transjugular intrahepatic portosystemic shunt	
	· Portal venous system
	· Distal splenorenal shunt procedure
	· Interventional radiology
	1. `What You Need to Know about the Transjugular intrahepatic portosystemic shunt .`. Cleveland Clinic. http://www.clevelandclinic.org/health/health-info/docs/0200/0237.asp?index=4956..

Chapter 2. PART II: Chapter 19 - Chapter 36

Vasopressin	Arginine Vasopressin argipressin or antidiuretic hormone (ADH), is a hormone found in most mammals, including humans. Vasopressin is a peptide hormone which controls the reabsorbtion of molecules in the tubules of the kidneys by affecting the tissue`s permeability. It plays a key role in homeostasis, and the regulation of water, glucose and salts in the blood.
Sclerotherapy	Sclerotherapy is a procedure used to treat blood vessels or blood vessel malformations (vascular malformations) and also those of the lymphatic system. A medicine is injected into the vessels, which makes them shrink. It is used for children and young adults with vascular or lymphatic malformations.
Biliary tract	The Biliary tract is the common anatomy term for the path by which bile is secreted by the liver on its way to the duodenum, or small intestine, of most members of the mammal family. It is referred to as a tree because it begins with many small branches which end in the common bile duct, sometimes referred to as the trunk of the biliary tree. The duct is present along with the branches of the hepatic artery and the portal vein forming the central axis of the portal triad.
Gallstone	In medicine, Gallstones (choleliths) are crystalline bodies formed within the body by accretion or concretion of normal or abnormal bile components. Gallstones can occur anywhere within the biliary tree, including the gallbladder and the common bile duct. Obstruction of the common bile duct is choledocholithiasis; obstruction of the biliary tree can cause jaundice; obstruction of the outlet of the pancreatic exocrine system can cause pancreatitis.
Cholecystitis	Cholecystitis is inflammation of the gall bladder. Cholecystitis is often caused by cholelithiasis (the presence of choleliths, or gallstones, in the gallbladder), with choleliths most commonly blocking the cystic duct directly. This leads to inspissation (thickening) of bile, bile stasis, and secondary infection by gut organisms, predominantly E. coli and Bacteroides species.
Choledocholithiasis	Choledocholithiasis is the presence of gallstones in the common bile duct. This condition causes jaundice and liver cell damage, and is a medical emergency, requiring the endoscopic retrograde cholangiopancreatography (ERCP) procedure or surgical treatment. A tendency for this disease can be inherited.
Gastroesophageal reflux disease	Gastroesophageal reflux disease (GERD), gastro-oesophageal reflux disease (GORD), gastric reflux disease, or acid reflux disease is defined as chronic symptoms or mucosal damage produced by the abnormal reflux in the esophagus.

Chapter 2. PART II: Chapter 19 - Chapter 36

	This is commonly due to transient or permanent changes in the barrier between the esophagus and the stomach. This can be due to incompetence of the lower esophageal sphincter, transient lower esophageal sphincter relaxation, impaired expulsion of gastric reflux from the esophagus, or a hiatal hernia.
Achalasia	Achalasia, also known as esophageal Achalasia, Achalasia cardiae, cardiospasm, and esophageal aperistalsis, is an esophageal motility disorder: The smooth muscle layer of the esophagus loses normal peristalsis (muscular ability to move food down the esophagus), and the lower esophageal sphincter (LES) fails to relax properly in response to swallowing. Achalasia is characterized by difficulty swallowing, regurgitation, and sometimes chest pain. Diagnosis is reached with esophageal manometry and barium swallow X-ray studies.
Esophagus	The layers of the esophagus are as follows: · mucosa (mucus) · nonkeratinized stratified squamous epithelium: is rapidly turned over, and serves a protective effect due to the high volume transit of food, saliva and mucus. · lamina propria: sparse. · muscularis mucosae: smooth muscle · submucosa: Contains the mucous secreting glands (esophageal glands), and connective structures termed papillae. · muscularis externa (or `muscularis propria`): composition varies in different parts of the esophagus, to correspond with the conscious control over swallowing in the upper portions and the autonomic control in the lower portions: · upper third, or superior part: striated muscle · middle third, smooth muscle and striated muscle · inferior third: predominantly smooth muscle

· adventitia

The junction between the esophagus and the stomach (the gastroesophageal junction or GE junction) is not actually considered a valve, although it is sometimes called the cardiac sphincter, cardia or cardias, although it is actually better resembles a stricture.

In most fish, the esophagus is extremely short, primarily due to the length of the pharynx (which is associated with the gills). However, some fish, including lampreys, chimaeras, and lungfish, have no true stomach, so that the oesophagus effectively runs from the pharynx directly to the intestine, and is therefore somewhat longer.

Reflux	Reflux is a technique involving the condensation of vapors and the return of this condensate to the system from which it originated. It is used in industrial and laboratory distillations. It is also used in chemistry to supply energy to reactions over a long period of time.
Diverticula	A diverticulum is medical or biological term for an outpouching of a hollow structure in the body.
	In medicine the term usually implies that the structure is not normally present, i.e., pathological. However, in the embryonic stage, some normal structures begin development as a diverticulum arising from another structure.
	An alphabetical listing of some frequently encountered Diverticula follows:
	· Bladder diverticulum: Balloon-like growths on the bladder commonly associated with a chronic outflow obstruction, such as benign prostatic hyperplasia in older males.
Hernia	A Hernia is a protrusion of a tissue, structure, or part of an organ through the muscle tissue or the membrane by which it is normally contained. The Hernia has three parts: the orifice through which it Herniates, the Hernial sac, and its contents. By far the most common Hernias develop in the abdomen, when a weakness in the abdominal wall evolves into a localized hole, or `defect`, through which adipose tissue, or abdominal organs covered with peritoneum, may protrude.

Chapter 2. PART II: Chapter 19 - Chapter 36

Stomach — The stomach is a hollow muscular, sac-shaped digestive organ. between the esophagus and the small intestine. It is involved in the second phase of digestion, following mastication (chewing).

Carcinoma — A Carcinoma is any malignant cancer that arises from epithelial cells. Carcinomas invade surrounding tissues and organs and may metastasize, or spread, to lymph nodes and other sites.

Carcinoma in situ (CIS) is a pre-malignant condition, in which some cytological signs of malignancy are present, but there is no histological evidence of invasion through the epithelial basement membrane.

Colitis — Colitis is a chronic digestive disease characterized by inflammation of the colon. Colitis is one of a group of conditions which are inflammatory and auto-immune, affecting the tissue that lines the gastrointestinal system (the large and small intestine). It is classed as an inflammatory bowel disease (IBD), not to be confused with irritable bowel syndrome (IBS).

Peptic ulcer — A Peptic ulcer PUD or Peptic ulcer disease, is an ulcer (defined as mucosal erosions equal to or greater than 0.5 cm) of an area of the gastrointestinal tract that is usually acidic and thus extremely painful. As many as 80% of ulcers are associated with Helicobacter pylori, a spiral-shaped bacterium that lives in the acidic environment of the stomach, however only 40% of those cases go to a doctor. Ulcers can also be caused or worsened by drugs such as aspirin and other NSAIDs.

Peptic ulcer disease — A peptic ulcer, also known as ulcus pepticum, peptic ulcer disease , is an ulcer (defined as mucosal erosions equal to or greater than 0.5 cm) of an area of the gastrointestinal tract that is usually acidic and thus extremely painful. As many as 80% of ulcers are associated with Helicobacter pylori, a spiral-shaped bacterium that lives in the acidic environment of the stomach, however only 40% of those cases go to a doctor. Ulcers can also be caused or worsened by drugs such as aspirin and other NSAIDs.

Zollinger-Ellison syndrome — Zollinger-Ellison syndrome is a disorder where increased levels of the hormone gastrin are produced, causing the stomach to produce excess hydrochloric acid. Often the cause is a tumor (gastrinoma) of the duodenum or pancreas producing the hormone gastrin. Gastrin then causes an excessive production of acid which can lead to peptic ulcers in almost 95% of patients.

Afferent — Afferent is an anatomical term with the following meanings:

· Conveying towards a center, for example the Afferent arterioles conveying blood towards the Bowman's capsule in the Kidney. Opposite to Efferent.

· Something that so conducts, see Afferent nerve fiber

· Afferent lymphatic vessels

Gastrostomy	Gastrostomy refers to a surgical opening into the stomach. Creation of an artificial external opening into the stomach for nutritional support or gastrointestinal compression. Typically this would include an incision in the patient`s epigastrium as part of a formal operation.
Peritoneum	The Peritoneum is the serous membrane that forms the lining of the abdominal cavity or the coelom -- it covers most of the intra-abdominal (or coelomic) organs -- in higher vertebrates and some invertebrates (annelids, for instance). It is composed of a layer of mesothelium supported by a thin layer of connective tissue. The Peritoneum both supports the abdominal organs and serves as a conduit for their blood and lymph vessels and nerves.
Peritonitis	Peritonitis is defined as inflammation of the peritoneum (the serous membrane which lines part of the abdominal cavity and some of the viscera it contains). It may be localised or generalised, generally has an acute course, and may depend on either infection (often due to rupture of a hollow organ as may occur in abdominal trauma) or on a non-infectious process. The main manifestations of Peritonitis are acute abdominal pain, abdominal tenderness, and abdominal guarding, which are exacerbated by moving the peritoneum, e.g. coughing (forced cough may be used as a test), flexing one`s hips, or eliciting the Blumberg sign (a.k.a. rebound tenderness, meaning that pressing a hand on the abdomen elicits less pain than releasing the hand abruptly, which will aggravate the pain, as the peritoneum snaps back into place).
Inflammatory bowel disease	In medicine, Inflammatory bowel disease is a group of inflammatory conditions of the colon and small intestine. The major types of Inflammatory bowel disease are Crohn`s disease and ulcerative colitis.. The main forms of Inflammatory bowel disease are Crohn`s disease and ulcerative colitis (UC).
Tyrosine	Tyrosine or 4-hydroxyphenylalanine, is one of the 20 amino acids that are used by cells to synthesize proteins. It is a non-essential amino acid with a polar side group. The word `Tyrosine` is from the Greek tyros, meaning cheese, as it was first discovered in 1846 by German chemist Justus von Liebig in the protein casein from cheese.
Ulcerative colitis	Ulcerative colitis (Colitis ulcerosa, Ulcerative colitis) is a form of inflammatory bowel disease (IBD). Ulcerative colitis is a form of colitis, a disease of the intestine, specifically the large intestine or colon, that includes characteristic ulcers, or open sores, in the colon. The main symptom of active disease is usually constant diarrhea mixed with blood, of gradual onset.

Chapter 2. PART II: Chapter 19 - Chapter 36

Abdominal compartment syndrome	Abdominal compartment syndrome refers to organ dysfunction caused by increased intra-abdominal pressure (IAP). Etiology of Abdominal compartment syndrome may be categorized into the following: · Primary or acute Abdominal compartment syndrome occurs when the compartment syndrome is directly and proximally caused by intra-abdominal pathology. · Secondary Abdominal compartment syndrome occurs when injuries outside the abdomen cause intra-abdominal fluid accumulation.
Diverticulitis	Diverticulitis is a common digestive disease particularly found in the large intestine. Diverticulitis develops from diverticulosis, which involves the formation of pouches (diverticula) on the outside of the colon. Diverticulitis results if one of these diverticula becomes inflamed.
Diverticulosis	Diverticulosis, otherwise known as `diverticular disease,` is the condition of having diverticula in the colon, which are outpocketings of the colonic mucosa and submucosa through weaknesses of muscle layers in the colon wall. These are more common in the sigmoid colon, which is a common place for increased pressure. This is uncommon before the age of 40 for some unknown reason Diverticulosis is being treated in patients as young as 35 years old, and increases in incidence after that age.
Polyp	A Polyp in zoology is one of two forms found in the phylum Cnidaria, the other being the medusa. Polyps are approximately cylindrical in shape and elongated at the axis of the body. In solitary Polyps, the aboral end is attached to the substrate by means of a disc-like holdfast, while in colonies of Polyps it is connected to other Polyps, either directly or indirectly.
Volvulus	A Volvulus is a bowel obstruction in which a loop of bowel has abnormally twisted on itself. · Volvulus Neonatorum · Volvulus Small Intestine · Volvulus Caecum

	· Volvulus Sigmoid Colon Midgut Volvulus occurs in patients (usually in infants) that are predisposed because of congenital intestinal malrotation. Segmental Volvulus occurs in patients of any age, usually with a predisposition because of abnormal intestinal contents (e.g. meconium ileus) or adhesions. Volvulus of the cecum, transverse colon, or sigmoid colon occurs, usually in adults, with only minor predisposing factors such as redundant (excess, inadequately supported) intestinal tissue and constipation.
Anacin	Anacin is a family of branded over-the-counter pharmaceutical agents used to combat pain and headaches. The Anacin brand is currently owned by Insight Pharmaceuticals. Anacin's active ingredients are aspirin and caffeine.
Appendicitis	Appendicitis is a condition characterized by inflammation of the appendix. It is a medical emergency. All cases require removal of the inflamed appendix, either by laparotomy or laparoscopy.
Enteritis	In medicine, Enteritis refers to inflammation of the small intestine. It is most commonly caused by the ingestion of substances contaminated with pathogenic microorganisms. Symptoms include abdominal pain, cramping, diarrhea, dehydration and fever.
Pseudomembranous colitis	Pseudomembranous colitis is an infection of the colon. It is often, but not always, caused by the bacterium Clostridium difficile. Because of this, the informal name C. difficile colitis is also commonly used.
Carcinoid	Carcinoid is a slow-growing type of neuroendocrine tumour, originating in the cells of the neuroendocrine system. In 2000, the World Health Organization redefined `Carcinoid`, but this new definition has not been accepted by all practitioners. This has led to some complexity in distinguishing between Carcinoid and neuroendocrine tumors in the literature.
Carcinoid syndrome	Carcinoid syndrome refers to the array of symptoms that occur secondary to carcinoid tumors. Carcinoid tumors are discrete, yellow, well-circumscribed tumors that can occur anywhere along the gastrointestinal tract and in the lung. They most commonly affect the appendix, ileum, and rectum.

Chapter 2. PART II: Chapter 19 - Chapter 36

349

Chapter 2. PART II: Chapter 19 - Chapter 36

Splenectomy	A Splenectomy is a surgical procedure that partially or completely removes the spleen.

The spleen, similar in structure to a large lymph node, acts as a blood filter. Current knowledge of its purpose includes the removal of old red blood cells and platelets, and the detection and fight against certain bacteria. |
Liver transplantation	Liver transplantation or hepatic transplantation is the replacement of a diseased liver with a healthy liver allograft. The most commonly used technique is orthotopic transplantation, in which the native liver is removed and the donor organ is placed in the same anatomic location as the original liver. Liver transplantation nowadays is a well accepted treatment option for end-stage liver disease and acute liver failure.
Embolism	In medicine, an Embolism (plural Embolisms) occurs when an object migrates from one part of the body (through circulation) and causes a blockage (occlusion) of a blood vessel in another part of the body. The term was coined in 1848 by Rudolph Carl Virchow. This is in contrast with a thrombus, or clot, which forms at the blockage point within a blood vessel and is not carried from somewhere else.
Subcutaneous emphysema	Subcutaneous emphysema or Sub Q air occurs when gas or air is present in the subcutaneous layer of the skin. Subcutaneous refers to the tissue beneath the cutis of the skin, and emphysema refers to trapped air. Since the air generally comes from the chest cavity, Subcutaneous emphysema usually occurs on the chest, neck and face, where it is able to travel from the chest cavity along the fascia.
Hypercapnia	Hypercapnia or hypercapnea , also known as hypercarbia, is a condition where there is too much carbon dioxide in the blood. Carbon dioxide is a gaseous product of the body`s metabolism and is normally expelled through the lungs.
Hypercapnia normally triggers a reflex which increases breathing and access to oxygen, such as arousal and turning the head during sleep.
Mechanical ventilation	In medicine, Mechanical ventilation is a method to mechanically assist or replace spontaneous breathing.
This may involve a machine called a ventilator or the breathing may be assisted by a physician or other suitable person compressing a bag or set of bellows. Traditionally divided into negative-pressure ventilation, where air is essentially sucked into the lungs, or positive pressure ventilation, where air (or another gas mix) is pushed into the trachea.
Postoperative nausea and vomiting	Postoperative nausea and vomiting (PONV) is an unpleasant complication affecting about a third of the 10% of the population undergoing general anaesthesia each year. This equates to about two million people in the United Kingdom annually.

	On average the incidence of nausea or vomiting after general anesthesia ranges between 25 and 30% [Cohen 1994].
Nausea	Nausea is the sensation of unease and discomfort in the stomach with an urge to vomit. Nausea is also an adverse effect of many drugs, opiates in particular, and may also be a side-effect of a large intake of sugary foods.
	Nausea is not a sickness, but rather a symptom of several conditions, many of which are unrelated to the stomach.
Neuromuscular junction	A Neuromuscular junction is the synapse or junction of the axon terminal of a motoneuron with the motor end plate, the highly-excitable region of muscle fiber plasma membrane responsible for initiation of action potentials across the muscle`s surface, ultimately causing the muscle to contract. In vertebrates, the signal passes through the Neuromuscular junction via the neurotransmitter acetylcholine.
	Upon the arrival of an action potential at the presynaptic neuron terminal, voltage-dependent calcium channels open and Ca^{2+} ions flow from the extracellular fluid into the presynaptic neuron`s cytosol.
Synthesis	In general, the noun Synthesis refers to the combining of two or more entities to form something new. The corresponding verb, to Synthesise , means to make or form a Synthesis.
	Synthesis or Synthesise may also refer to:
	· Chemical Synthesis, the execution of chemical reactions to form a more complex molecule from chemical precursors
	· Organic Synthesis, the chemical Synthesis of organic compounds
	· Total Synthesis, the complete organic Synthesis of complex organic compounds, usually without the aid of biological processes

· Convergent Synthesis or linear Synthesis, a strategy to improve the efficiency of multi-step chemical syntheses

· Dehydration Synthesis, a chemical Synthesis resulting in the loss of a water molecule

· BioSynthesis, the creation of an organic compound in a living organism, usually aided by enzymes

· PhotoSynthesis, a biochemical reaction using a carbon molecule to produce an organic molecule, using sunlight as a catalyst

· ChemoSynthesis, the Synthesis of biological compounds into organic waste, using methane or an oxidized molecule as a catalyst

· Amino acid Synthesis, the Synthesis of an amino acid from its constituents*

· Peptide Synthesis, the biochemical Synthesis of peptides using amino acids

· Protein bioSynthesis, the multi-step biochemical Synthesis of proteins (long peptides)

· DNA Synthesis several biochemical processes for making DNA

· DNA replication, DNA bioSynthesis in vivo

· RNA Synthesis, the Synthesis of RNA from nucleic acids, using another nucleic acid chain as a template

· ATP Synthesis, the biochemical Synthesis of ATP

·

· [tyler wayne covington is the hottest motocrosser everrrrrr!]

· the process of converting a higher-level form of a design into a lower-level implementation

· Logic Synthesis

· High-level Synthesis

· Sound Synthesis, various methods of sound generation in audio electronics

· Subtractive Synthesis

· Frequency modulation Synthesis

· Speech Synthesis, the artificial production of human speech

· in philosophy, the end result of a dialectic, as in thesis, antithesis, Synthesis

· a cognitive skill in Benjamin Bloom`s Taxonomy of Educational Objectives.

· In philosophy and science, a higher a priori process than analysis

· Synthesis a web site and magazine covering popular culture

· Synthesis a journal of chemical Synthesis. .

Myofibrils	Myofibrils are cylindrical organelles. They are found within muscle cells. They are bundles of actomyosin filaments that run from one end of the cell to the other and are attached to the cell surface membrane at each end.

Chapter 2. PART II: Chapter 19 - Chapter 36

Sarcomere	A Sarcomere is the basic unit of a muscle's cross-striated myofibril. Sarcomeres are multi-protein complexes composed of three different filament systems. · The thick filament system is composed of Myosin protein which is connected from the M-line to the Z-disc by titin. It also contains myosin-binding protein C which binds at one end to the thick filament and the other to Actin. · The thin filaments are assembled by Actin monomers bound to nebulin, which also involves tropomyosin (a dimer which coils itself around the F-actin core of the thin filament) and troponin. · Nebulin and titin give stability and structure to the Sarcomere.
Cycling	Cycling, also called biCycling or biking, is the use of bicycles for transport, recreation, or for sport. Persons engaged in Cycling are cyclists or bicyclists. Apart from ordinary two-wheeled bicycles, Cycling also includes riding a unicycle, tricycle, quadracycle, and other similar human-powered vehicles (HPVs).
Actin	Actin is a globular, roughly 42-kDa protein found in all eukaryotic cells (the only known exception being nematode sperm) where it may be present at concentrations of over 100 μM. It is also one of the most highly-conserved proteins, differing by no more than 20% in species as diverse as algae and humans. Actin is the monomeric subunit of two types of filaments in cells: microfilaments, one of the three major components of the cytoskeleton, and thin filaments, part of the contractile apparatus in muscle cells. Thus, Actin participates in many important cellular processes including muscle contraction, cell motility, cell division and cytokinesis, vesicle and organelle movement, cell signaling, and the establishment and maintenance of cell junctions and cell shape.
Transverse	The transverse or costal processes of a vertebra, two in number, project one at either side from the point where the lamina joins the pedicle, between the superior and inferior articular processes. They serve for the attachment of muscles and ligaments.
Grading	In pathology, grading is a measure of the progress of tumors and other neoplasms. Some pathology grading systems apply only to malignant neoplasms (cancer); others apply also to benign neoplasms.

Pathology grading systems are used to classify neoplasms in terms of how abnormal the cells appear microscopically and what may be the outcome in terms of rate of growth, invasiveness, and dissemination.

Carbamazepine	Carbamazepine is an anticonvulsant and mood stabilizing drug used primarily in the treatment of epilepsy and bipolar disorder, as well as trigeminal neuralgia. It is also used off-label for a variety of indications, including attention-deficit hyperactivity disorder (ADHD), schizophrenia, phantom limb syndrome, paroxysmal extreme pain disorder, and post-traumatic stress disorder.
Energy	In physics, Energy is a scalar physical quantity that describes the amount of work that can be performed by a force, an attribute of objects and systems that is subject to a conservation law. Different forms of Energy include kinetic, potential, thermal, gravitational, sound, light, elastic, and electromagnetic Energy. The forms of Energy are often named after a related force.
Fatty acid	In chemistry, especially biochemistry, a fatty acid is a carboxylic acid often with a long unbranched aliphatic tail (chain), which is either saturated or unsaturated. Carboxylic acids as short as butyric acid (4 carbon atoms) are considered to be fatty acids, whereas fatty acids derived from natural fats and oils may be assumed to have at least eight carbon atoms, caprylic acid (octanoic acid), for example. The most abundant natural fatty acids have an even number of carbon atoms because their biosynthesis involves acetyl-CoA, a coenzyme carrying a two-carbon-atom group .
Fatty acids	Fatty acids are an important source of energy for many organisms. Excess glucose can be stored efficiently as fat. Triglycerides yield more than twice as much energy for the same mass as do carbohydrates or proteins.
Carbohydrate	A Carbohydrate is an organic compound with general formula $C_m(H_2O)_n$, that is, consisting only of carbon, hydrogen and oxygen, the last two in the 2:1 atom ratio. Carbohydrates can be viewed as hydrates of carbon, hence their name. The term is most used in biochemistry, where it is a synonym of saccharide.
Embolization	Embolization is a non-surgical, minimally-invasive procedure performed by an interventional radiologist and interventional neuroradiologists. It involves the selective occlusion of blood vessels by purposely introducing emboli. Embolisation is used to treat a wide variety of conditions affecting different organs of the human body.

Chapter 2. PART II: Chapter 19 - Chapter 36

Skeletal muscle	Skeletal muscle is a form of striated muscle tissue existing under control of the somatic nervous system. It is one of three major muscle types, the others being cardiac and smooth muscle. As its name suggests, most Skeletal muscle is attached to bones by bundles of collagen fibers known as tendons.
Tetanus	Tetanus is a medical condition characterized by a prolonged contraction of skeletal muscle fibers. The primary symptoms are caused by tetanospasmin, a neurotoxin produced by the Gram-positive, obligate anaerobic bacterium Clostridium tetani. Infection generally occurs through wound contamination and often involves a cut or deep puncture wound.
Cholinergic crisis	A Cholinergic crisis is an over-stimulation at a neuromuscular junction due to an excess of acetylcholine (ACh), as of a result of the inactivity (perhaps even inhibition) of the AChE enzyme, which normally breaks down acetylcholine. This is a consequence of some types of nerve gas, (e.g. sarin gas). In medicine, this is seen in patients with myasthenia gravis who take too high a dose of their cholinergic treatment medications, or seen in some surgical cases, when too high a dose of a cholinesterase inhibitor is given to reverse surgical muscle paralysis.
Gravis	Gravis can have multiple meanings: · Gramin Vikas Vigyan Samiti, an Indian NGO · Advanced Gravis Computer Technology, manufacturer of computer peripherals and joysticks
Myasthenia gravis	Myasthenia gravis is a neuromuscular disease leading to fluctuating muscle weakness and fatiguability. It is an autoimmune disorder, in which weakness is caused by circulating antibodies that block acetylcholine receptors at the post-synaptic neuromuscular junction, inhibiting the stimulative effect of the neurotransmitter acetylcholine. Myasthenia is treated medically with cholinesterase inhibitors or immunosuppressants, and, in selected cases, thymectomy.
Becker muscular dystrophy	Becker muscular dystrophy is an X-linked recessive inherited disorder characterized by slowly progressive muscle weakness of the legs and pelvis.

	It is a type of dystrophinopathy, which includes a spectrum of muscle diseases in which there is insufficient dystrophin produced in the muscle cells, resulting in instability in the structure of muscle cell membrane. This is caused by mutations in the dystrophin gene, which encodes the protein dystrophin.
Muscular dystrophy	Muscular dystrophy refers to a group of genetic, hereditary muscle diseases that weaken the muscles that move the human body. Muscular dystrophies are characterized by progressive skeletal muscle weakness, defects in muscle proteins, and the death of muscle cells and tissue. Nine diseases including Duchenne, Becker, limb girdle, congenital, facioscapulohumeral, myotonic, oculopharyngeal, distal, and Emery-Dreifuss are always classified as Muscular dystrophy but there are more than 100 diseases in total with similarities to Muscular dystrophy.
Myotonia	Myotonia is a symptom of a small handful of certain neuromuscular disorders characterized by the slow relaxation of the muscles after voluntary contraction or electrical stimulation. Generally, repeated effort is needed to relax the muscles, and the condition improves after the muscles have warmed-up. However, prolonged, rigorous exercise may also trigger the condition.
Myotonic dystrophy	Myotonic dystrophy (dystrophia myotonica, DM) is a chronic, slowly progressing, highly variable inherited multisystemic disease that can manifest at any age from birth to old age. It is characterized by wasting of the muscles (muscular dystrophy), posterior subcapsular iridescent cataracts (opacity of the lens of the eyes), heart conduction defects, endocrine changes and myotonia (difficulty relaxing a muscle). Most notably, the highly variable age of onset decreases with successive generations.
Thomsen disease	Thomsen disease, a form of Myotonia congenita, is a muscular genetic disorder characterized by muscle stiffness (cramp) and an inability of the muscle to relax after a voluntary contraction. The affected muscle functions normally after a few repetitions. It is associated with mutations in the chloride channel gene CLCN1.
Disease-modifying antirheumatic drugs	Disease-modifying antirheumatic drugs (DMARDs) is a category of otherwise unrelated drugs defined by their use in rheumatoid arthritis to slow down disease progression. The term is often used in contrast to non-steroidal anti-inflammatory drug, which refers to agents that treat the inflammation but not the underlying cause. The term `antirheumatic` can be used in similar contexts, but without making a claim about an effect on the course.

Chapter 2. PART II: Chapter 19 - Chapter 36

Myositis	Myositis is a general term for inflammation of the muscles. Many such conditions are considered likely to be caused by autoimmune conditions, rather than directly due to infection (although autoimmune conditions can be activated or exacerbated by infections). It is also a documented side effect of the lipid-lowering drugs statins and fibrates.
Exocrine	Exocrine glands are glands that secrete their products (excluding hormones and other chemical messengers) into ducts (duct glands) which lead directly into the external environment. They are the counterparts to endocrine glands, which secrete their products (hormones) directly into the bloodstream (ductless glands) or release hormones (paracrines) that affect only target cells nearby the release site. Typical Exocrine glands include sweat glands, salivary glands, mammary glands, stomach, liver, pancreas.
Endocrine glands	Endocrine glands are glands of the endocrine system that secrete their products, hormones, directly into the blood rather than through a duct. The main Endocrine glands include the pituitary gland, pancreas, ovaries, testes, thyroid gland, and adrenal glands. The hypothalamus is a neuroendocrine organ.
Exocrine glands	Exocrine glands are glands that secrete their products (excluding hormones and other chemical messengers) into ducts (duct glands) which lead directly into the external environment. They are the counterparts to endocrine glands, which secrete their products (hormones) directly into the bloodstream (ductless glands) or release hormones (paracrines) that affect only target cells nearby the release site. Typical Exocrine glands include sweat glands, salivary glands, mammary glands, stomach, liver, pancreas.
Thyroid Hormone	The Thyroid hormones, thyroxine (T_4) and triiodothyronine (T_3), are tyrosine-based hormones produced by the thyroid gland primarily responsible for regulation of metabolism. An important component in the synthesis of Thyroid hormones is iodine. The major form of Thyroid hormone in the blood is thyroxine (T_4), which has a longer half life than T_3.

Chapter 2. PART II: Chapter 19 - Chapter 36

Biorhythm	Biorhythm is an attempt to predict various aspects of a person's life through simple mathematical cycles. The notion has no more predictive power than chance, and is now considered a classic example of pseudoscience by modern science. Beliefs According to believers in biorhythms, a person's life is affected by rhythmic biological cycles which affect one's ability in various domains, such as mental, physical, and emotional activity.
Hypothalamus	The Hypothalamus is a portion of the brain that contains a number of small nuclei with a variety of functions. One of the most important functions of the Hypothalamus is to link the nervous system to the endocrine system via the pituitary gland (hypophysis). The Hypothalamus is located below the thalamus, just above the brain stem.
Pituitary gland	The pituitary gland, or hypophysis, is an endocrine gland about the size of a pea and weighing 0.5 g (0.02 oz).. It is a protrusion off the bottom of the hypothalamus at the base of the brain, and rests in a small, bony cavity (sella turcica) covered by a dural fold (diaphragma sellae). The pituitary fossa, in which the pituitary gland sits, is situated in the sphenoid bone in the middle cranial fossa at the base of the brain.
Adrenocorticotropic hormone	Adrenocorticotropic hormone is a polypeptide tropic hormone produced and secreted by the anterior pituitary gland. It is an important component of the hypothalamic-pituitary-adrenal axis and is often produced in response to biological stress . Its principal effects are increased production of corticosteroids and, as its name suggests, cortisol from the adrenal cortex.
Luteinizing hormone	Luteinizing hormone is a hormone produced by the anterior pituitary gland. · In the female, an acute rise of Luteinizing hormone - the Luteinizing hormone surge - triggers ovulation and corpus luteum development. · In the male, where Luteinizing hormone had also been called Interstitial Cell Stimulating Hormone , it stimulates Leydig cell production of testosterone.

Luteinizing hormone is a heterodimeric glycoprotein. Each monomeric unit is a glycoprotein molecule; one alpha and one beta subunit make the full, functional protein.

Thyroid-stimulating hormone	Thyroid-stimulating hormone is a peptide hormone synthesized and secreted by thyrotrope cells in the anterior pituitary gland, which regulates the endocrine function of the thyroid gland.
	TSH stimulates the thyroid gland to secrete the hormones thyroxine and triiodothyronine (T_3). TSH production is controlled by thyrotropin-releasing hormone (TRH), which is manufactured in the hypothalamus and transported to the anterior pituitary gland via the superior hypophyseal artery, where it increases TSH production and release.
Prolactin	Prolactin or Luteotropic hormone (LTH) is a peptide hormone discovered by Dr. Henry Friesen, primarily associated with lactation. In breastfeeding, the act of an infant suckling the nipple stimulates the production of Prolactin, which fills the breast with milk via a process called lactogenesis, in preparation for the next feed. Oxytocin, another hormone, is also released, which triggers milk let-down.
Vessels	Vessels are a post-rock band from Leeds, UK. Vessels were born from the ashes of A Day Left in September 2005. In 2006 the band self-released a five track eponymous EP, and played many gigs, including the unsigned stage at Leeds Festival as one of the six winners of the Futuresound competition.
	On 5 March 2007, the band released a limited 7` single (Yuki/Forever the Optimist) through Cuckundoo Records, and have been tipped by BBC Radio One as one of the hottest new bands in the country. The band recorded a session for Huw Stephens `s show on BBC Radio 1, which was broadcast on 29 March.
Parathyroid gland	The parathyroid glands are small endocrine glands in the neck that produce parathyroid hormone. Humans have four parathyroid glands, which are usually located behind the thyroid gland, and, in rare cases, within the thyroid gland or in the chest. parathyroid glands control the amount of calcium in the blood and within the bones.
Islet	An Islet is a small island.
	As suggested by its origin as Islette, an Old French diminutive of `isle`, use of the term implies small size, but little attention is given to drawing an upper limit on its applicability.

· Rock - A `rock`, in the sense of a type of Islet, is a landform composed of rock, lying offshore, uninhabited, and having at most minimal vegetation.

· Sandbar - An exposed sandbar is another type of Islet.

· Sea stack - A thin, vertical landform jutting out of a body of water.

· Subsidiary Islets - A more technical application is to small land features, isolated by water, lying off the shore of a larger island. Likewise, any emergent land in an atoll is also called an Islet.

· Tidal island - Often small islands which lie off the mainland of an area, being connected to it in low tide and isolated in high tide.

· River island - A small Islet within the current of a river.

· Ait - A term for river islands that occur within the River Thames in England.

· Towhead - A Middle American term used to describe small river-bound Islets of vegetation, most often within the Mississippi River.

· Holm or Holmen is a common suffix too in Nordic and northern European countries .

· In the Caribbean and West Atlantic, Islets are often called cays or keys.

| Islets of Langerhans | The Islets of Langerhans are the regions of the pancreas that contain its endocrine (i.e., hormone-producing) cells. Discovered in 1869 by German pathological anatomist Paul Langerhans at the age of 22, the Islets of Langerhans constitute approximately 1 to 2% of the mass of the pancreas. There are about one million islets in a healthy adult human pancreas, which are distributed throughout the organ; their combined mass is 1 to 1.5 grams. |

Chapter 2. PART II: Chapter 19 - Chapter 36

Parathyroid hormone	Parathyroid hormone is secreted by the parathyroid glands as a polypeptide containing 84 amino acids. It acts to increase the concentration of calcium (Ca^{2+}) in the blood, whereas calcitonin (a hormone produced by the parafollicular cells (C cells) of the thyroid gland) acts to decrease calcium concentration. PTH acts to increase the concentration of calcium in the blood by acting upon Parathyroid hormone receptor in three parts of the body: PTH half-life is approximately 4 minutes.
Calcitonin	Calcitonin is a 32-amino acid linear polypeptide hormone that is produced in humans primarily by the parafollicular cells (also known as C-cells) of the thyroid, and in many other animals in the ultimobranchial body. It acts to reduce blood calcium (Ca^{2+}), opposing the effects of parathyroid hormone (PTH). It has been found in fish, reptiles, birds, and mammals.
Hyperparathyroidism	Hyperparathyroidism is overactivity of the parathyroid glands resulting in excess production of parathyroid hormone (PTH). The parathyroid hormone regulates calcium and phosphate levels and helps to maintain these levels. Excessive PTH secretion may be due to problems in the glands themselves, in which case it is referred to as primary hyperparathryroidism and which leads to hypercalcemia (raised calcium levels).
Hypoparathyroidism	In medicine (endocrinology), Hypoparathyroidism is decreased function of the parathyroid glands, leading to decreased levels of parathyroid hormone (PTH). The consequence, hypocalcaemia, is a serious medical condition. · Tingling lips, fingers, and toes · Muscle cramps · Pain in the face, legs, and feet · Abdominal pain · Dry hair · Brittle nails · Dry, scaly skin · Cataracts

· Weakened tooth enamel (in children)

· Muscle spasms called tetany (can lead to spasms of the larynx, causing breathing difficulties)

· Convulsions (seizures)

· Tetanic contractions
Additional symptoms that may be associated with this disease include:

· Painful menstruation

· Hand or foot spasms

· Decreased consciousness

· Delayed or absent tooth formation
In contrast to hyperparathyroidism (hyperfunction of the parathyroids), Hypoparathyroidism does not have consequences for bone.

Diagnosis is by measurement of calcium, serum albumin (for correction) and PTH in blood.

Primary hyperparathyroidism	Primary hyperparathyroidism causes hypercalcemia (elevated blood calcium levels) through the excessive secretion of parathyroid hormone (PTH), usually by an adenoma (benign tumors) of the parathyroid glands. Its incidence is approximately 42 per 100,000 people. It is almost exactly three times as common in women as men.
Secondary hyperparathyroidism	Secondary hyperparathyroidism refers to the excessive secretion of parathyroid hormone (PTH) by the parathyroid glands in response to hypocalcemia (low blood calcium levels) and associated hypertrophy of the glands. This disorder is especially seen in patients with chronic renal failure. It is often--although not consistently--abbreviated as SHPT in medical literature.

Chapter 2. PART II: Chapter 19 - Chapter 36

Bone	Bones are rigid organs that form part of the endoskeleton of vertebrates. They function to move, support, and protect the various organs of the body, produce red and white blood cells and store minerals. bone tissue is a type of dense connective tissue.
Pancreas	The pancreas is a gland organ in the digestive and endocrine system of vertebrates. It is both an endocrine gland producing several important hormones, including insulin, glucagon, and somatostatin, as well as an exocrine gland, secreting pancreatic juice containing digestive enzymes that pass to the small intestine. These enzymes help in the further breakdown of the carbohydrates, protein, and fat in the chyme.
Energy balance	In biology, energy balance is the biological homeostasis of energy in living systems. It is measured with the following equation: Energy intake = internal heat produced + external work + storage. It is also an aspect of bioenergetics, concerning energy flow through living systems.
Lipolysis	Lipolysis is the breakdown of fat stored in fat cells. During this process, free fatty acids are released into the bloodstream and circulate throughout the body. Ketones are produced, and are found in large quantities in ketosis (a state in metabolism occurring when the liver converts fat into fatty acids and ketone bodies which can be used by the body for energy).
Ketone	In organic chemistry, a Ketone is a type of compound that features one carbonyl group (C=O) bonded to two other carbon atoms, i.e., $R_3CCO\text{-}CR_3$ where R can be a variety of atoms and groups of atoms. With carbonyl carbon bonded to two carbon atoms, Ketones are distinct from many other functional groups, such as carboxylic acids, aldehydes, esters, amides, and other oxygen-containing compounds. The double-bond of the carbonyl group distinguishes Ketones from alcohols and ethers.
Glucagon	Glucagon is an important hormone involved in carbohydrate metabolism. Produced by the pancreas, it is released when blood glucose levels start to fall too low, causing the liver to convert stored glycogen into glucose and release it into the bloodstream, raising blood glucose levels and ultimately preventing the development of hypoglycemia. The action of Glucagon is thus opposite to that of insulin, which instructs the body`s cells to take in glucose from the blood.
Acetone	Acetone is the organic compound with the formula $OC(CH_3)_2$. This colorless, mobile, flammable liquid is the simplest example of the ketones. Owing to the fact that Acetone is miscible with water it serves as an important solvent in its own right, typically as the solvent of choice for cleaning purposes in the laboratory.

Chapter 2. PART II: Chapter 19 - Chapter 36

Polydipsia	Polydipsia is a medical symptom in which the patient displays excessive thirst. An etymologically related term is dipsomaniac, meaning an alcoholic. This symptom is characteristically found in diabetics, often as one of the initial symptoms, and in those who fail to take their anti-diabetic medications or whose dosages have become inadequate.
Polyuria	In medicine, Polyuria is a condition characterized by the passage of large volumes of urine (at least 2.5 L over 24 hours in adults). Polyuria often appears in conjunction with polydipsia (increased thirst), though it is possible to have one without the other, and the latter may be a cause or an effect. Psychogenic polydipsia may lead to Polyuria.
Deficiency	A Deficiency is a lack of something. Example there is a Deficiency of oxygen in the air and we shall soon suffocate. · In mathematics, a deficient number is a number n for which $\sigma(n) < 2n$. · In medicine there are a variety of nutrient deficiencies: · Avitaminosis is a Deficiency of vitamins. · Boron Deficiency · Chromium Deficiency · Iron Deficiency · Iodine Deficiency · Magnesium Deficiency · Micronutrient Deficiency

· In construction, a Deficiency is an item, or condition that is considered sub-standard, or below minimum expectations, such as those mandated by either drawings or specifications or the building code or the fire code, and/or any combination of the foregoing. Deficiencies are routinely discussed and dealt with in construction site meetings.

· In genetics, a genetic deletion is also called a Deficiency.

· In real estate law, a Deficiency in the ability to pay off a debt is called a Deficiency judgment or Deficiency judgement.

Glucose	Glucose a monosaccharide (or simple sugar) also known as grape sugar, blood sugar, or corn sugar, is a very important carbohydrate in biology. The living cell uses it as a source of energy and metabolic intermediate. Glucose is one of the main products of photosynthesis and starts cellular respiration in both prokaryotes (bacteria and archaea) and eukaryotes (animals, plants, fungi, and protists).
Acarbose	Acarbose is an anti-diabetic drug used to treat type 2 diabetes mellitus and, in some countries, prediabetes. It is sold in Europe under the brand name Glucobay (Bayer AG), in North America as Precose (Bayer Pharmaceuticals), and in Canada as Prandase (Bayer AG). It is an inhibitor of alpha glucosidase, an enteric enzyme that releases glucose from larger carbohydrates.
Biguanide	Biguanide can refer to a molecule, or to a class of drugs based upon this molecule. Biguanides can function as oral antihyperglycemic drugs used for diabetes mellitus or prediabetes treatment. They are also used as antimalarial drugs.
Metformin	Metformin is an oral anti-diabetic drug in the biguanide class. It is the first-line drug of choice for the treatment of type 2 diabetes, particularly in overweight and obese people and those with normal kidney function. Evidence is also mounting for its efficacy in gestational diabetes, although safety concerns still preclude its widespread use in this setting.
Pioglitazone	Pioglitazone is a prescription drug of the class thiazolidinedione (TZD) with hypoglycemic (antihyperglycemic, antidiabetic) action. Pioglitazone is marketed as trademarks Actos in the USA and UK, Glustin in Europe, and Zactos in Mexico by Takeda Pharmaceuticals. Actos was the tenth-best selling drug in the U.S. in 2008, with sales exceeding $2.4 billion.
Pramlintide	Pramlintide acetate (Symlin) is a relatively new adjunct treatment for diabetes (both type 1 and 2), developed by Amylin Pharmaceuticals.

	Pramlintide is an analogue of amylin, a small peptide hormone that is released into the bloodstream by the β-cells of the pancreas along with insulin, after a meal. Like insulin, amylin is deficient in individuals with diabetes.
Rosiglitazone	Rosiglitazone is an anti-diabetic drug in the thiazolidinedione class of drugs. It works as an insulin sensitizer, by binding to the PPAR receptors in fat cells and making the cells more responsive to insulin. It is marketed by the pharmaceutical company GlaxoSmithKline as a stand-alone drug (Avandia) and in combination with metformin (Avandamet) or with glimepiride (Avandaryl).
Sitagliptin	Sitagliptin is an oral antihyperglycemic (anti-diabetic drug) of the dipeptidyl peptidase-4 (DPP-4) inhibitor class, Sitagliptin being the only second generation DPP-4 inhibitor currently available in the USA. This enzyme-inhibiting drug is used either alone or in combination with other oral antihyperglycemic agents (such as metformin or a thiazolidinedione) for treatment of diabetes mellitus type 2. The benefit of this medicine is its lower side-effects (e.g., less hypoglycemia, less weight gain) in the control of blood glucose values. Exenatide (Byetta) also works by its effect on the incretin system.
	In clinical trials, adverse effects were as common with Sitagliptin as they were with placebo, except for extremely rare nausea and common cold-like symptoms.
Thiazolidinedione	The medication class of Thiazolidinedione was introduced in the late 1990s as an adjunctive therapy for diabetes mellitus (type 2) and related diseases.
	Thiazolidinediones or TZDs act by binding to PPARs (peroxisome proliferator-activated receptors), a group of receptor molecules inside the cell nucleus, specifically PPARγ (gamma). The ligands for these receptors are free fatty acids (FFAs) and eicosanoids.
Glimepiride	Glimepiride is a medium-to-long acting sulfonylurea anti-diabetic drug. It is marketed as Amaryl by Sanofi-Aventis and Glista OD by Cadila Pharmaceuticals Ltd. Glimepiride is the first third-generation sulfonylurea, and is very potent.
Glipizide	Glipizide is an oral medium-to-long acting anti-diabetic drug from the sulfonylurea class. It is classified as a second generation sulfonylurea, which means that it undergoes enterohepatic circulation. The structure on the R2 group is a much larger cyclo or aromatic group compared to the 1st generation sulfonylureas.

Chapter 2. PART II: Chapter 19 - Chapter 36

Naproxen	Naproxen Sodium (INN) is a non-steroidal anti-inflammatory drug commonly used for the reduction of mild to moderate pain, fever, inflammation and stiffness caused by conditions such as osteoarthritis, rheumatoid arthritis, psoriatic arthritis, gout, ankylosing spondylitis, menstrual cramps, tendinitis, bursitis, and the treatment of primary dysmenorrhea. It works by inhibiting both the COX-1 and COX-2 enzymes. Naproxen and Naproxen sodium are marketed under various trade names including: Aleve, Anaprox, Antalgin, Feminax Ultra, Flanax, Inza, Midol Extended Relief, Miranax, Naprelan, Naprogesic, Naprosyn, Narocin, Proxen, Synflex, Xenobid.
Renin	Renin, also known as angiotensinogenase is an enzyme that participates in the body's Renin-angiotensin system (RAS) that mediates extracellular volume (i.e. that of the blood plasma, lymph and interstitial fluid), and arterial vasoconstriction. Thus it regulates the body's mean arterial blood pressure. Renin was discovered, characterized and named in 1898 by Robert Tigerstedt, Professor of Physiology at the Karolinska Institute in Stockholm.
Renin-angiotensin system	The Renin-angiotensin system or the renin-angiotensin-aldosterone system (RAAS) is a hormone system that regulates blood pressure and water (fluid) balance. When blood volume is low, the kidneys secrete renin. Renin stimulates the production of angiotensin.
Secretagogue	A Secretagogue is a substance that causes another substance to be secreted. One example is gastrin which stimulates secretion of gastric acid by the stomach. Sulfonylureas are insulin Secretagogues, triggering insulin release by direct action on the K_{ATP} channel of the pancreatic beta cells.
Tizanidine	Tizanidine is a drug that is used as a muscle relaxant. It is a centrally acting α-2 adrenergic agonist. It is used to treat the spasms, cramping, and tightness of muscles caused by medical problems such as multiple sclerosis, spastic diplegia, back pain, or certain other injuries to the spine or central nervous system.
Diabetic ketoacidosis	Diabetic ketoacidosis is a potentially life-threatening complication in patients with diabetes mellitus. It happens predominantly in those with type 1 diabetes, but it can occur in those with type 2 diabetes under certain circumstances. DKA results from an absolute shortage of insulin; in response the body switches to burning fatty acids and producing acidic ketone bodies that cause most of the symptoms and complications.

Chapter 2. PART II: Chapter 19 - Chapter 36

Adrenal glands	In mammals, the adrenal glands are the star-shaped endocrine glands that sit on top of the kidneys. They are chiefly responsible for releasing hormones in conjunction with stress through the synthesis of corticosteroids and catecholamines, including cortisol and adrenaline (epinephrine), respectively.
	Anatomically, the adrenal glands are located in the retroperitoneum situated atop the kidneys, one on each side.
Endocarditis	Endocarditis is an inflammation of the inner layer of the heart, the endocardium. It usually involves the heart valves (native or prosthetic valves). Other structures which may be involved include the interventricular septum, the chordae tendinae, the mural endocardium, or even on intracardiac devices.
Adrenal cortex	Situated along the perimeter of the adrenal gland, the adrenal cortex mediates the stress response through the production of mineralocorticoids and glucocorticoids, including aldosterone and cortisol respectively. It is also a secondary site of androgen synthesis.
	The cortex can be divided into three distinct layers of tissue based on their organisation.
Cortisol	Cortisol is a corticosteroid hormone or glucocorticoid produced by zona fasciculata of the adrenal cortex, which is a part of the adrenal gland. It is usually referred to as the `stress hormone` as it is involved in response to stress and anxiety, controlled by CRH. It increases blood pressure and blood sugar, and reduces immune responses. Various synthetic forms of Cortisol are used to treat a variety of different illnesses.
Glucocorticoid	Glucocorticoids (GC) are a class of steroid hormones that bind to the Glucocorticoid receptor (GR), which is present in almost every vertebrate animal cell. The name Glucocorticoid derives from their role in the regulation of the metabolism of glucose, their synthesis in the adrenal cortex, and their steroidal structure .
	GCs are part of the feedback mechanism in the immune system that turns immune activity (inflammation) down.
Mineralocorticoid	Mineralocorticoids are a class of steroid hormones characterised by their similarity to aldosterone and their influence on salt and water balance.

Full:

The name Mineralocorticoid derives from early observations that these hormones were involved in the retention of sodium, a mineral. The primary endogenous Mineralocorticoid is aldosterone, although a number of other endogenous hormones (including progesterone and deoxycorticosterone) have Mineralocorticoid function.

Primary aldosteronism

Primary aldosteronism, also known as primary hyperaldosteronism, is characterized by the overproduction of the mineralocorticoid hormone aldosterone by the adrenal glands. Aldosterone causes increase in sodium and water retention and potassium excretion in the kidneys, leading to arterial hypertension (high blood pressure). An increase in the production of mineralocorticoid from the adrenal gland is evident.

Replacement

Replacement means:

· Replacements, Tuttle, Lisa

· Axiom schema of Replacement

· Text Replacement, a feature of word processors correcting automatically common misspellings and typos

· Replacement rate

· Sampling (statistics) with Replacement .

Adrenal medulla

The Adrenal medulla is part of the adrenal gland. It is located at the center of the gland, being surrounded by the adrenal cortex.

The Adrenal medulla consists of irregularly shaped cells grouped around blood vessels.

Pheochromocytoma

A phaeochromocytoma (PCC) , is a neuroendocrine tumor of the medulla of the adrenal glands (originating in the chromaffin cells), or extra-adrenal chromaffin tissue that failed to involute after birth and secretes excessive amounts of catecholamines, usually adrenaline and noradrenaline. Extra-adrenal paragangliomas (often described as extra-adrenal Pheochromocytomas) are closely related, though less common, tumors that originate in the ganglia of the sympathetic nervous system and are named based upon the primary anatomical site of origin.

Traditionally it is known as the `10% tumor` - however this description is now flawed, as below:

· About 10% of adrenal cases are bilateral (suggesting hereditary disease)

· About 10% of adrenal cases occur in children (also suggesting hereditary disease)

· About 10% are extra-adrenal (located in any orthosympathetic tissue): of these 9% are in the abdomen and 1% are located elsewhere.

Rule

A rule is:

· Rewrite rule, in generative grammar and computer science

· Standardization, a formal and widely-accepted statement, fact, definition, or qualification

· Operation, a determinate rule (method) for performing a mathematical operation and obtaining a certain result (Mathematics, Logic)

· Unary operation

· Binary operation

· rule of inference, a function from sets of formulae to formulae (Mathematics, Logic)

· rule of thumb, principle with broad application that is not intended to be strictly accurate or reliable for every situation. Also often simply referred to as a rule

· Moral, an atomic element of a moral code for guiding choices in human behavior

· Heuristic, a quantized `rule` which shows a tendency or probability for successful function

· A regulation, as in sports

· A Production rule, as in computer science

· Procedural law, a ruleset governing the application of laws to cases

· A law, which may informally be called a `rule`

· A court ruling, a decision by a court

· In the U.S. Government, a regulation mandated by Congress, but written or expanded upon by the Executive Branch.

· Norm (sociology), an informal but widely accepted rule, concept, truth, definition, or qualification (social norms, legal norms, coding norms)

· Norm (philosophy), a kind of sentence or a reason to act, feel or believe

· `rulership` is the concept of governance by a government:

· Military rule, governance by a military body

· Monastic rule, a collection of precepts that guides the life of monks or nuns in a religious order where the superior holds the place of Christ

· Slide rule

· `rule,` a song by Ayumi Hamasaki

· `rule,` a song by rapper Nas

· `rules,` an album by the band The Whitest Boy Alive

· rules: Pyaar Ka Superhit Formula, a 2003 Bollywood film

· ruler, an instrument for measuring lengths

· rule, a component of an astrolabe, circumferator or similar instrument

· The rules, a bestselling self-help book

· rule Project (Run Up-to-date Linux Everywhere), a project that aims to use up-to-date Linux software on old PCs

· rule engine, a software system that helps managing business rules

· Ja rule, a hip hop artist

· R.U.L.E., a 2005 greatest hits album by rapper Ja rule

· `rules,` a KMFDM song

Codeine

Codeine or methylmorphine is an opiate used for its analgesic, antitussive, and antidiarrheal properties.

Codeine is a natural alkaloid found in opium poppy, a plant in the papaveraceae family. Opium poppy has been cultivated and utilized throughout human history for a variety of medicinal (analgesic, anti-tussive, anti-diarrheal..).

Thyroxine

Thyroxine, or 3,5,3`,5`-tetraiodothyronine , a form of thyroid hormones is the major hormone secreted by the follicular cells of the thyroid gland. Thyroxine is synthesized via the iodination and covalent bonding of the phenyl portions of tyrosine residues found in an initial peptide, thyroglobulin, which is secreted into thyroid granules. These iodinated diphenyl compounds are cleaved from their peptide backbone upon being stimulated by thyroid stimulating hormone.

Triiodothyronine

Triiodothyronine, $C_{15}H_{12}I_3NO_4$, also known as T_3, is a thyroid hormone.

Thyroid-stimulating hormone activates the production of thyroxine (T_4) and T_3. This process is under regulation.

CramIOI

Chapter 2. PART II: Chapter 19 - Chapter 36

Thyroidectomy	A Thyroidectomy is an operation that involves the surgical removal of all or part of the thyroid gland. Surgeons often perform a Thyroidectomy when a patient has thyroid cancer or some other condition of the thyroid gland (such as hyperthyroidism). Other indications for surgery include cosmetic (very enlarged thyroid), or symptomatic obstruction (causing difficulties in swallowing or breathing).
Storm	A Storm is any disturbed state of an astronomical body's atmosphere, especially affecting its surface, and strongly implying severe weather. It may be marked by strong wind, thunder and lightning (a thunderStorm), heavy precipitation, such as ice (ice Storm), or wind transporting some substance through the atmosphere (as in a dust Storm, snowStorm, hailStorm, etc).
	Storms are created when a center of low pressure develops, with a system of high pressure surrounding it.
Myxedema	Hypothyroid type Myxedema describes a specific form of cutaneous and dermal non-pitting edema secondary to increased deposition of connective tissue matrix components . In Graves' disease the Myxedema is secondary to lymphocytic infiltrate and secondary swelling from inflammatory reactions and is typically located in the periorbital tissues, extraocular muscles and in the lower legs, mostly below the knee (pretibial Myxedema).[535] While both hyper- and hypo-thyroidism have forms of Myxedema their etiologies are pathophysiologically distinct.
	The word originates from μῖξα, taken from ancient Greek to convey 'mucus' or 'slimy substance' and ά½ Γ δημα for swelling.
D-Dimer	D-dimer is a fibrin degradation product, a small protein fragment present in the blood after a blood clot is degraded by fibrinolysis. D-dimer concentration may be determined by a blood test to help diagnose thrombosis. Since its introduction in the 1990s, it has become an important test performed in patients suspected of thrombotic disorders.
Hemostasis	Hemostasis or haemostasis is a complex process which causes the bleeding process to stop. It refers to the process of keeping blood within a damaged blood vessel (the opposite of Hemostasis is hemorrhage). Most of the time this includes the changing of blood from a fluid to a solid state.

Chapter 2. PART II: Chapter 19 - Chapter 36

Von Willebrand factor	Von Willebrand factor is a blood glycoprotein involved in hemostasis. It is deficient or defective in von Willebrand disease and is involved in a large number of other diseases, including thrombotic thrombocytopenic purpura, Heyde`s syndrome, and possibly hemolytic-uremic syndrome. vWF is a large multimeric glycoprotein present in blood plasma and produced constitutively in endothelium (in the Weibel-Palade bodies), megakaryocytes (α-granules of platelets), and subendothelial connective tissue.
Anticoagulant	An Anticoagulant is a substance that prevents coagulation; that is, it stops blood from clotting. A group of pharmaceuticals called Anticoagulants can be used in vivo as a medication for thrombotic disorders. Some chemical compounds are used in medical equipment, such as test tubes, blood transfusion bags, and renal dialysis equipment.
Thrombin	Thrombin also commonly called pro-Thrombin is a coagulation protein in the blood stream that has many effects in the coagulation cascade. It is a serine protease (EC 3.4.21.5) that converts soluble fibrinogen into insoluble strands of fibrin, as well as catalyzing many other coagulation-related reactions. The Thrombin gene is located on the eleventh chromosome (11p11-q12).
Vasodilation	Vasodilation refers to the widening of blood vessels resulting from relaxation of smooth muscle cells within the vessel walls, particularly in the large arteries, smaller arterioles and large veins. The process is essentially the opposite of vasoconstriction, or the narrowing of blood vessels. When vessels dilate, the flow of blood is increased due to a decrease in vascular resistance.
Tissue factor	Tissue factor factor III, thrombokinase, or CD142 is a protein present in subendothelial tissue, platelets, and leukocytes necessary for the initiation of thrombin formation from the zymogen prothrombin. An incorrect synonym is thromboplastin. Historically, thromboplastin was a lab reagent, usually derived from placental sources, used to assay prothrombin times (PT time).
Celecoxib	Celecoxib is a sulfa non-steroidal anti-inflammatory drug used in the treatment of osteoarthritis, rheumatoid arthritis, acute pain, painful menstruation and menstrual symptoms, and to reduce numbers of colon and rectum polyps in patients with familial adenomatous polyposis. It is marketed by Pfizer. It is known under the brand name Celebrex or Celebra for arthritis and Onsenal for polyps.

Chapter 2. PART II: Chapter 19 - Chapter 36

Fibrinolysis	Fibrinolysis is the process wherein a fibrin clot, the product of coagulation, is broken down. Its main enzyme plasmin cuts the fibrin mesh at various places, leading to the production of circulating fragments that are cleared by other proteases or by the kidney and liver.
	Plasmin is produced in an inactive form, plasminogen, in the liver.
Malnutrition	Malnutrition is the insufficient, excessive or imbalanced consumption of nutrients. A number of different nutrition disorders may arise, depending on which nutrients are under or overabundant in the diet.
	The World Health Organization cites Malnutrition as the gravest single threat to the world`s public health.
Vitamin E	Vitamin E is a generic term for tocopherols and tocotrienols. Vitamin E is a family of α-, β-, γ-, and δ-tocopherols and corresponding four tocotrienols. Vitamin E is a fat-soluble antioxidant that stops the production of reactive oxygen species formed when fat undergoes oxidation.
Bleeding diathesis	In medicine (hematology), Bleeding diathesis is an unusual susceptibility to bleeding (hemorrhage) due to a defect in the system of coagulation. Several types are distinguished, ranging from mild to lethal. Some examples of bleeding diatheses:
	· Haemophilia
	· von Willebrand disease
	· Glanzmann thrombasthenia
	· Bernard-Soulier syndrome
	· Scurvy
	· Leukemia
	· Wiskott-Aldrich syndrome

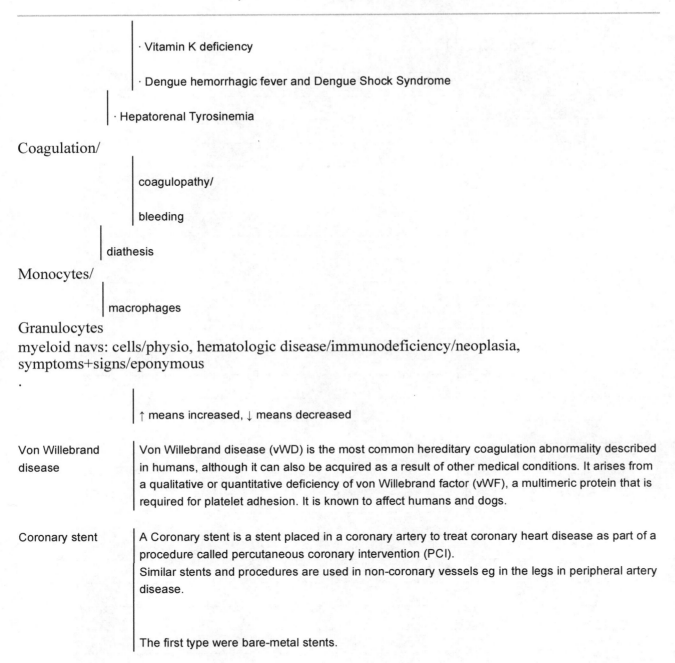

· Vitamin K deficiency

· Dengue hemorrhagic fever and Dengue Shock Syndrome

· Hepatorenal Tyrosinemia

Coagulation/

coagulopathy/

bleeding

diathesis

Monocytes/

macrophages

Granulocytes

myeloid navs: cells/physio, hematologic disease/immunodeficiency/neoplasia, symptoms+signs/eponymous

.

↑ means increased, ↓ means decreased

Von Willebrand disease	Von Willebrand disease (vWD) is the most common hereditary coagulation abnormality described in humans, although it can also be acquired as a result of other medical conditions. It arises from a qualitative or quantitative deficiency of von Willebrand factor (vWF), a multimeric protein that is required for platelet adhesion. It is known to affect humans and dogs.
Coronary stent	A Coronary stent is a stent placed in a coronary artery to treat coronary heart disease as part of a procedure called percutaneous coronary intervention (PCI). Similar stents and procedures are used in non-coronary vessels eg in the legs in peripheral artery disease. The first type were bare-metal stents.

Chapter 2. PART II: Chapter 19 - Chapter 36

Drug-eluting stent	A Drug-eluting stent (DES) is a coronary stent (a scaffold) placed into narrowed, diseased coronary arteries that slowly releases a drug to block cell proliferation. This prevents fibrosis that, together with clots (thrombus), could otherwise block the stented artery, a process called restenosis. The stent is usually placed within the coronary artery by an Interventional cardiologist during an angioplasty procedure.
Antiplatelet drug	An Antiplatelet drug is a member of a class of pharmaceuticals that decreases platelet aggregation and inhibits thrombus formation. They are effective in the arterial circulation, where anticoagulants have little effect. They are widely used in primary and secondary prevention of thrombotic cerebrovascular or cardiovascular disease.
Argatroban	Argatroban is an anticoagulant that is a small molecule direct thrombin inhibitor. In 2000, Argatroban was licensed by the Food and Drug Administration (FDA) for prophylaxis or treatment of thrombosis in patients with heparin-induced thrombocytopenia (HIT). In 2002, it was approved for use during percutaneous coronary interventions in patients who have HIT or are at risk for developing it.
Bivalirudin	Bivalirudin (Angiomax) is a drug that belongs to the anticoagulant class and acts as a direct thrombin inhibitor. Chemically it constitutes a synthetic congener of the naturally occurring drug hirudin (found in the saliva of the medicinal leech Hirudo medicinalis). Both Bivalirudin and Hirudin directly inhibit thrombin by specifically binding as well to the catalytic site and to the anion-binding exosite of circulating and clot- or thrombus-bound thrombin.
Dalteparin	Dalteparin is a low molecular weight heparin. It is marketed as Fragmin by Pfizer Inc. Like other low molecular weight heparins, Dalteparin is used for prophylaxis or treatment of deep vein thrombosis and pulmonary embolism.
Fondaparinux	Fondaparinux (Arixtra) is an anticoagulant medication. It is marketed by GlaxoSmithKline. .

Chapter 2. PART II: Chapter 19 - Chapter 36

Heparin-induced thrombocytopenia	Heparin-induced thrombocytopenia (HIT) without or with thrombosis (HITT) is the development of thrombocytopenia (low platelet counts) due to the administration of the anticoagulant (blood clotting inhibitor) heparin, either in its `unfractionated` or `low molecular weight` form. It predisposes to thrombosis, the formation of abnormal blood clots inside a blood vessel. If someone receiving heparin develops new or worsening thrombosis, or if the platelet count falls, HIT can be confirmed with specific blood tests.
Abciximab	Abciximab, manufactured by Centocor and distributed by Eli Lilly under the trade name ReoPro, is a platelet aggregation inhibitor mainly used during and after coronary artery procedures like angioplasty to prevent platelets from sticking together and causing thrombus (blood clot) formation within the coronary artery. Its mechanism of action is inhibition of glycoprotein IIb/IIIa.
	While Abciximab has a short plasma half life, due to its strong affinity for its receptor on the platelets, it may occupy some receptors for weeks.
Eptifibatide	Eptifibatide, is an antiplatelet drug that selectively blocks the platelet glycoprotein IIb/IIIa receptor. Eptifibatide is a cyclic heptapeptide derived from a protein found in the venom of the southeastern pygmy rattlesnake (Sistrurus miliarius barbouri). It belongs to the class of the so called arginin-glycin-aspartat-mimetics and reversibly binds to platelets.
Tinzaparin	Tinzaparin is an antithrombotic drug in the heparin group. It is a low molecular weight heparin marketed as Innohep or innohep world wide. It has been approved by the U.S. Food and Drug Administration (FDA) for once daily treatment of deep vein thrombosis and pulmonary embolism.
Tirofiban	Tirofiban is an antiplatelet drug. It belongs to a class of anticoagulants named glycoprotein IIb/IIIa inhibitors. Tirofiban is the first drug candidate whose origins can be traced to a pharmacophore-based virtual screening lead.
Warfarin	Warfarin is an anticoagulant. It was initially marketed as a pesticide against rats and mice and is still popular for this purpose, although more potent poisons such as brodifacoum have since been developed. A few years after its introduction, Warfarin was found to be effective and relatively safe for preventing thrombosis and embolism (abnormal formation and migration of blood clots) in many disorders.
American College of Chest Physicians	The American College of Chest Physicians (ACCP) is a medical organization consisting of physicians and non-physician specialists in the field of chest medicine, which includes pulmonology, thoracic surgery, and critical care medicine.

Fellow of the College of Chest Physicians (FCCP) is a title given to a doctor who specializes in pulmonology, thoracic surgery, and critical care medicine. FCCP is used as a post-nominal title, such as John Citizen, MD, FCCP. To be eligible for the Fellowship, a physician in the United States of America or Canada must be board certified in both a primary board and an applicable subspecialty board, have at least 18 months experience in the field, and be sponsored by two Fellows of the College.

Disseminated intravascular coagulation	Disseminated intravascular coagulation , also known as consumptive coagulopathy, is a pathological activation of coagulation (blood clotting) mechanisms that happens in response to a variety of diseases. As its name suggests, it leads to the formation of small blood clots inside the blood vessels throughout the body. As the small clots consume all the available coagulation proteins and platelets, normal coagulation is disrupted and abnormal bleeding occurs from the skin , the digestive tract, the respiratory tract and surgical wounds.
Physician	A Physician -- also known as medical practitioner, doctor of medicine, medical doctor which is concerned with maintaining or restoring human health through the study, diagnosis, and treatment of disease or injury. This properly requires both a detailed knowledge of the academic disciplines underlying diseases and their treatment -- the science of medicine -- and also a decent competence in its applied practice -- the art or craft of medicine. Both the role of the Physician and the meaning of the word itself vary significantly around the world, but as generally understood, the ethics of medicine require that Physicians show consideration, compassion and benevolence for their patients.
Thrombosis	Thrombosis is the formation of a blood clot (thrombus) inside a blood vessel, obstructing the flow of blood through the circulatory system. When a blood vessel is injured, the body uses platelets and fibrin to form a blood clot, because the first step in repairing it (hemostasis) is to prevent loss of blood. If that mechanism causes too much clotting, and the clot breaks free, an embolus is formed.
Superficial	Superficial is an adjective generally meaning `regarding the surface`, often metaphorically. Both in the literal as in the metaphorical sense the term has often a negative connotation based on the idea that deeper parts are also important to consider. · In human anatomy, Superficial describes objects near the body`s surface as compared to other objects that may be deep. For example, skin is a Superficial structure of the body and muscles are deep to skin.

Chapter 2. PART II: Chapter 19 - Chapter 36

Total body surface area	Total body surface area is an assessment measure of burns of the skin. In adults, the `rule of nines` is used to determine the total percentage of area burned for each major section of the body. In some cases, the burns may cover more than one body part, or may not fully cover such a part - in these cases, burns are measured by using the casualty`s palm as a reference point for 1% of the body.
Heat	In physics and thermodynamics, Heat is the process of energy transfer from one body or system due to thermal contact, which in turn is defined as an energy transfer to a body in any other way than due to work performed on the body. When an infinitesimal amount of Heat δQ is transferred to a body in thermal equilibrium at absolute temperature T in a reversible way, then it is given by the quantity TdS, where S is the entropy of the body. A related term is thermal energy, loosely defined as the energy of a body that increases with its temperature.
Chemical Burn	A Chemical burn occurs when living tissue is exposed to a corrosive substance such as a strong acid or base. Chemical burns follow standard burn classification and may cause extensive tissue damage. The main types of irritant and/or corrosive products are: acids, bases, oxidizers, solvents, reducing agents and alkylants.
Carbon monoxide	Carbon monoxide, with the chemical formula CO, is a colorless, odorless and tasteless, yet highly toxic gas. Its molecules consist of one carbon atom and one oxygen atom, connected by a covalent double bond and a dative covalent bond. It is the simplest oxocarbon, and can be viewed as the anhydride of formic acid (CH_2O_2).
Carbon monoxide poisoning	Carbon monoxide poisoning occurs after enough inhalation of carbon monoxide (CO). Carbon monoxide is a toxic gas, but, being colorless, odorless, tasteless, and non-irritating, it is very difficult for people to detect. Carbon monoxide is a product of incomplete combustion of organic matter with insufficient oxygen supply to enable complete oxidation to carbon dioxide (CO_2) and is often produced in domestic or industrial settings by motor vehicles and other gasoline-powered tools, heaters, and cooking equipment.

413

Debridement	Debridement is the medical removal of a patient's dead, damaged, or infected tissue to improve the healing potential of the remaining healthy tissue. Removal may be surgical, mechanical, chemical, autolytic (self-digestion), and by maggot therapy, where certain species of live maggots selectively eat only necrotic tissue.
	In oral hygiene and dentistry, Debridement refers to the removal of plaque and calculus that have accumulated on the teeth.

Chapter 3. PART III: Chapter 37 - Chapter 54

Adrenocorticotropic hormone	Adrenocorticotropic hormone is a polypeptide tropic hormone produced and secreted by the anterior pituitary gland. It is an important component of the hypothalamic-pituitary-adrenal axis and is often produced in response to biological stress . Its principal effects are increased production of corticosteroids and, as its name suggests, cortisol from the adrenal cortex.
Schwann cell	Schwann cells are glia of the peripheral nervous system (PNS). They are involved in many important aspects of peripheral nerve biology; the conduction of nervous impulses along axons, nerve development and regeneration, trophic support for neurons, production of the nerve extracellular matrix and presentation of antigens to T-lymphocytes. Charcot-Marie-Tooth disease (CMT), Guillain-Barré syndrome (GBS), schwannomatosis and chronic inflammatory demyelinating polyneuropathy (CIDP) are all neuropathies involving Schwann cells.
Schwann cells	Schwann cells are glia of the peripheral nervous system (PNS). They are involved in many important aspects of peripheral nerve biology; the conduction of nervous impulses along axons, nerve development and regeneration, trophic support for neurons, production of the nerve extracellular matrix and presentation of antigens to T-lymphocytes. Charcot-Marie-Tooth disease (CMT), Guillain-Barré syndrome (GBS), schwannomatosis and chronic inflammatory demyelinating polyneuropathy (CIDP) are all neuropathies involving Schwann cells.
Spinal cord	The Spinal cord is a long, thin, tubular bundle of nervous tissue and support cells that extends from the brain. The brain and Spinal cord together make up the central nervous system. The Spinal cord extends down to the space in between the first and second lumbar vertebrae.
Trauma	Trauma can represent: · Physical Trauma, an often serious and body-altering physical injury, such as the removal of a limb · Blunt Trauma, a type of physical Trauma caused by impact or other force applied from or with a blunt object · Penetrating Trauma, a type of physical Trauma in which the skin or tissues are pierced by an object · Psychological Trauma, an emotional or psychological injury, usually resulting from an extremely stressful or life-threatening situation

417

CRAM101

· Post-cult Trauma, the intense emotional problems that some members of cults and new religious movements experience upon disaffection and disaffiliation

· Trauma team, a group of healthcare workers who attend to seriously ill or injured casualties who arrive at a hospital emergency department

· Trauma center, a hospital equipped to provide comprehensive emergency medical services to patients suffering Traumatic injuries

· Trauma, a character associated with Avengers: The Initiative in the Marvel Universe

· Trauma a psychological thriller directed by Marc Evans and starring Colin Firth

· Trauma a horror film directed by Dario Argento

· Trauma a medical drama set in San Francisco

· Also see Troma Entertainment, a film company specializing in independent, horror, and exploitation films

· Trauma Studios, an American computer game development company

· Trauma Center (series), a surgical based video game.

· `Day Twelve: Trauma`, a song by Ayreon on the album The Human Equation

· `Trauma` (song) by Ayumi Hamasaki

· Trauma by rapper/producer DJ Quik

· Trauma Records, a record label

· Trauma an American Heavy-metal band

CRAM101

Chapter 3. PART III: Chapter 37 - Chapter 54

	· Trauma Flintstone, drag performer and actress
	· Baltimore Trauma, professional paintball team from North Carolina
Burn	A burn is a type of skin injury that may be caused by heat, electricity, chemicals, light, radiation, or friction. Most burns only affect the skin (epidermal tissue and dermis). Rarely deeper tissues, such as muscle, bone, and blood vessel can also be injured.
Pneumocephalus	Pneumocephalus is the presence of air or gas within the cranial cavity. It is usually associated with disruption of the skull: after head and facial trauma, tumors of the skull base, after neurosurgery or otorhinolaryngology, and rarely, spontaneously. Pneumocephalus can occur in scuba diving, but is very rare in this context.
Pneumoperitoneum	Pneumoperitoneum is air or gas in the abdominal (peritoneal) cavity. It is often seen on X-ray, but small amounts are often missed, and CT is nowadays regarded as a criterion standard in the assessment of a Pneumoperitoneum. CT can visualize quantities as small as 5 cmÂ³ of air or gas.
Pneumothorax	In medicine (pulmonology), a Pneumothorax is a potential medical emergency wherein air or gas is present in the pleural cavity. A Pneumothorax can occur spontaneously. It can also occur as the result of disease or injury to the lung, or due to a puncture to the chest wall.
Stabilization	Stabilizer may mean:
	· Stabilizer (aircraft), surfaces to help keep aircraft under control. Includes:
	· Vertical stabilizer of airplanes
	· Tailplane or horizontal stabilizer
	· Stabilizer (ship), fins on ships to counteract roll

· Stabilizer (Music Breakbeat UK), UK-based breakbeat producer

· Stabilizer (chemistry), a substance added to prevent unwanted change in state of another substance

· Stabilization (medical) is a process to help prevent shock in sick or injured people

· Stabilization (architecture) of worn or damaged foundations of a structure

· Stabilizer subgroup, a concept in abstract mathematics

· Automatic stabilizer, an economics term

· Gun stabilizer, or gyrostabilizer, a device that helps a moving tank`s gunner to aim the gun

· Mood stabilizer, a kind of psychiatric medication

· Stabilizer, another name for bicycle training wheels

· Stabilizer is a type of food additive

· Stabilizer is a kind of voltage regulator in electronics

· Sway bar, a bar linking the two sides of an automotive suspension

· `Stabilizer`, an unofficially released song by Step Zero

· Clarification and Stabilization of wine

Airway management	In cardiopulmonary resuscitation, anaesthesia, emergency medicine, intensive care medicine and first aid, Airway management is the process of ensuring that:

· there is an open pathway between a patient's lungs and the outside world, and

· the lungs are safe from aspiration.

Chapter 3. PART III: Chapter 37 - Chapter 54

	In nearly all circumstances Airway management is the highest priority for clinical care. This is because if there is no airway, there can be no breathing, hence no oxygenation of blood and therefore circulation (and hence all the other vital body processes) will soon cease.
Cardiopulmonary resuscitation	Cardiopulmonary resuscitation (CPR) is an emergency medical procedure for a victim of cardiac arrest or, in some circumstances, respiratory arrest. CPR is performed in hospitals, or in the community by laypersons or by emergency response professionals. CPR involves physical interventions to create artificial circulation through rhythmic pressing on the patient`s chest to manually pump blood through the heart, called chest compressions, and usually also involves the rescuer exhaling into the patient (or using a device to simulate this) to inflate the lungs and pass oxygen in to the blood, called artificial respiration.
Leukemia inhibitory factor	Leukemia inhibitory factor an interleukin 6 class cytokine, is a chemical in cells that affects their growth and development. Leukemia inhibitory factor derives its name from its ability to induce the terminal differentiation of myeloid leukaemic cells. Other properties attributed to the cytokine include: the growth promotion and cell differentiation of different types of target cells, influence on bone metabolism, cachexia, neural development, embryogenesis and inflammation.
Life Support	Life support, in medicine is a broad term that applies to any therapy used to sustain a patients life while they are critically ill or injured. There are many therapies and techniques that may be used by clinicians to achieve the goal of sustaining life. Some examples include: · feeding tubes · Inotropes · total parenteral nutrition · mechanical ventilation · heart/lung bypass · urinary catheterization · dialysis · Cardiopulmonary resuscitation

· Defibrillation

· Artificial pacemaker
These techniques are applied most commonly in the Emergency Department, Intensive Care Unit and, Operating Rooms.

Monitoring | To monitor or Monitoring generally means to be aware of the state of a system. Below are specific examples:

· to observe a situation for any changes which may occur over time, using a monitor or measuring device of some sort:

· Baby monitor, medical monitor, Heart rate monitor

· BioMonitoring

· Cure Monitoring for composite materials manufacturing

· Deformation Monitoring

· Election Monitoring

· Mining Monitoring

· Natural hazard Monitoring

· Network Monitoring

· Structural Monitoring

· Website Monitoring

· Futures Monitoring, Media Monitoring service

· to observe the behaviour or communications of individuals or groups

· Monitoring competence at a task.

· Clinical Monitoring for new medical drugs
Monitoring Integration Platform

· Indiktor - Monitoring Integration Platform

·

Procedures

An ASC is a health care facility that specializes in providing surgery, including certain pain management and diagnostic (e.g., colonoscopy) services in an outpatient setting. Overall, the services provided can be generally called procedures. In simple terms, ASC-qualified procedures can be considered procedures that are more intensive than those done in the average doctor's office but not so intensive as to require a hospital stay.

Shock

· Shock (circulatory), a circulatory medical emergency

· Acute stress reaction, often termed `Shock` by laypersons, a psychological condition in response to terrifying events

· Post-traumatic stress disorder, a long-term complication of acute stress reaction

· Shock (economics), an unexpected or unpredictable event that affects an economy

· Shocks (Image Processing)

· Electric Shock

· Shock (mechanics)

· short for `Shock absorber`

· Shock wave, one example being a sonic boom

· Shock site, a website that is intended to be offensive or Shocking to most viewers

· Shock tactics, a close quarter battle tactic, usually done by specially trained Shock troops.

· Shock troops, troops trained for Shock tactics, usually heavy cavalry or infantry

· The Detroit Shock, a professional women's basketball team

· Shock (Cooking Technique), to quickly stop the cooking process of blanched items by plunging them in ice water.

· Aaron Schock, member of the U.S. House of Representatives representing the 18th district of Illinois.

Fluid	A fluid or water deprivation test is a medical test for the purposes of diagnosing the causes of polydipsia, a condition of excessive thirst that causes an excessive intake of water. The patient is required, for a prolonged period, to forgo intake of water completely, to determine the cause of the thirst. This test measures changes in body weight, urine output, and urine composition when fluids are withheld.
Thrombocytopenia	Thrombocytopenia (, or thrombopenia in short) is the presence of relatively few platelets in blood. Generally speaking, in humans, a normal platelet count ranges from 150,000 and 450,000 per mm^3. These limits, however, are determined by the 2.5th lower and upper percentile, and a deviation does not necessarily imply any form of disease.
Diabetes	Diabetes mellitus --often referred to as diabetes--is a condition in which the body either does not produce enough, or does not properly respond to, insulin, a hormone produced in the pancreas. Insulin enables cells to absorb glucose in order to turn it into energy. This causes glucose to accumulate in the blood , leading to various potential complications. Many types of diabetes are recognized: The principal three are:

· Type 1: Results from the body`s failure to produce insulin.

Blunt trauma

In medical terminology, Blunt trauma, blunt injury, non-penetrating trauma or blunt force trauma refers to a type of physical trauma caused to a body part, either by impact, injury or physical attack; the latter usually being referred to as blunt force trauma. The term itself is used to refer to the precursory trauma, from which there is further development of more specific types of trauma, such as concussions, abrasions, lacerations, and/or bone fracturing. Blunt trauma is contrasted with penetrating trauma, in which an object such as a bullet enters the body.

PAD

Pad or Pad can be either a word, an abbreviation or a three letter acronym.

· A keyPad is a set of buttons which usually bear digits (numPad)

· A GamePad or joyPad for a computer or console

· A paper tablet

· Part of an animal paw

· A bachelor Pad

· An abbreviation for maxi Pad, sanitary napkin (US), or `towel` (UK)

· Launch Pad, in rocketry, the platform from which an orbital vehicle is launched

· HeliPad, for helicopters

· One of the transliterations of the fourth syllable in the Buddhist six syllable mantra Om mani Padme hum
Protective gear

· Elbow Pads

· Hip Pads

· Knee Pads

· Shoulder Pads

· Pads (in baseball, cricket, and hockey)
Electronics

· In electronics manufacturing, a flat surface used to make electrical contact. A special case is bonding Pads, to which components are soldered

· In audio and RF electronics, an attenuator

· Pressure Pad, sensitive to pressure

· The iPad is a tablet released by Apple Inc.
Music

· Pad button, found on some mixing consoles, used for lowering input gain

· Synth Pad, in electronic music, is a sound (timbre), which is a harmonic background sound

· electronic drum Pad
Computing

· A graphics Pad, another term for a graphics tablet.

· Word-processing programs such as NotePad and WordPad

435

· MousePad, a Pad/mat used in computing for a mouse

· Pad field, in networking, part of the ethernet frame that fills in the data field (if necessary) to ensure that it meets the minimum length (64 bytes)

· Packet Assembler/Disassembler, an interface that connects an asynchronous terminal to an X.25 network

· Paderborn Lippstadt Airport`s airport code

· Payphone Antifraud Device, an electronic circuit that monitors the telephone line connected to a payphone

· People`s Alliance for Democracy, political group in Thailand

· Peripheral Artery Disease, the more common form of PVD, a term for the condition of having poor circulation in the legs, less frequently arms

· Peter Allen David, a comic book writer

· Philemon Arthur and the Dung, a Swedish folk song duet

· Poker After Dark a late night poker television program on NBC

· Portable Application Description, a machine-readable document format for providing product descriptions and specifications

· Program Associated Data, usually data sent along with a high-definition radio program

· Punjab Archaeology Department

· Phi Alpha Delta, Law Fraternity

· The Pad control character in the C1 control code set

· Prithvi Air Defense, an anti-ballistic missile for high altitude interception

437

	City Planning
	· Planned Area Development, originally approved permitted uses
	·
Energy	In physics, Energy is a scalar physical quantity that describes the amount of work that can be performed by a force, an attribute of objects and systems that is subject to a conservation law. Different forms of Energy include kinetic, potential, thermal, gravitational, sound, light, elastic, and electromagnetic Energy. The forms of Energy are often named after a related force.
Fan death	Fan death is a South Korean urban legend which states that an electric fan, if left running overnight in a closed room, can cause the death of those inside (by suffocation, poisoning,). Fans manufactured and sold in Korea are equipped with a timer switch that turns them off after a set number of minutes, which users are frequently urged to set when going to sleep with a fan on. The specifics behind belief in the myth of fan-death often offer several explanations for the precise mechanism by which the fan kills.
Abdominal trauma	Abdominal trauma is an injury to the abdomen. It may be blunt or penetrating and may involve damage to the abdominal organs. Signs and symptoms include abdominal pain, tenderness, rigidity, and bruising of the external abdomen.
Bronchus	A Bronchus is a passage of airway in the respiratory tract that conducts air into the lungs. No gas exchange takes place in this part of the lungs.
	The trachea divides into two main bronchi (also mainstem bronchi), the left and the right, at the level of the sternal angle at the anatomical point known as the carina. The right main Bronchus is wider, shorter, and more vertical than the left main Bronchus. The right main Bronchus subdivides into three lobar bronchi while the left main Bronchus divides into two.
Hemothorax	A Hemothorax is a condition that results from blood accumulating in the pleural cavity. Its cause is usually traumatic, from a blunt or penetrating injury to the thorax, resulting in a rupture of the serous membrane either lining the thorax or covering the lungs. This rupture allows blood to spill into the pleural space, equalizing the pressures between it and the lungs.

Chapter 3. PART III: Chapter 37 - Chapter 54

Orthopedic	Orthopedic surgery or Orthopedics (also spelled orthopaedics) is the branch of surgery concerned with conditions involving the musculoskeletal system. Orthopedic surgeons use both surgical and non-surgical means to treat musculoskeletal trauma, sports injuries, degenerative diseases, infections, tumors, and congenital conditions. Nicholas Andry coined the word `orthopaedics`, derived from Greek words for orthos and paideion (`child`), when he published Orthopaedia: or the Art of Correcting and Preventing Deformities in Children in 1741.
Spinal shock	Spinal shock was first defined by Whytt in 1750 as a loss of sensation accompanied by motor paralysis with initial loss but gradual recovery of reflexes, following a spinal cord injury (SCI) – most often a complete transection. Reflexes in the spinal cord caudal to the SCI are depressed (hyporeflexia) or absent (areflexia), while those rostral to the SCI remain unaffected. Note that the `shock` in Spinal shock does not refer to circulatory collapse.
Suxamethonium	Suxamethonium, also known as succinylcholine, is a paralytic drug used to induce muscle relaxation and short term paralysis, usually to make endotracheal intubation possible. Suxamethonium is sold under the trade names Anectine and Scoline. Suxamethonium acts as a depolarizing neuromuscular blocker.
Microshock	Microshock is a risk in patients with intracardiac conductors, such as external pacemaker electrodes, saline filled catheters, or weak or old heart tissue within the heart. A current as low as 10uAmps directly through the heart, may send a patient directly into ventricular fibrillation.
Muscle	Muscle is the contractile tissue of animals and is derived from the mesodermal layer of embryonic germ cells. Muscle cells contain contractile filaments that move past each other and change the size of the cell. They are classified as skeletal, cardiac, or smooth Muscles.
Sign	A sign is an entity which signifies another entity. A natural sign is an entity which bears a causal relation to the signified entity, as thunder is a sign of storm. A conventional sign signifies by agreement, as a full stop signifies the end of a sentence.

441

Chapter 3. PART III: Chapter 37 - Chapter 54

Symptoms	A symptom is a departure from normal function or feeling which is noticed by a patient, indicating the presence of disease or abnormality. A symptom is subjective, observed by the patient, and not measured. Symptoms may be chronic, relapsing or remitting.
Ketamine	Ketamine is a drug used in human and veterinary medicine developed by Parke-Davis (today a part of Pfizer) in 1962. Its hydrochloride salt is sold as Ketanest, Ketaset, and Ketalar. Pharmacologically, Ketamine is classified as an NMDA receptor antagonist. At high, fully anesthetic level doses, Ketamine has also been found to bind to opioid μ receptors and sigma receptors.
Anesthesia	Anesthesia has traditionally meant the condition of having sensation blocked or temporarily taken away. This allows patients to undergo surgery and other procedures without the distress and pain they would otherwise experience. The word was coined by Oliver Wendell Holmes, Sr.
Hyperreflexia	Hyperreflexia is defined as overactive or overresponsive reflexes. Examples of this can include twitching or spastic tendencies, which are indicative of upper motor neuron disease as well as the lessening or loss of control ordinarily exerted by higher brain centers of lower neural pathways (disinhibition).
Reflex	A Reflex action, also known as a Reflex, is an involuntary and nearly instantaneous movement in response to a stimulus. In most contexts, in particular those involving humans, Reflex actions are mediated via the Reflex arc; this is not always true in other animals, nor does it apply to casual uses of the term `Reflex`. For a Reflex, reaction time or latency is the time from the onset of a stimulus until the organism responds.
Surgical	Surgery is a medical specialty that uses operative manual and instrumental techniques on a patient to investigate and/or treat a pathological condition such as disease or injury, to help improve bodily function or appearance, or sometimes for some other reason. An act of performing surgery may be called a surgical procedure, operation, or simply surgery. In this context, the verb operating means performing surgery.

Chapter 3. PART III: Chapter 37 - Chapter 54

Perspective	Perspective erspective in the graphic arts, such as drawing, is an approximate representation, on a flat surface , of an image as it is seen by the eye. The two most characteristic features of perspective are that objects are drawn: · Smaller as their distance from the observer increases · Foreshortened: the size of an object`s dimensions along the line of sight are relatively shorter than dimensions across the line of sight . Linear perspective works by representing the light that passes from a scene through an imaginary rectangle (the painting), to the viewer`s eye. It is similar to a viewer looking through a window and painting what is seen directly onto the windowpane.
Hepatitis	Hepatitis (plural hepatitides) implies injury to the liver characterized by the presence of inflammatory cells in the tissue of the organ. The name is from ancient Greek hepar , the root being hepat- (á¼¡πατ-), meaning liver, and suffix -itis, meaning `inflammation` (c. 1727).
Infant	An Infant or baby is the term used to refer to the very young offspring of humans. The term Infant derives from the Latin word infans, meaning `unable to speak.` It is typically applied to children between the ages of 1 month and 12 months; however, definitions vary between birth and 3 years of age. `Infant` is also a legal term referring to any child under the age of legal adulthood.
Disease	A Disease or medical condition is an abnormal condition of an organism that impairs bodily functions, associated with specific symptoms and signs. It may be caused by external factors, such as invading organisms, or it may be caused by internal dysfunctions, such as autoimmune Diseases. In human beings, `Disease` is often used more broadly to refer to any condition that causes pain, dysfunction, distress, social problems, and/or death to the person afflicted, or similar problems for those in contact with the person.
Health	At the time of the creation of the World Health Organization (WHO), in 1948, Health was defined as being `a state of complete physical, mental, and social well-being and not merely the absence of disease or infirmity`.

This definition invited nations to expand the conceptual framework of their Health systems beyond issues related to the physical condition of individuals and their diseases, and it motivated us to focus our attention on what we now call social determinants of Health. Consequently, WHO challenged political, academic, community, and professional organizations devoted to improving or preserving Health to make the scope of their work explicit, including their rationale for allocating resources.

Cystic fibrosis	Cystic fibrosis (also known as Cystic fibrosis, mucovoidosis,) is a genetic disorder known to be an inherited disease of the secretory glands, including the glands that make mucus and sweat. The hallmarks of Cystic fibrosis are salty tasting skin, normal appetite but poor growth and poor weight gain, excess mucus production, frequent chest infections and coughing/shortness of breath. Males can be infertile due to the condition Congenital absence of the vas deferens.
Malignant hyperthermia	Malignant hyperthermia (Malignant hyperthermia , or `malignant hyperpyrexia due to anaesthesia`) is a rare life-threatening condition that is triggered by exposure to certain drugs used for general anesthesia (specifically all volatile anesthetics), nearly all gas anesthetics, and the neuromuscular blocking agent succinylcholine. In susceptible individuals, these drugs can induce a drastic and uncontrolled increase in skeletal muscle oxidative metabolism, which overwhelms the body`s capacity to supply oxygen, remove carbon dioxide, and regulate body temperature, eventually leading to circulatory collapse and death if not treated quickly. Susceptibility to Malignant hyperthermia is often inherited as an autosomal dominant disorder, for which there are at least 6 genetic loci of interest, most prominently the ryanodine receptor gene (RYR1).
General anaesthetic	A General anaesthetic drug is an anaesthetic drug that brings about a reversible loss of consciousness. These drugs are generally administered by an anesthesia provider in order to induce or maintain general anaesthesia to facilitate surgery. · Drugs given to induce or maintain general anaesthesia are either given as: · Gases or vapors (inhalational anaesthetics) · Injections (intravenous anaesthetics) Most commonly these two forms are combined, with an injection given to induce anaesthesia and a gas used to maintain it, although it is possible to deliver anaesthesia solely by inhalation or injection.

Chapter 3. PART III: Chapter 37 - Chapter 54

Diagnostic test	A Diagnostic test is any kind of medical test performed to aid in the diagnosis or detection of disease. For example: · to diagnose diseases · to measure the progress or recovery from disease · to confirm that a person is free from disease A drug test can be a specific medical test to ascertain the presence of a certain drug in the body (for example, in drug addicts). Some medical tests are parts of a simple physical examination which require only simple tools in the hands of a skilled practitioner, and can be performed in an office environment.
Pelvic inflammatory disease	Pelvic inflammatory disease is a generic term for inflammation of the female uterus, fallopian tubes, and/or ovaries as it progresses to scar formation with adhesions to nearby tissues and organs. This may lead to tissue necrosis and sometimes abscess formation whereby pus can be released into the peritoneum. Pelvic inflammatory disease is often associated with sexually transmitted infections, as it is a common result of such infections.
Apnea	Apnea, apnoea, or apnÅ"a is a term for suspension of external breathing. During Apnea there is no movement of the muscles of respiration and the volume of the lungs initially remains unchanged. Depending on the patency (openness) of the airways there may or may not be a flow of gas between the lungs and the environment; gas exchange within the lungs and cellular respiration is not affected.
Positive airway pressure	Positive airway pressure is a method of respiratory ventilation used primarily in the treatment of sleep apnea, for which it was first developed. Positive airway pressure ventilation is also commonly used for critically ill patients in hospital with respiratory failure, and in newborn infants (neonates). In these patients, Positive airway pressure ventilation can prevent the need for endotracheal intubation, or allow earlier extubation.

Chapter 3. PART III: Chapter 37 - Chapter 54

Reactive Airways Dysfunction Syndrome	Reactive Airways Dysfunction Syndrome is a term proposed by S.M. Brooks and colleagues in 1985 to describe an asthma-like syndrome developing after a single exposure to high levels of an irritating vapor, fume, or smoke. In time, however, it has evolved to be mistakenly used as a synonym for asthma. Current usage of the term in the medical community is to describe an asthma-like syndrome in infants that may later be confirmed to be asthmatics when they become old enough to participate in diagnostic tests such as the bronchial challenge test.
Sleep apnea	Sleep apnea is a sleep disorder characterized by pauses in breathing during sleep. Each episode, called an apnea , from α- (a-), privative, πνῖειν (pnéein), to breathe), lasts long enough so that one or more breaths are missed, and such episodes occur repeatedly throughout sleep. The standard definition of any apneic event includes a minimum 10 second interval between breaths, with either a neurological arousal (a 3-second or greater shift in EEG frequency, measured at C3, C4, O1, or O2), a blood oxygen desaturation of 3-4% or greater, or both arousal and desaturation.
Assertive community treatment	Assertive community treatment is a highly intensive and integrated approach for community mental health service delivery. Assertive community treatment programs serve people whose symptoms of mental illness result in severe functional difficulties that interfere with their ability to achieve personally meaningful recovery goals in several major areas of life: working, having friends, living independently, and so forth. The defining characteristics of Assertive community treatment include: · a clear focus on those participants (clients) who require the most help from the service delivery system; · an explicit mission to promote the participants' independence, rehabilitation, and recovery, and in so doing to prevent homelessness and unnecessary hospitalization; · a primary emphasis on home visits and other in vivo (out-of-the-office) interventions, eliminating the need to transfer learned behaviors from an artificial rehabilitation or treatment setting to the 'real world'; · a participant-to-staff ratio that is low enough to allow the Assertive community treatment 'core services team' to perform virtually all of the necessary rehabilitation, treatment, and community support tasks themselves in a coordinated and efficient manner -- unlike traditional case managers, who broker or 'farm out' most of the work to other professionals; · a 'total team approach' in which all of the staff work with all of the participants;

· an interdisciplinary assessment and service planning process that typically involves a psychiatrist and one or more nurses, social workers, substance abuse specialists, vocational rehabilitation specialists, and peer recovery specialists (individuals who have had personal, successful experience with the recovery process);

· a willingness on the part of the team to take ultimate professional responsibility for the participants' well-being in all areas of community functioning, including most especially the 'nitty-gritty' aspects of everyday life;

· a conscious effort to help people avoid crisis situations in the first place or, if that proves impossible, to intervene at any time of the day or night to keep crises from turning into unnecessary hospitalizations; and

· a promise to work with people on a time-unlimited basis, as long as they demonstrate a continuing need for this highly intensive and integrated form of professional help.

Aspirin	Aspirin is a salicylate drug, often used as an analgesic to relieve minor aches and pains, as an antipyretic to reduce fever, and as an anti-inflammatory medication. Aspirin also has an antiplatelet effect by inhibiting the production of thromboxane, which under normal circumstances binds platelet molecules together to create a patch over damage of the walls within blood vessels. Because the platelet patch can become too large and also block blood flow, locally and downstream, Aspirin is also used long-term, at low doses, to help prevent heart attacks, strokes, and blood clot formation in people at high risk for developing blood clots.
Medical Device	A Medical device is a product which is used for medical purposes in patients, in diagnosis, therapy or surgery. If applied to the body, the effect of the Medical device is primarily physical, in contrast to pharmaceutical drugs, which exert a biochemical effect. Specific regional definitions of Medical device vary slightly as detailed below.
Patient education	Patient education is the process by which health professionals and others impart information to patients that will alter their health behaviors or improve their health status. Education providers may include: physicians, registered dietitians, nurses, hospital discharge planners, medical social workers, psychologists, disease or disability advocacy groups, special interest groups, and pharmaceutical companies.

	Health education is also a tool used by managed care plans, and may include both general preventive education or health promotion and disease or condition specific education.
Physical examination	Physical examination or clinical examination is the process by which a health care provider investigates the body of a patient for signs of disease. It generally follows the taking of the medical history -- an account of the symptoms as experienced by the patient. Together with the medical history, the Physical examination aids in determining the correct diagnosis and devising the treatment plan.
Obstetric	Obstetrics is the surgical specialty dealing with the care of women and their children during pregnancy, childbirth and postnatal. Midwifery is the non-medical equivalent. Veterinary Obstetrics is the same concept for veterinary medicine.
Pregnancy	Pregnancy is the carrying of one or more offspring, known as a fetus or embryo, inside the uterus of a female. In a pregnancy, there can be multiple gestations, as in the case of twins or triplets. Human pregnancy is the most studied of all mammalian pregnancies.
Pregnancy test	A Pregnancy test attempts to determine whether or not a woman is pregnant. Records of attempts at Pregnancy testing have been found as far back as the ancient Greek and ancient Egyptian cultures. Modern Pregnancy tests look for chemical markers associated with pregnancy.
Chest radiograph	In medicine, a Chest radiograph, commonly called a chest x-ray (CXR), is a projection radiograph of the chest used to diagnose conditions affecting the chest, its contents, and nearby structures. Chest radiographs are among the most common films taken, being diagnostic of many conditions. Like all methods of radiography, Chest radiography employs ionizing radiation in the form of x-rays to generate images of the chest.
Electrocardiography	Electrocardiography (ECG or EKG) is a transthoracic interpretation of the electrical activity of the heart over time captured and externally recorded by skin electrodes. It is a noninvasive recording produced by an electrocardiographic device. The etymology of the word is derived from electro, because it is related to electrical activity, cardio, Greek for heart, and graph, a Greek root meaning `to write`.
Fasting	Fasting is primarily the act of willingly abstaining from some or all food, drink, or both, for a period of time. An absolute fast is normally defined as abstinence from all food and liquid for a defined period, usually a single day (24 hours), or several daytime periods. Other fasts may be only partially restrictive, limiting particular foods or substance.

Regurgitation	Regurgitation, Regurgiate or Regurgitate can refer to: · Regurgitation · Vomiting · Regurgitation · Regurgitate (band), a goregrind band `
Rhinorrhea	Rhinorrhea, commonly referred to as runny nose, consists of an unusually significant amount of nasal fluid. It is a symptom of the common cold and of allergies (hay fever). The term is a combination of the Greek words `rhinos` meaning `of the nose` and `-rrhea` meaning `discharge or flow`.
Heart	The Heart is a muscular organ found in most vertebrates that is responsible for pumping blood throughout the blood vessels by repeated, rhythmic contractions. The term cardiac (as in cardiology) means `related to the Heart` and comes from the Greek καρδιî¬, kardia, for `Heart.` The vertebrate Heart is composed of cardiac muscle, an involuntary striated muscle tissue which is found only within this organ. The average human Heart, beating at 72 beats per minute, will beat approximately 2.5 billion times during a lifetime (about 66 years).
Heart murmur	Murmurs are extra heart sounds that are produced as a result of turbulent blood flow which is sufficient to produce audible noise. Most murmurs can only be heard with the assistance of a stethoscope (`on auscultation`). A functional murmur or `physiologic murmur` is a Heart murmur that is primarily due to physiologic conditions outside the heart, as opposed to structural defects in the heart itself.
Tetracaine	Tetracaine is a potent local anesthetic of the ester group. It is mainly used topically in ophthalmology and as an antipruritic, and it has been used in spinal anesthesia. In biomedical research, Tetracaine is used to alter the function of calcium release channels (ryanodine receptors) that control the release of calcium from intracellular stores.

Chapter 3. PART III: Chapter 37 - Chapter 54

Warfarin	Warfarin is an anticoagulant. It was initially marketed as a pesticide against rats and mice and is still popular for this purpose, although more potent poisons such as brodifacoum have since been developed. A few years after its introduction, Warfarin was found to be effective and relatively safe for preventing thrombosis and embolism (abnormal formation and migration of blood clots) in many disorders.
Premedication	Premedication refer to a drug treatment given to a patient before a (surgical or invasive) medical procedure. These drugs are typically sedative or analgesic. Premedication before chemotherapy for cancer often refers to special drug regimens (usually 2 or more drugs, eg dexamethasone, diphenhydramine and omeprazole) given to a patient minutes to hours before the chemotherapy to avert side effects or hypersensitivity reactions (i.e. allergic reactions).
Arthroplasty	Joint replacement consists of replacing painful, arthritic, worn or cancerous parts of the joint with artificial surfaces shaped in such a way as to allow joint movement. Arthroplasty [from Greek arthron, joint, limb, articulate, + -plassein, to form, mould, forge, feign, make an image of] is a procedure of orthopedic surgery, in which the arthritic or dysfunctional joint surface is replaced with something better or by remodelling or realigning the joint by osteotomy or some other procedure. Previously, a popular form of Arthroplasty was interpositional Arthroplasty with interposition of some other tissue like skin, muscle or tendon to keep inflammatory surfaces apart or excisional Arthroplasty in which the joint surface and bone was removed leaving scar tissue to fill in the gap.
Infection	An Infection is the detrimental colonization of a host organism by a foreign species. In an Infection, the infecting organism seeks to utilize the host`s resources to multiply, usually at the expense of the host. The infecting organism, or pathogen, interferes with the normal functioning of the host and can lead to chronic wounds, gangrene, loss of an infected limb, and even death.
Antacids	Antacids perform a neutralization reaction, i.e. they buffer gastric acid, raising the pH to reduce acidity in the stomach. When gastric hydrochloric acid reaches the nerves in the gastrointestinal mucosa, they signal pain to the central nervous system. This happens when these nerves are exposed, as in peptic ulcers.

Chapter 3. PART III: Chapter 37 - Chapter 54

Gastroprokinetic agent	A Gastroprokinetic agent, gastrokinetic, or prokinetic, is a type of drug which enhances gastrointestinal motility by increasing the frequency of contractions in the small intestine or making them stronger, but without disrupting their rhythm. They are used to relieve gastrointestinal symptoms such as abdominal discomfort, bloating, constipation, heart burn, nausea, and vomiting. They are used to treat a number of gastrointestinal disorders, including irritable bowel syndrome, gastritis, acid reflux disease, gastroparesis, and functional dyspepsia.
Histamine	Histamine is a biogenic amine involved in local immune responses as well as regulating physiological function in the gut and acting as a neurotransmitter. Histamine triggers the inflammatory response. As part of an immune response to foreign pathogens, Histamine is produced by basophils and by mast cells found in nearby connective tissues.
Humulin	Humulin is the brand name for a group of biosynthetic human insulin products, originally developed by Genentech in 1978 (Generic name insulin isophane) and later acquired by Eli Lilly and Company, the company who arguably facilitated the product's approval with the U.S. Food and Drug Administration. Humulin is synthesized in a laboratory strain of Escherichia coli bacteria which has been genetically altered to produce biosynthetic human insulin. The synthesized insulin is then combined with other compounds or types of insulin which affect its shelf life and absorption.
Lansoprazole	Lansoprazole is a proton-pump inhibitor (PPI) which prevents the stomach from producing gastric acid. It is manufactured by a number of companies worldwide under several brand names . It was first approved by the U.S. Food and Drug Administration (FDA) in 1995.
Proton pump inhibitors	Proton pump inhibitors are a group of drugs whose main action is a pronounced and long-lasting reduction of gastric acid production. They are the most potent inhibitors of acid secretion available today. The group followed and has largely superseded another group of pharmaceuticals with similar effects, but different mode-of-action, called H_2-receptor antagonists.
Cimetidine	Cimetidine is a histamine H_2-receptor antagonist that inhibits the production of acid in the stomach. It is largely used in the treatment of heartburn and peptic ulcers. It is marketed by GlaxoSmithKline under the trade name Tagamet .

Chapter 3. PART III: Chapter 37 - Chapter 54

Omeprazole	Omeprazole is a proton pump inhibitor used in the treatment of dyspepsia, peptic ulcer disease , gastroesophageal reflux disease (GORD/GERD) and Zollinger-Ellison syndrome. It was first marketed in the US in 1989 by AstraZeneca under the brand names Losec and Prilosec, and is now also available from generic manufacturers under various brand names. AstraZeneca markets Omeprazole as Losec, Antra, Gastroloc, Mopral, Omepral, and Prilosec.
Brachial plexus	The Brachial plexus is an arrangement of nerve fibers, running from the spine, formed by the ventral rami of the lower four cervical and first thoracic nerve roots (C5-T1). It proceeds through the neck, the axilla (armpit region), and into the arm.
	The Brachial plexus is responsible for cutaneous and muscular innervation of the entire upper limb, with two exceptions: the trapezius muscle innervated by the spinal accessory nerve (CN XI) and an area of skin near the axilla innervated by the intercostobrachial nerve.
Sedation	Sedation is a medical procedure involving the administration of sedative drugs, generally to facilitate a medical procedure with local anaesthesia. Sedation is now typically used in procedures such as endoscopy, vasectomy, RSI (Rapid Sequence Intubation), or minor surgery and in dentistry for reconstructive surgery, some cosmetic surgeries, removal of wisdom teeth, or for high-anxiety patients. Sedation methods in dentistry include inhalation Sedation (using nitrous oxide), oral Sedation, and intravenous (IV) Sedation.
Epidural	Epidural or extradural hematoma (haematoma) is a type of traumatic brain injury (TBI) in which a buildup of blood occurs between the dura mater (the tough outer membrane of the central nervous system) and the skull. The dura mater also covers the spine, so Epidural bleeds may also occur in the spinal column. Often due to trauma, the condition is potentially deadly because the buildup of blood may increase pressure in the intracranial space and compress delicate brain tissue.
Headache	In medicine a Headache or cephalalgia is a symptom of a number of different conditions of the head. Some of the causes are benign while others are medical emergencies. There are a number of different classification systems for Headaches.
Nerve	A Nerve is an enclosed, cable-like bundle of peripheral axons (the long, slender projections of neurons). A Nerve provides a common pathway for the electrochemical Nerve impulses that are transmitted along each of the axons. Nerves are found only in the peripheral nervous system.

Chapter 3. PART III: Chapter 37 - Chapter 54

Nerve block	Regional Nerve blockade, or more commonly Nerve block, is a general term used to refer to the injection of local anesthetic onto or near nerves for temporary control of pain. It can also be used as a diagnostic tool to identify specific nerves as pain generators. Permanent Nerve block can be produced by destruction of nerve tissue.
Orthostatic hypotension	Orthostatic hypotension (also known as postural hypotension, and, colloquially, as head rush or a dizzy spell and to some people `the elevator effect`) is a form of hypotension in which a person`s blood pressure suddenly falls when the person stands up. The decrease is typically greater than 20/10 mm Hg, and may be most pronounced after resting. The incidence increases with age.
Glasgow coma scale	Glasgow Coma Scale or Glasgow Coma Scale, is a neurological scale which aims to give a reliable, objective way of recording the conscious state of a person, for initial as well as subsequent assessment. A patient is assessed against the criteria of the scale, and the resulting points give a patient score between 3 (indicating deep unconsciousness) and either 14 (original scale) or 15 (the more widely used modified or revised scale). Glasgow Coma Scale was initially used to assess level of consciousness after head injury, and the scale is now used by first aid, EMS and doctors as being applicable to all acute medical and trauma patients.
Coma	In medicine, a Coma is a profound state of unconsciousness. A Comatose person cannot be awakened, fails to respond normally to pain or light, does not have sleep-wake cycles, and does not take voluntary actions. Coma may result from a variety of conditions, including intoxication, metabolic abnormalities, central nervous system diseases, acute neurologic injuries such as stroke, and hypoxia.
Retention	Retention can have the following meanings: · retention basin, instance retaining (e.g. water in the ground) · In learning: it is the ability to retain facts and figures in memory (spaced repetition) · Grade retention, in schools, keeping a student in the same grade for another year (that is, not promoting the student to the next higher grade with his/her classmates) · retention period, in Usenet, the time a news server holds a newsgroup posting before deleting it as no longer relevant · Judicial retention, in the United States court system, a process whereby a judge is periodically subject to a vote in order to remain in the position of judge

· Urinary retention, the lack or inability to urinate

· Employment retention, the ability to keep employees within an organization

· retention agent is a process chemical

Urinary retention	Urinary retention also known as ischuria is a lack of ability to urinate. It is a common complication of benign prostatic hypertrophy (also known as benign prostatic hyperplasia or BPH), although anticholinergics may also play a role, and requires a catheter or prostatic stent. Various pharmaceuticals can cause Urinary retention, including some antidepressants, COX-2 inhibitors, amphetamines and opiates.
Postoperative nausea and vomiting	Postoperative nausea and vomiting (PONV) is an unpleasant complication affecting about a third of the 10% of the population undergoing general anaesthesia each year. This equates to about two million people in the United Kingdom annually. On average the incidence of nausea or vomiting after general anesthesia ranges between 25 and 30% [Cohen 1994].
Hospital	.

· Jean Manco, The Heritage of Mercy

· Last Resort: Hospital Care in Canada (an illustrated historical essay)

· Medieval Hospitals of England, by Rotha Mary Clay (1909 book, now in the public domain)

· Directory and Ranking of more than 17000 Hospitals worldwide

.

· Haute Autorité de santé or French National Authority for Health

Nausea	Nausea is the sensation of unease and discomfort in the stomach with an urge to vomit. Nausea is also an adverse effect of many drugs, opiates in particular, and may also be a side-effect of a large intake of sugary foods.

Chapter 3. PART III: Chapter 37 - Chapter 54

	Nausea is not a sickness, but rather a symptom of several conditions, many of which are unrelated to the stomach.
Risk factor	A Risk factor is a variable associated with an increased risk of disease or infection. Risk factors are correlational and not necessarily causal, because correlation does not imply causation. For example, being young cannot be said to cause measles, but young people are more at risk as they are less likely to have developed immunity during a previous epidemic.
Dolasetron	Dolasetron is a serotonin 5-HT$_3$ receptor antagonist used to treat nausea and vomiting following chemotherapy. Its main effect is to reduce the activity of the vagus nerve, which is a nerve that activates the vomiting center in the medulla oblongata. It does not have much antiemetic effect when symptoms are due to motion sickness.
Ephedrine	Ephedrine is a sympathomimetic amine commonly used as a stimulant, appetite suppressant, concentration aid, decongestant, and to treat hypotension associated with anaesthesia.
	Ephedrine is similar in structure to the (semi-synthetic) derivatives amphetamine and methamphetamine. Chemically, it is an alkaloid derived from various plants in the genus Ephedra (family Ephedraceae).

Acupressure

· Acupressure

· Body work

· Chiropractic

· Manipulative therapy

· Massage therapy

· Manual lymphatic drainage

· Naprapathy

· Structural Integration

· Shiatsu

NCCAM classifications	· Tui na
	· Alternative Medical Systems · Mind-Body Intervention · Biologically Based Therapy · Manipulative Methods · Energy Therapy
Desflurane	Desflurane is a highly fluorinated methyl ethyl ether used for maintenance of general anesthesia. Together with sevoflurane, it is gradually replacing isoflurane for human use, except in the third world where its high cost precludes its use. It has the most rapid onset and offset of the volatile anesthetic drugs used for general anesthesia due to its low solubility in blood.
Dexamethasone	Dexamethasone is a potent synthetic member of the glucocorticoid class of steroid drugs. It acts as an anti-inflammatory and immunosuppressant. Its potency is about 20-30 times that of the naturally occuring hormone hydrocortisone and 4-5 times of prednisone.
Laparoscopic surgery	Laparoscopic surgery, also called minimally invasive surgery (MIS), bandaid surgery, keyhole surgery is a modern surgical technique in which operations in the abdomen are performed through small incisions (usually 0.5-1.5cm) as compared to larger incisions needed in traditional surgical procedures. Practicioners of `open` surgery sometimes use the misleading defensive term `microscopic` surgery, which implies a small incision. However, open surgery typically requires an incision large enough for the surgeon`s hands to enter the patient, while the term microscopic refers to various magnifying devices used during open surgery.

Chapter 3. PART III: Chapter 37 - Chapter 54

Metoclopramide	Metoclopramide is an antiemetic and gastroprokinetic agent. Thus it is primarily used to treat nausea and vomiting, and to facilitate gastric emptying in patients with gastroparesis. It is also a primary treatment for migraine headaches.
Midazolam	Midazolam is a short-acting drug in the benzodiazepine class that is used for treatment of acute seizures and for inducing sedation and amnesia before medical procedures. It has potent anxiolytic, amnestic, hypnotic, anticonvulsant, skeletal muscle relaxant, and sedative properties. Midazolam has a fast recovery time and is the most commonly used benzodiazepine as a premedication for sedation; less commonly it is used for induction and maintenance of anesthesia.
Pain management	Pain management is the medical discipline concerned with the relief of pain. Acute pain, such pain resulting from trauma, often has a reversible cause and may require only transient measures and correction of the underlying problem. In contrast, chronic pain often results from conditions that are difficult to diagnose and treat, and that may take a long time to reverse.
Promethazine	Promethazine is a first-generation H_1 receptor antagonist of the phenothiazine chemical class used medically as an antihistamine and antiemetic. It can also have strong sedative effects and in some countries is prescribed for insomnia when benzodiazepines are contraindicated. It is a prescription drug in the United States but is available over the counter in the United Kingdom, Australia, Canada, Switzerland, and many other countries (brand names Phenergan, Promethegan, Romergan, Fargan, Farganesse, Prothiazine, Avomine, Atosil, Receptozine, Lergigan).
Rocuronium	Rocuronium is an aminosteroid non-depolarizing (that is, it does not cause initial stimulation of muscles before weakening them) neuromuscular blocker or muscle relaxant used in modern anaesthesia, to facilitate endotracheal intubation and to provide skeletal muscle relaxation during surgery or mechanical ventilation. Introduced in 1994, Rocuronium has rapid onset, and intermediate duration of action. It is marketed under the trade name of Zemuron in the United States and Esmeron in most other countries.
Caregiver	Carer (UK, NZ, Australian usage) and Caregiver are words normally used to refer to unpaid relatives or friends who support people with disabilities. The words may be prefixed with `family` `spousal`, `child` to distinguish between different care situations. The general term dependent/dependant care is also used for the service provided.

Chapter 3. PART III: Chapter 37 - Chapter 54

Anatomy	Anatomy is a branch of biology and medicine that is the consideration of the structure of living things. It is a general term that includes human Anatomy, animal Anatomy and plant Anatomy (phytotomy). In some of its facets Anatomy is closely related to embryology, comparative Anatomy and comparative embryology, through common roots in evolution.
Cardiovascular system	The circulatory system is an organ system that passes nutrients (such as amino acids and electrolytes), gases, hormones, blood cells, etc. to and from cells in the body to help fight diseases and help stabilize body temperature and pH to maintain homeostasis. This system may be seen strictly as a blood distribution network, but some consider the circulatory system as composed of the Cardiovascular system, which distributes blood, and the lymphatic system, which distributes lymph.
Central nervous system	The Central nervous system is the part of the nervous system that functions to coordinate the activity of all parts of the bodies of multicellular organisms. In vertebrates, the Central nervous system is enclosed in the meninges. It contains the majority of the nervous system and consists of the brain and the spinal cord.
Ear	The Ear is the organ that detects sound. The vertebrate Ear shows a common biology from fish to humans, with variations in structure according to order and species. It not only acts as a receiver for sound, but plays a major role in the sense of balance and body position.
Larynx	The Larynx , colloquially known as the `voice box`, is an organ in the neck of mammals involved in protection of the trachea and sound production. It manipulates pitch and volume. The Larynx houses the vocal folds, which are an essential component of phonation.
Laser surgery	Laser surgery is surgery using a laser to cut tissue instead of a scalpel. Examples include the use of a laser scalpel in otherwise conventional surgery, and soft tissue Laser surgery, in which the laser beam vaporizes soft tissue with high water content. Laser resurfacing is a technique in which molecular bonds of a material are dissolved by a laser.
Nasopharynx	The Nasopharynx is the uppermost part of the pharynx. It extends from the base of the skull to the upper surface of the soft palate; it differs from the oral and laryngeal parts of the pharynx in that its cavity always remains patent (open). In front it communicates through the choanae with the nasal cavities.
Oropharynx	The Oropharynx reaches from the Uvula to the level of the hyoid bone.

It opens anteriorly, through the isthmus faucium, into the mouth, while in its lateral wall, between the two palatine arches, is the palatine tonsil.

Although older resources have stated that Fusobacterium is a common occurrence in the human Oropharynx, the current consensus is that Fusobacterium should always be treated as a pathogen.

The name is formed from their initials:

· Haemophilus

· Actinobacillus actinomycetemcomitans

· Cardiobacterium hominis

· Eikenella corrodens

· Kingella
All of these organisms are part of the normal oropharyngeal flora which grow slowly, prefer a carbon dioxide-enriched atmosphere and share an enhanced capacity to produce endocardial infections, especially in young children.

Abdominal aorta	The Abdominal aorta is the largest artery in the abdominal cavity. As part of the aorta, it is a direct continuation of the descending aorta (of the thorax). It begins at the level of the diaphragm, crossing it via the aortic hiatus, technically behind the diaphragm, at the vertebral level of T12. It travels down the posterior wall of the abdomen in front of the vertebral column.
Fracture	A fracture is the (local) separation of an object or material into two, or more, pieces under the action of stress.

477

Chapter 3. PART III: Chapter 37 - Chapter 54

	The word fracture is often applied to bones of living creatures, or to crystals or crystalline materials, such as gemstones or metal. Sometimes, in crystalline materials, individual crystals fracture without the body actually separating into two or more pieces.
Physiology	Physiology is the study of the mechanical, physical, and biochemical functions of living organisms. Physiology has traditionally been divided between plant Physiology and animal and all living things Physiology but the principles of Physiology are universal, no matter what particular organism is being studied. For example, what is learned about the Physiology of yeast cells may also apply to human cells that one may be studying.
Sodium	Sodium is a metallic element with a symbol Na and atomic number 11. It is a soft, silvery-white, highly reactive metal and is a member of the alkali metals within `group 1` . It has only one stable isotope, ^{23}Na.
	Elemental Sodium was first isolated by Sir Humphry Davy in 1806 by passing an electric current through molten Sodium hydroxide.
Topical anesthetic	A Topical anesthetic is a local anesthetic that is used to numb the surface of a body part. They can be used to numb the front of the eye, the inside of the nose, the throat, the skin, the ear, the anus, and the genital area. Topical anesthetics are available in creams, ointments, aerosols, sprays, lotions, and jellies.
Adenoid	Adenoids (or pharyngeal tonsils, or nasopharyngeal tonsils) are a mass of lymphoid tissue situated at the very back of the nose, in the roof of the nasopharynx, where the nose blends into the mouth.
	Normally, in children, they make a soft mound in the roof and posterior wall of the nasopharynx, just above and behind the uvula.
	Enlarged Adenoids, hypertrophy, can become nearly the size of a ping pong ball and completely block airflow through the nasal passages.
Epiglottis	The Epiglottis is a flap of elastic cartilage tissue covered with a mucus membrane, attached to the root of the tongue. It projects obliquely upwards behind the tongue and the hyoid bone. The term is, like tonsils, often incorrectly used to refer to the uvula.

Chapter 3. PART III: Chapter 37 - Chapter 54

Palatine	A Palatine or palatinus was a high-level official attached to imperial or royal courts in Europe since Roman times. The term palatinus was first used in Ancient Rome for chamberlains of the Emperor due to their association with the Palatine Hill, the imperial palace guard after the rise of Constantine I were also called the Scholae Palatinae for the same reason. In the Early Middle Ages the title became attached to courts beyond the imperial one; the highest level of officials in the Roman Catholic Church were called the judices palatini.
Pharynx	The pharynx is the part of the neck and throat situated immediately posterior to the mouth and nasal cavity, and cranial, or superior, to the esophagus, larynx, and trachea. The pharynx is part of the digestive system and respiratory system of many organisms. Because both food and air pass through the pharynx, a flap of connective tissue called the epiglottis closes over the trachea when food is swallowed to prevent choking or aspiration.
Tonsils	The Tonsils are areas of lymphoid tissue on either side of the throat. An infection of the Tonsils is called tonsillitis. Most commonly, the term `Tonsils` refers to the palatine Tonsils that can be seen in the back of the throat.
Palatine tonsils	Palatine tonsils, occasionally called the faucial tonsils, are the tonsils that can be seen on the left and right sides at the back of the throat. Tonsillitis is an inflammation of the tonsils and will often, but not necessarily, cause a sore throat and fever. In chronic cases tonsillectomy may be indicated.
Sevoflurane	Sevoflurane is a sweet-smelling, non-flammable, highly fluorinated methyl isopropyl ether used for induction and maintenance of general anesthesia. Together with desflurane, it is replacing isoflurane and halothane in modern anesthesiology. It is often administered in a mixture of nitrous oxide and oxygen.
Large intestine	The large intestine is the second to last part of the digestive system--the final stage of the alimentary canal is the anus --in vertebrate animals. Its function is to absorb water from the remaining indigestible food matter, and then to pass useless waste material from the body
Laryngeal mask airway	The Laryngeal mask airway was invented in 1983 by British anaesthetist, Dr. Archie Brain. A laryngeal mask

Laryngeal masks are used in anaesthesia and in emergency medicine for airway management. They consist of a tube with an inflatable cuff that is inserted into the pharynx.

Anticholinergic

An Anticholinergic agent is a substance that blocks the neurotransmitter acetylcholine in the central and the peripheral nervous system. An example of an Anticholinergic is dicyclomine, and the classic example is atropine. Anticholinergics are administered to reduce the effects mediated by acetylcholine on acetylcholine receptors in neurons through competitive inhibition.

Steroid

A Steroid is a type of organic compound that contains a specific arrangement of four rings that are joined to each other. Examples of Steroids include cholesterol, the sex hormones estradiol and testosterone, and the anti-inflammatory drug dexamethasone.

The sterane core of Steroids is composed of seventeen carbon atoms bonded together to form four fused rings: three cyclohexane rings (designated as rings A, B, and C in the figure to the right) and one cyclopentane ring (the D ring).

Foreign body

In physiology, a Foreign body is any object originating outside the body. In machinery, it can mean any unwanted intruding object.
Most references to foreign bodies involve propulsion through natural orifices into hollow organs.

Jet ventilation

Jet ventilation is a special type of mechanical ventilation for surgical operations in the airway. Jet ventilation is characterized by the insufflation of gas portions with high velocity into the airway. The latter has to be open to the atmosphere in order to allow an unhindered gas egress and therefore to avoid overdistention (barotrauma) of the lungs.

Myringotomy

Myringotomy is a surgical procedure in which a tiny incision is created in the eardrum, so as to relieve pressure caused by the excessive build-up of fluid, or to drain pus. Myringotomy is often performed as a treatment for otitis media. If a patient requires Myringotomy for drainage or ventilation of the middle ear, this generally implies that the Eustachian tube is either partially or completely obstructed and is not able to perform this function in its usual physiologic fashion.

Middle ear

The Middle ear is the portion of the ear internal to the eardrum, and external to the oval window of the cochlea. The mammalian Middle ear contains three ossicles, which couple vibration of the eardrum into waves in the fluid and membranes of the inner ear. The hollow space of the Middle ear has also been called the tympanic cavity, or cavum tympani.

Chapter 3. PART III: Chapter 37 - Chapter 54

Nitrous oxide	Nitrous oxide, commonly known as laughing gas, is a chemical compound with the formula N_2O. It is an oxide of nitrogen. At room temperature, it is a colorless non-flammable gas, with a pleasant, slightly sweet odor and taste.
Tonsillectomy	A Tonsillectomy is a 2,000 year-old surgical procedure in which the tonsils are removed from either side of the throat. The procedure is performed in response to cases of repeated occurrence of acute tonsillitis or adenoiditis, obstructive sleep apnea, nasal airway obstruction, snoring, or peritonsillar abscess. Sometimes the adenoids are removed at the same time, a procedure called adenoidectomy.
Syndrome	In medicine and psychology, the term syndrome refers to the association of several clinically recognizable features, signs (observed by a physician), symptoms (reported by the patient), phenomena or characteristics that often occur together, so that the presence of one feature alerts the physician to the presence of the others. In recent decades the term has been used outside of medicine to refer to a combination of phenomena seen in association. The term syndrome derives from its Greek roots and means literally `run together`, as the features do.
Cleft palate	Cleft lip (cheiloschisis) and Cleft palate (colloquially known as harelip), which can also occur together as cleft lip and palate, are variations of a type of clefting congenital deformity caused by abnormal facial development during gestation. A cleft is a fissure or opening--a gap. It is the non-fusion of the body`s natural structures that form before birth.
Dental	The word Dental is used for things pertaining to teeth and could refer to: · Dentistry, a medical profession · Dental Auxiliary · Dental hygienist, a licensed practitioner · Dental technician · Any of a variety of other Dental professions, such as `Dental assistant`, someone who works in a dentist`s office, but may not be a licensed medical worker

· The American Dental Association

· Dental amalgam controversy

· Dental brace

· Dental cavities

· Dental consonant (linguistics)

· Dental extraction

· Dental restoration

· Dental implants

· Dental alveolus

· Dental caries

· Dental dam

· Dental drill

· Dental emergency

· Dental fillings

· Dental floss

· Dental fluorosis

· Dental insurance

· Dental implant

· Dental Key

· Dental pellicle

· Dental phobia

· Dental plaque

· Dental porcelain

· Dental restoration

· Dental sealant

· Dental surgery

· Dentalize
Other uses:

· Dental Records, a record label .

Facial trauma	Facial trauma is any physical trauma to the face. Facial trauma can involve soft tissue injuries such as burns, lacerations and bruises, or fractures of the facial bones such as nasal fractures and fractures of the jaw, as well as trauma such as eye injuries. Symptoms are specific to the type of injury; for example, fractures may involve pain, swelling, loss of function, or changes in the shape of facial structures.
Neck dissection	The Neck dissection is a surgical procedure for control of neck lymph node metastasis from squamous cell carcinoma (SCC) of the head and neck. The aim of the procedure is to remove lymph nodes from one side of the neck into which cancer cells may have migrated. Metastasis of squamous cell carcinoma into the lymph nodes of the neck reduce survival and is the most important factor in the spread of the disease.
Cranial nerves	Cranial nerves are nerves that emerge directly from the brain stem, in contrast to spinal nerves which emerge from segments of the spinal cord.

Clam\101

Chapter 3. PART III: Chapter 37 - Chapter 54

	Human Cranial nerves are evolutionarily homologous to those found in many other vertebrates. Cranial nerves XI and XII evolved in the common ancestor to amniotes (non-amphibian tetrapods) thus totaling twelve pairs.
Esthesiometer	An Esthesiometer (British spelling aEsthesiometer} is a device f, or eye, etc).. The measure of the degree of tactile sensitivity is called aesthesiometry. There are different types of aEsthesiometers depending on their particular function.
Blood	Blood is a specialized bodily fluid that delivers necessary substances to the body's cells -- such as nutrients and oxygen -- and transports waste products away from those same cells. In vertebrates, it is composed of Blood cells suspended in a liquid called Blood plasma. Plasma, which comprises 55% of Blood fluid, is mostly water (90% by volume), and contains dissolved proteins, glucose, mineral ions, hormones, carbon dioxide (plasma being the main medium for excretory product transportation), platelets and Blood cells themselves.
Cardiac surgery	Cardiac surgery is surgery on the heart and/or great vessels performed by a cardiac surgeon. Frequently, it is done to treat complications of ischemic heart disease (for example, coronary artery bypass grafting), correct congenital heart disease, or treat valvular heart disease created by various causes including endocarditis. It also includes heart transplantation.
Electrolyte	In chemistry, an Electrolyte is any substance containing free ions that make the substance electrically conductive. The most typical Electrolyte is an ionic solution, but molten Electrolytes and solid Electrolytes are also possible. Electrolytes commonly exist as solutions of acids, bases or salts.
Endocrine system	The Endocrine system is a system of glands, each of which secretes a type of hormone to regulate the body. The field of study that deals with disorders of endocrine glands is endocrinology, a branch of the wider field of internal medicine. The Endocrine system is an information signal system much like the nervous system.
Extraocular muscles	The Extraocular muscles are the six muscles that control the movements of the (human) eye. The actions of the Extraocular muscles depend on the position of the eye at the time of muscle contraction. Since only the fovea provides sharp distinct vision, the eye must move to follow a target.

Eyelid	An Eyelid is a thin fold of skin that covers and protects an eye. With the exception of the prepuce and the labia minora, it has the thinnest skin of the whole body. The levator palpebrae superioris muscle retracts the Eyelid to `open` the eye.
Geriatric anesthesia	Geriatric anesthesia is the branch of medicine that studies anesthesia approach in elderly. The perioperative care of elderly patients differs from that of younger patients for a number of reasons. Some of these can be attributed to the changes that occur in the process of aging, but many are also caused by diseases that accompany seniority.
Immune system	An immune system is a system of biological structures and processes within an organism that protects against disease by identifying and killing pathogens and tumour cells. It detects a wide variety of agents, from viruses to parasitic worms, and needs to distinguish them from the organism`s own healthy cells and tissues in order to function properly. Detection is complicated as pathogens can evolve rapidly, producing adaptations that avoid the immune system and allow the pathogens to successfully infect their hosts.
Ischemia	In medicine, Ischemia is a restriction in blood supply, generally due to factors in the blood vessels, with resultant damage or dysfunction of tissue. It may also be spelled ischaemia or ischæmia.
	Rather than hypoxia , Ischemia is an absolute or relative shortage of the blood supply to an organ, i.e. a shortage of oxygen, glucose and other blood-borne fuels.
Musculoskeletal system	A Musculoskeletal system is an organ system that gives animals (including humans) the ability to move using the muscular and skeletal systems. The Musculoskeletal system provides form, stability, and movement to the body.
	It is made up of the body`s bones (the skeleton), muscles, cartilage, tendons, ligaments, joints, and other connective tissue (the tissue that supports and binds tissues and organs together).
Podiatry	Podiatry is a branch of medicine devoted to the study, diagnosis and treatment of disorders of the foot, ankle and lower leg. A podiatrist treats the foot of a patient at a homeless shelter in Homestead, Florida. Within the United Kingdom, the titles `podiatrist` and `chiropodist` are to some extent interchangeable. Although the UK government-appointed regulator acknowledges both titles and makes no distinction between them, they are used differently within the occupation.

Chapter 3. PART III: Chapter 37 - Chapter 54

Respiratory system	The respiratory system's function is to allow gas exchange to all parts of the body. The space between the alveoli and the capillaries, the anatomy or structure of the exchange system, and the precise physiological uses of the exchanged gases vary depending on the organism. In humans and other mammals, for example, the anatomical features of the respiratory system include airways, lungs, and the respiratory muscles.
Seizure	An epileptic Seizure, occasionally referred to as a fit, is defined as a transient symptom of `abnormal excessive or synchronous neuronal activity in the brain`. The outward effect can be as dramatic as a wild thrashing movement (tonic-clonic Seizure) or as mild as a brief loss of awareness. It can manifest as an alteration in mental state, tonic or clonic movements, convulsions, and various other psychic symptoms (such as déjà vu or jamais vu).
Trochlear nerve	The Trochlear nerve is a motor nerve (a `somatic efferent` nerve) that innervates a single muscle: the superior oblique muscle of the eye. The Trochlear nerve is unique among the cranial nerves in several respects. It is the smallest nerve in terms of the number of axons it contains.
Vagus nerve	The Vagus nerve cranial nerve X, the Wanderer or sometimes the Rambler, is the tenth of twelve (excluding CN0) paired cranial nerves. Upon leaving the medulla between the olivary nucleus and the inferior cerebellar penduncle, it extends through the jugular foramen, then passing into the carotid sheath between the internal carotid artery and the internal jugular vein down below the head, to the neck, chest and abdomen, where it contributes to the innervation of the viscera. Besides output to the various organs in the body the Vagus nerve conveys sensory information about the state of the body's organs to the central nervous system. 80-90% of the nerve fibers in the Vagus nerve are afferent (sensory) nerves communicating the state of the viscera to the brain.
Abducens nerve	The Abducens nerve or abducent nerve (the sixth cranial nerve, also called the sixth nerve or simply VI) is a 'somatic efferent' nerve that controls the movement of a single muscle, the lateral rectus muscle of the eye. Homologous Abducens nerves are found in all vertebrates except lampreys and hagfishes.
Epinephrine	Epinephrine is a hormone and neurotransmitter. When produced in the body it increases heart rate, contracts blood vessels and dilates air passages and participates in the `fight or flight` response of the sympathetic nervous system. It is a catecholamine, a sympathomimetic monoamine produced only by the adrenal glands from the amino acids phenylalanine and tyrosine.

Chapter 3. PART III: Chapter 37 - Chapter 54

Phenylephrine	Phenylephrine or Neo-Synephrine is an α_1-adrenergic receptor agonist used primarily as a decongestant, as an agent to dilate the pupil, and to increase blood pressure. Phenylephrine has recently been marketed as a substitute for pseudoephedrine (e.g., Pfizer's Sudafed (Original Formulation)), but there are recent claims that oral Phenylephrine may be no more effective as a decongestant than a placebo . Phenylephrine is used as a decongestant sold as an oral medicine, as a nasal spray, or as eye drops.
Glaucoma	Glaucoma refers to a group of diseases that affect the optic nerve and involves a loss of retinal ganglion cells in a characteristic pattern. It is a type of optic neuropathy. Raised intraocular pressure is a significant risk factor for developing Glaucoma (above 22 mmHg or 2.9 kPa).
ACE inhibitors	ACE inhibitors or angiotensin-converting enzyme inhibitors, are a group of pharmaceuticals that are used primarily in treatment of hypertension and congestive heart failure, in some cases as the drugs of first choice. ACE inhibitors are used primarily in the treatment of hypertension,though they are also sometimes used in those with cardiac failure,renal disease,or systemic sclerosis This system is activated in response to hypotension, decreased sodium concentration in the distal tubule, decreased blood volume and renal sympathetic nerve stimulation. In such a situation, the kidneys release renin which cleaves the liver-derived angiotensinogen into angiotensin I. Angiotensin I is then converted to angiotensin II via the ACE in the pulmonary circulation as well as in the endothelium of blood vessels in many parts of the body.
Atropine	Atropine is a tropane alkaloid extracted from deadly nightshade (Atropa belladonna), jimsonweed (Datura stramonium), mandrake (Mandragora officinarum) and other plants of the family Solanaceae. It is a secondary metabolite of these plants and serves as a drug with a wide variety of effects. It is a competitive antagonist for the muscarinic acetylcholine receptor.
Cyclopentolate	Cyclopentolate is a mydriatic and cycloplegic agent commonly used during pediatric eye examinations. Cyclopentolate is also administered as an atropine substitute to reverse muscarinic and CNS effects of indirect cholinomimetic (anti-AChase) administration. When used in eye drops in pediatric eye examinations, Cyclopentolate 0.5% and 1.0% is used to stop the eye focusing at near distance, enabling the optometrist or ophthalmologist to obtain a more accurate reading of the focusing power of the eyes.

Chapter 3. PART III: Chapter 37 - Chapter 54

Clam101

Chapter 3. PART III: Chapter 37 - Chapter 54

Diuretic	A Diuretic is any drug that elevates the rate of urination and thus provides a means of forced diuresis. There are several categories of Diuretics. All Diuretics increase the excretion of water from bodies, although each class does so in a distinct way.
Timolol	Timolol maleate is a non-selective beta-adrenergic receptor blocker. In its oral form (Blocadren), it is used to treat high blood pressure and prevent heart attacks, and occasionally to prevent migraine headaches. In its ophthalmic form (brand names Timoptol in Italy; Timoptic), it is used to treat open-angle and occasionally secondary glaucoma by reducing aqueous humour production through blockage of the beta receptors on the ciliary epithelium.
Agonist	An Agonist is a chemical that binds to a receptor of a cell and triggers a response by the cell. An Agonist often mimics the action of a naturally occurring substance. An Agonist produces an action.
Magnesium	Magnesium is a chemical element with the symbol Mg, atomic number 12 and common oxidation number +2. It is an alkaline earth metal and the eighth most abundant element in the Earth's crust by mass, although ninth in the known Universe as a whole. This preponderance of Magnesium is related to the fact that it is easily built up in supernova stars from a sequential addition of three helium nuclei to carbon . Magnesium constitutes about 2% of the Earth's crust by mass, which makes it the eighth most abundant element in the crust.
Carbonic anhydrase	The Carbonic anhydrases form a family of enzymes that catalyze the rapid conversion of carbon dioxide to bicarbonate and protons, a reaction that occurs rather slowly in the absence of a catalyst. The active site of most Carbonic anhydrases contains a zinc ion; they are therefore classified as metalloenzymes. Several forms of Carbonic anhydrase occur in nature.
Carbonic anhydrase inhibitor	Carbonic anhydrase inhibitors are a class of pharmaceuticals that suppress the activity of carbonic anhydrase. Their clinical use has been established as antiglaucoma agents, diuretics, antiepileptics, in the management of mountain sickness, gastric and duodenal ulcers, neurological disorders, or osteoporosis. Acetazolamide is an inhibitor of carbonic anhydrase.

Chapter 3. PART III: Chapter 37 - Chapter 54

Echothiophate	Echothiophate is a parasympathomimetic and organophosphate. It is an acetylcholinesterase inhibitor.
	It is used as an ocular antihypertensive in the treatment of chronic glaucoma and, in some cases, accommodative esotropia.
Acetazolamide	Acetazolamide, sold under the trade name Diamox, is a carbonic anhydrase inhibitor that is used to treat glaucoma, epileptic seizures, benign intracranial hypertension (pseudotumor cerebri), altitude sickness, cystinuria, and dural ectasia. Acetazolamide is available as a generic drug and is also used as a diuretic.
	Acetazolamide is a carbonic anhydrase inhibitor, which means that it forces the kidneys to excrete bicarbonate (HCO_3^-), thus re-acidifying the blood.
Carbamazepine	Carbamazepine is an anticonvulsant and mood stabilizing drug used primarily in the treatment of epilepsy and bipolar disorder, as well as trigeminal neuralgia. It is also used off-label for a variety of indications, including attention-deficit hyperactivity disorder (ADHD), schizophrenia, phantom limb syndrome, paroxysmal extreme pain disorder, and post-traumatic stress disorder.
LASIK	LASIK or LASIK is a type of refractive surgery for correcting myopia, hyperopia, and astigmatism. LASIK is performed by ophthalmologists using a laser. LASIK is similar to other surgical corrective procedures such as photorefractive keratectomy, PRK, (also called ASA, Advanced Surface Ablation) though it provides benefits such as faster patient recovery.
Acetylcholine	The chemical compound Acetylcholine is a neurotransmitter in both the peripheral nervous system (PNS) and central nervous system (CNS) in many organisms including humans. Acetylcholine is one of many neurotransmitters in the autonomic nervous system (ANS) and the only neurotransmitter used in the motor division of the somatic nervous system. (Sensory neurons use glutamate and various peptides at their synapses).
Balance disorder	A Balance disorder is a disturbance that causes an individual to feel unsteady, giddy, woozy spinning, or floating. Balance is the result of a number of body systems working together. Specifically, in order to achieve balance, the eyes (visual system), ears (vestibular system) and the body's sense of where it is in space (proprioception) need to be intact.
Local	Local usually refers to something nearby, or in the immediate area.

501

	It may be used in many ways, some of which are related to this general meaning, others which are not: .
Local anesthetic	A Local anesthetic is a drug that causes reversible local anesthesia and a loss of nociception. When it is used on specific nerve pathways (nerve block), effects such as analgesia and paralysis can be achieved. Clinical Local anesthetics belong to one of two classes: aminoamide and aminoester Local anesthetics.
Prostaglandin	A prostaglandin is any member of a group of lipid compounds that are derived enzymatically from fatty acids and have important functions in the animal body. Every prostaglandin contains 20 carbon atoms, including a 5-carbon ring. They are mediators and have a variety of strong physiological effects, such as regulating the contraction and relaxation of smooth muscle tissue.
Sodium bicarbonate	Sodium bicarbonate or sodium hydrogen carbonate is the chemical compound with the formula $NaHCO_3$. Sodium bicarbonate is a white solid that is crystalline but often appears as a fine powder. It has a slightly salty, alkaline taste resembling that of washing soda (sodium carbonate).
Drop	A drop or straw is a small volume of liquid, bounded completely or almost completely by free surfaces. A drop may form when liquid accumulates at the lower end of a tube or other surface boundary, producing a hanging drop called a pendant drop. drops may also be formed by the condensation of a vapor or by atomization of a larger mass of liquid.
Intraocular pressure	Intraocular pressure is the fluid pressure of the aqueous humor inside the eye. Intraocular pressure is mainly determined by the coupling of the production of aqueous humor and the drainage of aqueous humor mainly through the trabecular meshwork located in the anterior chamber angle. Intraocular pressure is measured with a tonometer.

Chapter 3. PART III: Chapter 37 - Chapter 54

Clinical	Clinical can refer to:
	· clinical medical practice
	· Clinic
	· Illness
	· clinical waste, segregated for safety or security
	· clinical medical professions
	· clinical psychology
	· clinical examination; see Physical examination
	· clinical conditions, diagnosed from clinical examination alone

	· clinical death
	· clinical research
	· clinical governance of patient care within a health system
	· clinical trial, research involving patients
	· clinical linguistics, linguistics applied to speech therapy .
Oculocardiac reflex	The Oculocardiac reflex, Aschner phenomenon, Aschner reflex, or Aschner-Dagnini reflex, is a decrease in pulse rate associated with traction applied to extraocular muscles and/or compression of the eyeball. The reflex is mediated by nerve connections between the trigeminal cranial nerve and the vagus nerve of the parasympathetic nervous system. The afferent tracts are derived mainly from the ophthalmic division of the trigeminal nerve, although tracts from the maxillary and mandibular division have also been documented.
Ptosis	Ptosis (πτωσις `falling, a fall`) refers to droopiness of any body part. Specifically, it can refer to: · Ptosis (eyelid) · Ptosis (breasts) · NephroPtosis (kidney) · GastroPtosis (stomach) .
Corneal abrasion	Corneal abrasion is a medical condition involving the loss of the surface epithelial layer of the eye`s cornea.

	Corneal abrasions are generally a result of trauma to the surface of the eye. Common causes include jabbing a finger into an eye, walking into a tree branch, getting grit in the eye and then rubbing the eye or being hit with a piece of projectile metal.
Corneal abrasions	Corneal abrasion is a medical condition involving the loss of the surface epithelial layer of the eye`s cornea.
	Corneal abrasions are generally a result of trauma to the surface of the eye. Common causes include jabbing a finger into an eye, walking into a tree branch, getting grit in the eye and then rubbing the eye or being hit with a piece of projectile metal.
Artery	The arterial system is the higher-pressure portion of the circulatory system. Arterial pressure varies between the peak pressure during heart contraction, called the systolic pressure, and the minimum, or diastolic pressure between contractions, when the heart expands and refills. This pressure variation within the Artery produces the pulse which is observable in any Artery, and reflects heart activity.
Tourniquet	A Tourniquet is a constricting or compressing device used to control venous and arterial circulation to an extremity for a period of time. Pressure is applied circumferentially upon the skin and underlying tissues of a limb; this pressure is transferred to the walls of vessels, causing them to become temporarily occluded. It is generally used as a tool for a medical professional in applications such as cannulation or to stem the flow of traumatic bleeding, especially by military medics.
Arthroscopy	Arthroscopy is a minimally invasive surgical procedure in which an examination and sometimes treatment of damage of the interior of a joint is performed using an arthroscope, a type of endoscope that is inserted into the joint through a small incision. Arthroscopic procedures can be performed either to evaluate or to treat many orthopaedic conditions including torn floating cartilage, torn surface cartilage, ACL reconstruction, and trimming damaged cartilage.
	The advantage of Arthroscopy over traditional open surgery is that the joint does not have to be opened up fully.
Paresthesia	Paraesthesia is a sensation of tingling, pricking, or numbness of a person`s skin with no apparent long-term physical effect. It is more generally known as the feeling of `pins and needles` or of a limb `falling asleep`. The manifestation of Paresthesia may be transient or chronic.

Chapter 3. PART III: Chapter 37 - Chapter 54

509

| Supine position | The Supine position is a position of the body: lying down with the face up, as opposed to the prone position, which is face down, sometimes with the hands behind the head or neck. When used in surgical procedures, it allows access to the peritoneal, thoracic and pericardial regions; as well as the head, neck and extremities. |
| | Using terms defined in the anatomical position, the dorsal side is down, and the ventral side is up. |